Rebound 1990

Ethnicity & Race
CRITICAL CONCEPTS IN SOCIAL WORK

Carolyn Jacobs and Dorcas D. Bowles, Editors

Ethnicity & Race
CRITICAL CONCEPTS IN SOCIAL WORK

Carolyn Jacobs and Dorcas D. Bowles, Editors

National Association of Social Workers, Inc.
7981 Eastern Avenue
Silver Spring, MD 20910

Library of Congress Cataloging-in-Publication Data

Ethnicity and race.

  Bibliography: p.
  1. Social work with minorities—United States.
2. Social work education—United States. 3. Mental
health services—United States. 4. Mental health
services—Study and teaching—United States.
5. Ethnic attitudes—United States. 6. Race
awareness—United States. I. Jacobs, Carolyn,
1946- . II. Bowles, Dorcas D. III. National
Association of Social Workers.
HV3176.E83 1988 362.8′4′0973 88-28263
ISBN 0-87101-155-7

Printed in the United States of America

CONTENTS

130,448

FOREWORD

In the past three years, the National Association of Social Workers (NASW) has focused on the concept of unity through diversity as we have sought new ways to meet the needs of our members, many of whom are ethnic or racial minorities. This increased emphasis on the diversity of our membership and of the clients our members serve builds on a long history of NASW concern for and commitment to equity and justice issues. The 1957 *Social Work Yearbook,* the first produced by NASW, carried a major article on civil liberties and discrimination[1]; since then, NASW has produced several publications devoted to minority issues. Our goal has been to eliminate racism and to replace it with an understanding of the wealth of cultural differences among people of color.

Despite the efforts made by the profession in addressing racism and discrimination, mental health services generally remain "color blind," and they are provided with little regard for the cultural differences that have an impact on a client's needs. Furthermore, because of staffing patterns in mental health clinics and other agencies, frequently neither the client nor the agency staff has access to ethnic minority staff who could discuss issues of culture and race. The result is often treatment failure.

Ethnicity and Race: Critical Concepts in Social Work presents a new dimension in that the articles examine the link between social work education and ethnically sensitive practice. The distinguished authors critically review course content, practice, research, and public policy issues that will help us meet the particular mental health needs of clients of color.

It is our hope that *Ethnicity and Race: Critical Concepts in Social Work* will play a major role in changing the tenor and quality of mental health services provided to people of color. Social workers in mental health practice today will find the book an invaluable resource for the knowledge, skills, and techniques they need to work effectively with nonwhite clients. An even greater long-term effect will result from the use of the book in schools of social work, both as reading material for students and as a guide to changes in curriculum. As the schools adopt the authors' substantive recommendations for course outlines and teaching models, new social workers will emerge with the knowledge and sensitivity they need to provide appropriate services. In a different climate of service provision, we also can hope to see more people of color providing mental health services.

NASW's official policy on racism mandates that we strive for full representation of people of color at all levels of leadership and employment and that we implement affirmative action concepts in all facets of practice, education,

---

[1] National Association of Social Workers, Inc., *Social Work Yearbook* (New York: National Association of Social Workers, Inc., 1957).

and professional development. *Ethnicity and Race: Critical Concepts in Social Work* offers us an exciting, new tool to use in our work. We applaud the editors and authors, and we are pleased to be publishing the work.

SUZANNE DWORAK-PECK
President

MARK G. BATTLE
Executive Director

April 1988

ACKNOWLEDGMENTS

We are deeply indebted to the authors who, at our request, have written and contributed chapters to this book in their areas of specialized knowledge. The authors' devotion and commitment to people of color and their hopes that ethnic minorities will receive the best possible mental health services is remarkable. We extend warm thanks to Rosina Becerra, June Hopps, and Wyatt Jones who, as initial reviewers, read, re-read, edited, and selected the final papers that compose this book. Their wise counsel has been essential and important for completion of this work.

To Jill Ker Conway, President of Smith College from 1975 to 1985, whose leadership and vision for social work education at Smith College was an inspiration, we are deeply grateful. To Katherine Gabel, Dean of the Smith College School for Social Work from 1976 to 1985, we offer special thanks. She has supported and continues to support the values and importance of ethnicity to social work education. Her unstinting and unswerving commitment has been both affirming and strengthening.

Many others also have been instrumental and supportive in the development of this book. We appreciate the help and encouragement of our families, friends, and colleagues at Smith College—a support network that has been an anchor and a source of strength.

We also thank Marta Sotomayor, Neilson Smith, and others affiliated with the National Institute of Mental Health from 1978 to 1984, which funded the Smith College School for Social Work Ethnic Minority Manpower Development Grant No. 5T01MH15839-03 SWE, which made possible the publication of this book.

Finally, we express thanks to the staff of the Publications Department of the National Association of Social Workers for their efficiency, editorial suggestions, and sound advice.

INTRODUCTION

People of color comprise a large number of individuals served by social and mental health agencies (Chunn, Dunston, and Ross-Sheriff, 1983). Despite this fact, textbooks for social work, counseling, psychotherapy, and curricula often do not address their needs sufficiently. As a result of pressure exerted by ethnic groups during the 1960s and 1970s, educators in institutions offering training in the major mental health disciplines have become more aware of and have given increased attention to issues of ethnicity and race in their curricula. However, courses often have been "add-ons," which have not been given the same seriousness and importance as established courses, and issues of ethnicity and race usually have not been integrated in core course content. Hence, support for and inclusion of issues of ethnicity and race throughout the curricula have not become a part of the educational mission and training of professionals.

Mental health clinics, inpatient and outpatient hospital settings, child guidance clinics, school social work departments, family agencies, and college counseling centers, which serve ethnic minority groups, often do not have ethnic minority staff members with whom clients can identify or with whom agency personnel can consult to discuss issues of culture and difference. Despite what is known about the social and cultural backgrounds of people of color, educators and service providers often continue to approach diagnosis and treatment of people of color from a "color blind" and cultureless point of view. As a result, ethnic and racial differences between therapists and clients often go unrecognized, and therapists may treat clients of color using the norms used to diagnose and treat white middle-class clients. Often, these norms are diametrically opposed to the cultural values, behaviors, and family structures of ethnic minority families.

We propose that ethnicity and race are critical concepts in the formulation of diagnosis and treatment interventions. People of color deserve adequate, effective, and sensitively attuned treatment. Such treatment only is possible if educators and mental health workers consider the client's ethnic and racial frame of reference. Educators and service providers must have some understanding of the value systems, family interactions, and role assignments, including parent–child relationships, the role played by religion, the impact of immigration and cultural adjustment, the extended family network, and the help-seeking patterns and behaviors of ethnic groups. If issues of ethnicity and race are not regarded seriously, treatment failures for minority groups will be enormous.

This book comprises papers that were commissioned by the Smith College School for Social Work under the curriculum development component of the National Institute of Mental Health-funded Ethnic Minority Manpower Development Grant. The authors who have contributed to this book describe specific that areas educators and mental health professionals should consider in planning course content, in evolving an ethnically and racially sensitive practice, in formulating research questions, and in addressing public policy issues. Additionally, the authors provide ethnically and racially relevant knowledge, techniques, and skills that can be used during the various phases of the treatment process. The authors further provide a perspective on how the allocation of public resources can shape and influence social service organizations and service delivery. A chapter on Asian Americans was included in the initial draft manuscript of this publication. Its omission in the final version results from a decision by the author to publish the article elsewhere. With the constraints of an untimely notification to us and the publication deadline, we were unable to solicit another article. It is our hope that the reader would supplement any use of this publication with materials on Asian Americans.

Although a specific ethnic group is the focus of each chapter, many of the ideas presented are useful across ethnic groups, given the "duality of response" required of all minority groups (Chestang, 1972). The capacity to understand the subtle features of specific ethnic groups and simultaneously understand those facets and family life patterns that may be similar for each of the groups is important. This sensitivity to the unique qualities and differing values, child-rearing patterns, and life-styles found in each culture allows for a perspective that truly looks at the person in the context of his or her environment.

This book is divided into two parts: (1) practice issues and (2) curriculum issues. After reading this book, mental health educators and training center workers should see it as their professional responsibility to consider ethnic and racial factors in training, practice, service delivery, and policy formulation. We hope that this book will

■ raise one's awareness of his or her attitudes and the attitudes of others toward people of color and issues of difference;

■ help one to see how ethnicity affects development, including how one's sense of self as a person of color evolves and is shaped;

■ provide a framework encompassing individual, family, and group modalities for considering the special treatment and research needs of ethnic groups;

■ call attention to policy issues; and

■ enhance the integration of content on ethnicity throughout the social work curricula—treatment methods, human behavior and social environment, and social policy and research.

CAROLYN JACOBS
Smith College
School for Social Work
Northampton, Massachusetts

DORCAS D. BOWLES
Atlanta University
School of Social Work
Atlanta, Georgia

Works Cited

Chestang, L. *Character Development in a Hostile Society,* Occasional Paper, No. 3, School of Social Service Administration. Chicago: University of Chicago Press, 1972.

Chunn, J. C., P. J. Dunston, and F. Ross-Sheriff. *Mental Health and People of Color: Curriculum Development and Change.* Washington: Howard University Press, 1983.

Part 1
PRACTICE ISSUES

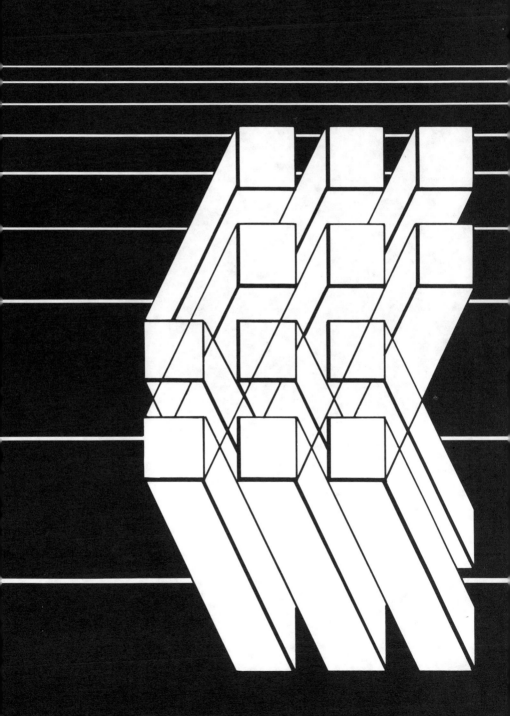

INTRODUCTION TO PART 1

Practice Issues

DORCAS D. BOWLES

he curriculum policy issued by the Council on Social Work Education (CSWE) for the master's and baccalaureate degree programs in social work education mandates the development and inclusion of content on ethnic minorities[1] by all schools so that after graduation, beginning professionals will be able to work with diverse populations regardless of their racial, ethnic, educational, socioeconomic, or religious background (*Handbook of Accreditation Standards and Procedures,* 1984). This complex task requires an understanding of the history of each ethnic minority group, as well as individual and institutional responses to ethnic minority groups over time and the effect of historical conditions on the development and socialization of ethnic minority children as females or males and as members of a subcultural group. That social work education will provide its students with a body of knowledge that will allow them to meet adequately the needs of people of color who are victimized by racism and oppression is assumed in the mandate. This means that the curriculum will need to incorporate the various practice modalities to include individual, family, groups, and the larger community, as well as the guidelines for policy planning and implementation.

Since the 1960s, social work educators and mental health professionals have struggled with ways to integrate ethnic minority content into the curriculum. Although gains have been made, the methods of integration and the degree

---

[1] *Ethnic minority* refers to people of color in the United States including African Americans, Asian Americans, Mexican Americans, American Indians, and Puerto Ricans.

1

to which the content is considered relevant are inconsistent. Some schools have offered elective courses, others have offered required courses, and still others a combination of elective and required courses. However, few, if any, schools have achieved an integrative approach that spans the total curriculum resulting in both cross-sequence and sequential compatibility and coherence. Additionally, as human service resources become more scarce, there is a trend toward lessening concerns over issues pertaining to ethnic minorities as other programmatic issues take precedence. Effective programs and treatment interventions demand that those providing the services understand and be sensitive to the values, culture, and special needs of all groups served, especially ethnic minorities. The social and political realities for people of color have led them to experience themselves and their world from a dual perspective—the perspective of one's ethnic minority group and the perspective of the majority group. An understanding of this duality is critical for all persons in the helping professions.

The editors and contributing authors in "Practice Issues" provide organizing theoretical frameworks for including content on people of color. This part contains theories of practice for working with individuals, families, and groups. These theories of practice are pertinent for educators and mental health professionals. In addition to providing a theoretical knowledge base, the authors provide specific and useful information pertaining to the range of ethnic minority groups. The authors emphasize the importance of understanding a group's history, values, culture, socialization patterns, and the effect of environmental and institutional arrangements on development and behavior. Students must be taught to pay attention to healthy and culturally adaptive behaviors by members of ethnic minorities so that those behaviors are not viewed erroneously as pathological. After reading the chapters in part 1, educators and those people involved in service delivery should be responsible for considering issues of ethnicity and race when developing curricula; when making diagnostic formulations and treatment plans; when formulating research questions, methodology, and design; when assessing the service needs of the community; and when critiquing social policies.

Using a social policy perspective, the author of chapter 1 focuses on the effect of current national policies on people of color. She examines the historical context in which policies are made and how those policies affect vulnerable populations. She clearly indicates in the chapter that the establishment of national goals that address the needs of minorities is needed to bring people of color into the overall national community.

The author of chapter 2 focuses on Asian Indian families and their social networks. The author suggests that for this population, relatives, friends, and co-workers are called on for service assistance while neighbors and formal organizations are used minimally for emotional and financial support. Social service programs must begin to augment, rather than ignore, natural support systems found in minority families. Working in collaboration with Asian Indian cultural and social organizations and involving helping professionals from this ethnic group is essential. Sensitivity to one's stance on dependency of adult children on their parents, male and female roles, arranged marriages, and care of the elderly is of critical importance. These areas, which are pertinent for other minority groups, must be understood within the context of their unique meaning for specific ethnic groups.

The use of group treatment as a significant form of mental health service delivery for Puerto Ricans in the United States is addressed in chapter 3. Folk beliefs and healing techniques, including spiritualism among Puerto Ricans, provide evidence of the importance of groups in achieving therapeutic change. An examination of folk beliefs and healing techniques supports this evidence, thereby affirming the importance of valuing and using what is unique within the culture of an ethnic group.

In chapter 4, the author focuses on the "use of time, space, and relationship with Puerto Rican families at risk" as a means of illustrating how significant components of traditional social work practice can be reshaped in ways that are more congruent with the culturally derived expectation of clients separated from their customary sources of support. Puerto Rican families at risk need and can be helped by a modified extended family system that provides structure, social cohesion, and competency in their daily lives.

The development of self-concepts for Chicanos and American Indians is the focus of chapters 5 and 6, respectively. Recent writings on identity formation have begun to address issues of self-concept for minorities and to show that, despite racism, minority children can and do develop positive self-regard. The effects of individual and institutional racism on Chicano children's self-concepts are described in chapter 5. Readers are shown how social work educative and organizing efforts can be used with Chicano families to promote positive self-esteem of Chicano children. Increasing political awareness, organizing communities, and recognizing and acknowledging ethnic group strengths and resources are important actions for ethnic minorities to learn and to take. Chapter 6 is an examination of contemporary variations in family and individual behavior. Although traditional family systems are used as a benchmark, the author does not assume that persistence of traditional beliefs is preferred over change.

Chapter 7 provides a theoretical framework for detailing how an ethnic sense of self evolves for the black child. The interaction between the black child and his or her parents is a key element in the development of an ethnic sense of self. Later, significant others within the black family and community with whom the black child interacts serve as "recharge units" for undergirding and strengthening the child's ethnic sense of self. Ethnic minorities have developed their own frames of reference for self-definition and use members of their group as significant role models.

In chapter 8, the concluding chapter for part 1, an argument for the promotion and practice of advocacy research by social workers is presented. The social worker (researcher) lends support to the world view of the client or client group, thereby empowering the client to act in his or her behalf individually, collectively, or both. The researcher is accountable not only to funding sources and colleagues but to the client group being studied. This accountability ensures that the research results likely will be used by community organizations, social agencies, and local policymakers.

The authors in part 1 agree that educators and professionals must respect differences. They agree that respect for differences will necessitate an examination of stereotypes about ethnic minorities and a willingness to honor the ethnic minority family life, values, and patterns that differ in subtle but important ways from the "model" white middle-class family. The ideas espoused by the authors in part 1 lead to the following recommendations:

■ The reaccreditation arm of CSWE should accredit only those schools whose curricula demonstrate the inclusion and integration of ethnic minority content across curriculum areas and whose faculties and student bodies reflect ethnic representation and diversity.

■ Foundations and other granting agencies, such as the Office of Education and National Institute of Mental Health, should include as part of their standard criteria for review of proposals a statement ensuring that content on ethnic minorities is included.

■ All professional schools and agencies that train students in the helping professions should have as part of their mission statement a firm commitment to train practitioners to work with ethnic minority groups and to serve an ethnically diverse clientele. Issues of ethnicity and race should become a required part of each psychosocial assessment and treatment plan in case discussions. Content on each minority group should be addressed and, where possible, cultural similarities and differences among ethnic groups noted.

■ At each school, the committee designated to deal with issues of curriculum should have as its mandate the review of all required courses by sequence to ensure that ethnic minority content is evident and that ethnic minority content demonstrates circular coherence, as is often the case with other content areas. Elective courses covering ethnic minority content should complement the core course offerings.

■ Professional schools should make every effort to support research on ethnic minorities by faculty members, interdisciplinary teams, and students.

■ Affiliated placement agencies should be pushed by schools who use them to have ethnic minority staff and supervisors and to have ethnic minority content addressed as part of case discussions.

■ Ethnic minority members should be invited to present papers, give lectures, and serve as consultants at schools and agencies.

■ CSWE should develop a directory of ethnic minority consultants by region for workshops and seminars on course revisions.

■ CSWE should take responsibility for the development of updated bibliographies on ethnic minorities, model course syllabi, and other teaching resources for distribution to all schools of social work.

Only through the demonstration of such measures will we be able to ensure that ethnic differences are appreciated, addressed, and incorporated in social work curricula, agency practice and service delivery, research, and public policy.

DORCAS D. BOWLES
Atlanta University
School of Social of Social Work
Atlanta

Works Cited

Handbook of Accreditation Standards and Procedures (rev. ed.). New York: Council on Social Work Education, Commission on Accreditation, July 1984, Appendix 1.

CHAPTER 1

FEDERALISM AND PEOPLE OF COLOR

MARTA SOTOMAYOR

Historically, the federal government occasionally championed the causes of people of color. Today, however, some view the "New Federalism," which is marked by the policies of the Reagan Administration, as "the boldest, most controversial attempt in 50 years to roll back the role of the federal government as a guarantor of equal opportunity and provider of social services," according to Pechman (1982). (P. 101.) To understand the government's ineffectiveness in addressing the needs of people of color, an examination of the meaning of federalism and the role of federalism in the shaping of legislation concerning people of color is essential. This chapter is an examination of federalism and its historical and current impact on people of color.

Federalism: A Historical Perspective

From the beginning, the federal government was designed to be a flexible mechanism for governace and to withstand tensions resulting from social change and economic development. Throughout the years, according to Elazar (1972), *American federalism* came to be defined as "a mode of political organization that unites different policies within an overarching political system by distributing power among general and constituent governments in a manner designed to protect the existence and authority of both." (P. 12.) In a larger sense, federalism became more than an arrangement of a system of governmental structures. Federalism became a mode of political activity requiring the establishment of certain kinds of cooperative relationships to be reflected in the decision-making and executive processes. Thus, federalism has become more

6

than a guiding principle; it has become the central characteristic of the American political system animating the relationships and political life of institutions, groups, and individuals. Now, public problems are addressed by these public and private sectors, and negotiations among them lead to the implementation of guiding policies (Elazar, 1972). According to this analysis, federalism is part of the problem of governmental ineffectiveness. The elements that determine the national goals and priorities of this country are elements that as a group people of color do not have: adequate representation, local control, and availability of or access to political and financial resources. Consequently, people of color have had to live with the results of legislation sponsored for state and national interests, rather than for self-interest, self-determination, and self-sufficiency.

Legislation and People

Generally, the interests of the various people of color have not been represented in the debates that promoted the establishment of governmental policies; rather than a concern for welfare of these groups, ideological beliefs, racism, and economic gain were the primary motivators for national policy-making throughout American history. Examples of national policies that negatively affected each of the people of color will be used to illustrate the various factors at play at the time of enactment. Expansionism, colonialism, and profit making often overshadowed racism as the main motivators of national objectives.

Policies Affecting Blacks

Even before the Civil War, the federal system of government, by allowing states to have rights, guaranteed that the needs of blacks could not be addressed and fulfilled from their perspective. As long as the states and federal government agreed on goals, progress could be expected. If they did not agree, government legislation and programs did not address the needs of blacks effectively.

According to Hawkins (1965), the stress and strain on federalism resulted from the issues of slavery before and during the Civil War and after the Supreme Court announced its decisions on desegregation and those decisions were implemented. The first issue of slavery was argued in terms of state's rights, the only rights other than federal rights known in the Constitution. The second issue was argued on the basis that federal intervention, in the form of a variety of programs initiated to help overcome racial discrimination, was managed on a state-by-state basis.

The emancipation of slaves at the end of the Civil War was followed by a brief challenge to white dominance. But, the emancipation was forced on Southerners and resulted in a large and costly federal program. In 1865, the Bureau of Refugees, Freedmen and Abandoned Lands was established for the economic rehabilitation of the freed slaves and to promote an educational program. The inadequate funding of the bureau made it impossible to accomplish its goals; it was abolished in 1872.

Soon after the war ended, eight southern states instituted the Black Codes, a series of statutes affecting apprenticeships, labor contracts, debts, and vagrancy, which reestablished the servile position of blacks (Frazier, 1957). Federal intervention became necessary when it was realized that the South was nullifying the Emancipation Proclamation.

The Fourteenth Amendment to the Constitution in 1886 and the supplementary Fifteenth Amendment in 1870 prohibited the abridgment of the full civil equality of all citizens and of the voting privilege on account of race, color, or previous condition of servitude. However, a biracial pattern of race relations in the South was allowed when the civil rights legislation of 1875 was declared unconstitutional. In the period of peaceful developments following the Reconstruction, the majority of the states that had fought over the issue of slavery did not make an issue of the overt system of discrimination based on race. The often used rationale for the failure of federal intervention was that the government attempted to accomplish sweeping goals in too short a time, against too strong a set of opposing forces, and with too little support from the northern states (Marden and Meyer, 1968).

The Supreme Court School Desegregation Decision of 1955 established that the matter of desegregation had to go beyond the schools alone. In effect, the court asserted that all state imposed racial segregation is unconstitutional. The civil rights legislation of 1957, which led to increased intervention by the federal government, exacerbated the southern crisis. Five months lapsed before the Commission on Civil Rights, authorized by the legislation, received a single complaint or testimony regarding the exent of the racist practices in the South. In the hearings held in Alabama and Louisiana, local authorities tried to resist the purpose of the commission by refusing to testify on the basis of state law (Marden and Meyer, 1968). While the civil rights legislation of 1960, 1964, and 1965 were enacted as federal mandates to all the states, the federal government and local officials failed to enforce them.

It can be argued that despite significant legislation enacted in the past decades to deal with discrimination and racism toward black populations in this country, policies supported by the new federalism ideology have and will continue to erode progress in years to come.

Policies Affecting American Indians

For the first 100 years of the U.S. government, the relationship of the Indian tribes to the federal government was characterized by the enactment of treaties negotiated with the various sovereign Indian nations. When American Indians failed to agree with the federal government, military force often was used. Local groups frequently moved against American Indians independent of the federal government. For example, the Georgia legislature passed an act confiscating all Cherokee land and declaring Cherokee tribal laws invalid within the state. In California, native Americans were forced off their land by the white Americans searching for gold. From 1851 on, the federal government negotiated treaties with many local tribes by which native Americans agreed to surrender more than half of California (Marden and Meyer, 1968).

The land allotment policy instituted by the Dawes Act of 1887 had disastrous effects for native Americans. Over the entire period in which this policy was in effect, 1887 to 1914, the lands held by native Americans were reduced from 138 million acres to 47 million acres (Shepard, 1942).

In 1924, Congress enacted a law that allowed native Americans to vote, yet as recently as 1940 there were seven states that barred them from voting either by discriminatory laws or interpretation of laws (Collier, 1947). Later, in 1941, Congress decreed that the American Indian tribes would be acknowledged and recognized as independent nations, tribes or powers, with whom the United States could make treaties (Billington, 1949). However, the established policy of the Indian office was aimed at weakening the tribal organization and forcing the native Americans' assimilation into the normative American way of life.

A significant reversal in the American Indian policy of the federal government occurred in the 1950s. In 1952, the Bureau of Indian Affairs attempted to relocate individuals or family groups to industrial centers for permanent employment and resettlement; this effort resulted in a large percentage of returnees to the reservation (Marden and Meyer, 1968).

A resolution passed by Congress in 1953 created a termination policy. Its intent was to initiate efforts to order or persuade tribes to request termination of their special relationship with the federal government. In the later part of the Eisenhower administration, the official policy veered back toward the principles embodied in the 1934 Indian Reorganization Act. This meant removing pressures on tribes to terminate their special relationship with the federal government. The groups in favor of the termination argued that the federal relationship was authoritarian and an infringement on Indian rights. It was argued that the U.S. government should not interfere with Indian business, but should free them so that they could have the same rights and privileges of other Americans (Wax and Buchanan, 1975).

While the intent of the various pieces of legislation affecting American Indians might have varied, the results are clear. The American Indians lost their lands, were robbed of their dignity and freedom, were belittled for their unique cultural and religious beliefs, and in general, were alienated from the mainstream of society.

Policies Affecting Mexican Americans

The annexation of the Southwest in 1948 resulted from the expansionist and colonialist ideologies of the time. However, the history of the U.S. immigration policy in relation to Mexican Americans was, more often than not, the result of the economic interests of the states.

Official hostilities between the U.S. and Mexican governments were terminated in 1848 by the Treaty of Guadalupe Hidalgo (Henry, 1950); the provisions of the treaty were extended to all residents of the conquered territories. Articles 8 and 9 accorded the Mexican population all the rights and privileges of citizenship; the articles specified that the Mexicans "would be maintained and protected in the free enjoyment of their liberty and property and secured in the free exercise of their religion without restriction" (Moquin, 1971). (P. 185.) In other words, "besides the rights and duties of American citizenship they would have some special privileges derived from their previous language, law and religion" (Perrigo, 1971). (P. 176.) With the exception of Article 10, which addressed land grants, the Congress of Mexico and the U.S. Congress ratified the provisions of the treaty. However, soon after, these provisions were rescinded. Within a few years, nearly 10,000 Spanish-speaking people within each southwestern state had taken on the characteristics of an oppressed people. Anglo Americans had assumed control of family and community land holdings and Mexicans were relegated to work as low-paid workers on their former lands (Swadesh, 1974). Officials appointed by the federal government helped to deprive the land heirs of their rights. Economic violations of the treaty took the form of fraudulent disposition of land grants, imposition of land taxes that the Mexicans could not pay, creation of vast public domain from community land grants, and appropriation of lands to create national forests (Swadesh, 1974).

In 1917 the Immigration Restriction League pressured Congress to pass an immigration law, which would require immigrants to pass a literacy test. The intent was to control the migration of non-English speaking groups to the United States. The law effectively cut off the supply of cheap European labor from mining, agriculture, and the railroad business. However, railroad and agricultural representatives lobbied in Congress to exempt Mexican labor from the Immigration Act of 1917 to ensure once again the availability of cheap labor from Mexico. Within six months of the passage of the act, Congress allowed the U.S. Secretary of Labor to suspend the literacy test and the contract labor clause to allow Mexican labor to come to the United States. The Secretary of Labor later extended the length of time allowed in the United States for Mexican workers involved in all the forms of mining and all government construction work in the various states (U.S. Bureau of Immigration, 1918).

Mexican American laborers served as the principal work force in the industrialization and development of agribusiness in the Southwest. Without their labor, high profits and large scale expansion in industry, transportation, and agribusiness would have been impossible (U.S. Bureau of Immigration, 1918). Because of economic interests the immigration laws were modified to meet the demands for a source of cheap labor.

The nationalism of the 1920s often was reflected in the belief that the Mexicans were inferior people and thus should be kept from entering the United States. The national quota system of 1924 that restricted the number of Mexicans who could immigrate into the United States was debated on the floor of both the U.S. Senate and the House of Representatives on this basis. Because of this belief, Mexicans were exempted from this system (Guzman, 1976).

The proposed immigration bills debated in Congress in the past years have addressed a number of issues that historically have determined immigration policy regarding Mexican Americans. For example, the provisions streamlining the procedures for employers to import temporary labor will increase greatly reliance on Mexican labor. Restrictions on "due process protection" in administrative proceedings might well result in increased legal challenges and judicial involvement in formulating national policies on the rights of immigrants and refugees (Schey, 1983).

Policies Affecting Puerto Ricans

At the close of the Spanish–American War, Puerto Rico became a United States dependent—another result of expansionist and colonialist ideologies. Before 1932, the federal government assumed a "laissez-faire" approach to the island's economy. As a result of this approach, mostly private American citizens invested capital in the development of Puerto Rico. In 1930, sugar was 60 percent absentee controlled; fruit, 31 percent or more; tobacco, 85 percent; banks, 60 percent; public utilities, 50 percent; and steamship lines, approximately 100 percent. This situation, further complicated by Puerto Rico's dependency on the mainland, forced Puerto Ricans to import most of their clothing, machinery, chemicals, and other necessities. The control of the absentee owner seemed complete with the aid of the Coastwide Shipping Act and the American Tariff provisions that allowed all of the profitable enterprise to become absorbed by American private businesses (Pattee, 1942).

Franklin Roosevelt launched a governmental effort to reorient the Puerto Rican economy by establishing the Puerto Rico Relief Administration. This was succeeded by the Puerto Rico Reconstruction Administration, which initiated irrigation, highway, school, housing, and other development projects. Despite efforts by the federal government to intervene in the economy of the island, conditions did not improve markedly, and great numbers of Puerto Ricans were forced to migrate to the mainland (Senior, 1961). They often settled in crowded urban areas where they experienced discrimination and poverty. While there is a degree of self-government in Puerto Rico today, the economic dependence on the U.S. mainland continues to perpetuate innumerable economic problems, which have serious sociopolitical consequences.

Policies Affecting Chinese Americans

Early federal and state policies regarding Chinese immigrants began with the discovery of gold in California when accusations that the Chinese had depressed the wages and the living standards of the white majority were made. Antagonism toward Chinese Americans soon turned into violence, and discriminatory city ordinances and state legislation were passed. California levied special taxes to prohibit Chinese people from entering the state. California also levied special taxes on Chinese residents based on ownership and use of vehicles. It became a misdemeanor for the Chinese residents to carry baskets suspended on a pole across their shoulders when Chinese who owned laundries commonly used no vehicles and used such baskets as a common practice (Davie, 1936). Following California's lead, Congress passed the Chinese Exclusion Act in 1882, suspending all Chinese immigration for 10 years (McWilliams, 1943). The provisions of this act were extended for an additional 10 years in 1892 and extended indefinitely in 1902.

In 1943, China was added to the list of immigrant nations on the quota system and allotted 105 annual entries. Exclusion of the Chinese from entering the United States by federal legislation was the result of a series of interrelated factors that included the national elections of the 1870s, the collapse of Reconstruction, and the joining of forces by the Southerners and Californians motivated by the same discriminatory attitudes toward blacks in the South and toward Chinese in California. Further, the lack of knowledge about the Chinese by most white Americans throughout the country led to the failure to recognize the issue as having national significance (McWilliams, 1943).

While the Chinese are a relatively small minority in terms of numbers, their vulnerability cannot be minimized. For example, as a whole, the Chinese have a higher proportion of individuals who have completed four or more years of college. Yet, they are not equally represented in managerial or other high level positions and their salaries are not comparable with those of the majority society with the same qualifications. They still suffer from many subtle forms of racism and discrimination and stereotyping.

Policies Affecting Japanese Americans

The Japanese were welcomed by residents of the West Coast at a time when that region was unsettled and in need of labor for economic development and growth. By 1890, labor unions began expressing antagonism toward Japanese Americans. By 1892, anti-Japanese activity was growing steadily in California, and by 1906, the school board of San Francisco passed a resolution requiring the segregation of all Asian children in one school. The famous Gentlemen's Agreement between the Imperial Government of Japan and the United States was signed after the Japanese government protested this matter.

The Japanese success in agriculture precipitated passage by the California legislature of the first land holding act in 1913, which allowed foreigners to lease land for a specific period, but not to own it. Further, legislation was enacted in several western states to prohibit the Japanese from purchasing stock in land-owning corporations in the names of their children who were born in the United States. The constitutionality of this legislation was upheld by the U.S. Supreme Court in a test case in 1923 (Ichihashi, 1932).

In 1942, over 110,000 Japanese Americans were transferred to 10 hastily built centers of detention in the Rocky Mountains and in Arkansas. The influence exerted by several groups, which prompted the evacuation, represented economic, nationalistic, and antiforeign interests.

The evacuation resulted from the interaction of a series of well-known factors: the established pattern of majority–minority relations, the need to project a united national antagonism toward those racially identified with an enemy nation, the pressure exerted by some interest groups antagonistic to the Japanese Americans because of their economic gains, and the inability of the federal government to exert leadership through any type of national policy that could have prevented an activity of this nature. Afterward, the federal government established the War Relocation Authority to plan for the supervision of Japanese Americans under detention. But, while the government took some steps to protect the property owned by Japanese Americans, most of their belongings, real and personal, had to be sold quickly; the sale resulted in substantial losses (Leighton, 1945).

The economic losses suffered by Japanese Americans have been estimated to run into the millions of dollars to include income and property losses because of forced sale of assets and loss of business goodwill (Bloom and Riemer, 1949). (P. 144.) While payment of compensation for a portion of those losses has been prompted by the passage of different acts of Congress, no financial settlement can compensate for the suffering of Japanese Americans during the war and postwar period. More favorable circumstances encountered by Japanese Americans recently have led to a greater degree of accommodation into the mainstream of American life and access into the avenues of opportunity in the United States.

Federalism: Its Role and Effects

The U.S. federal system of government proved to be adaptable and flexible in dealing with economic and political problems (although not always for the benefit of people of color). Problems arose that were solved by the ordinary interplay of democratic politics.

Unlike other countries, and despite the different backgrounds of U.S. immigrants, the American federation has been the mode of government of a single undifferentiated nation. One reason for this is that early in the history of the United States, English was named the official language of the country. If nothing else, this decision prevented perceived problems of separatism along language lines. The possibilities of the development of large distinct enclaves based on separate cultural or ethnic identities were prevented early by the high mobility of the populations. Black, Mexican American, Asian American enclaves, and American Indian reservations were nonentities and generally were ignored. The United States thus became a geographical federation rather than a federation of populations, which eventually were standardized by the modern consumer economy, the system of mass communication, and by an educational system whose primary function has been to perpetuate the one culture from generation to generation.

The growing conflicts between groups and classes that resulted from industrialization, science, and technology revived the notion of nationalism. It became crucial to emphasize the themes of solidarity, the essential unity of the country, national planning, the interdependence of the nation's various parts, a sound national economy, and federal mode of action. The values of liberty and equality inherent in a democratic system were taken for granted as the then recent white ethnic immigrants won a new degree of acceptance in everyday social activities and political participation greatly supported by a growing labor union movement. Rooseveltian reforms brought about a redistribution of power in favor of these immigrants, but not for people of color.

In the 1960s, Congress enacted a series of legislative policies, which established new relationships among federal, state, and local governments and asserted the national authority. Through the Economic Opportunity Act of 1964 and the Model Cities Act of 1966, Congress for the first time authorized aid to local communities for a virtually unrestricted range of functions. Characteristic of this legislation was the forthright declaration of the national purpose—close federal supervision and control to assure that the national purposes on behalf of the poor were served. Before the 1960s, typical federal assistance programs did not involve an expressly stated national purpose nor did the programs emerge from a coherent design. Rather, they were instituted as a means of helping state or local governments accomplish their objectives. Federal assistance programs accumulated, piece by piece, through a process of disjointed incrementalism as a response to a variety of different, uncoordinated pressures from interest groups (*Welfare Policy,* 1982).

Statute after statute of the Great Society era reflected the belief that the country's problems were national problems and that there was no limit on the extent of the federal responsibility to resolve these problems (Sundquist, 1968). While one can argue that none of the ideas embodied in the War on Poverty programs really was new (the ideas had been acknowledged in the New Deal and Fair Deal eras), the commitment to end poverty was perceived by most as new (Lampman, 1974; and Aaron, 1978). Supporters argued that any effective policy had to deal with the root causes of the problem. The federal government then had to design policy measures to improve the performance of the economy, the productivity of the poor, and the attitude of those who could hire them.

Except for the concern articulated by the civil rights movement with the unemployment and economic conditions faced by blacks, there had not been before this time organized interest groups advocating for the needs of the poor, nor had this issue been prioritized by any political platform. Problems of economic equality, poverty, and discrimination were considered largely outside the proper realm of public policy. With the civil rights movement of the sixties and seventies, the problems of poverty and racial discrimination were linked closely and blended.

The common view is that many programs of the Great Society were over-sold, vaguely legislated, and hastily created. The implementation of these programs went beyond the capacities of the federal, state, and local governments to administer. It is argued that the resulting red tape, confusion, and waste revealed the limits and the capacities of the federal government to deal with local problems. However, to think of the War on Poverty merely as a set of programs that concerned the poor alone is to miss the point. For people of color, the War on Poverty programs meant that there was national recognition that to be of one ethnic, racial, or linguistic group rather than of another could make a difference concerning the availability and access to life chances. There was agreement among the various minority groups that a national effort guided by clearly articulated goals was needed to bring them into the overall national community.

While this national effort shaped a different allocation of roles among the different levels of government, it also forced policymakers to define public problems. The allocation of roles, following clearly established national goals, gave direction to the national mobilization of public opinion and sentiment in support of specific vulnerable groups. Values such as fairness, equity, and social justice were integrated into a public philosophy that guided policy decisions and programs.

The events that emerged from the involvement of the various levels of government on behalf of people of color created a tremendous impact on the self-awareness and mobilization of these groups.

New Federalism and People of Color

The legislation of the 1960s raised the issues of income redistribution and opportunity to a national forum. It also suggested solutions to the difficult and chronic forms of poverty long experienced by people of color. Solutions included programs such as cash transfers, health care and nutrition, subsidized housing, job training, and compensatory education. People of color perceive these programs to be fundamental to their well-being and necessary to augment their opportunities for a better standard of living.

But, the New Federalism has diminished such chances. This new ideological position purported to address the allocation of responsibility among the various levels of government and to determine how government services should be provided and by whom. However, many in the service professions doubt that government, at any level, has been effective or efficient in the delivery of the wide range of services necessary to improve the quality of life of the most vulnerable populations. Instead, the government is viewed as a competitor to the nonprofit sector that traditionally assumed a key role in seeking their welfare.

In reality, the New Federalism has raised fundamental questions about who should pay for needed social services for poor people; but more important, it has raised questions about whether the goals and strategies such as the ones sponsored under the War on Poverty legislation have indeed been realized or effective. Thus, new strategies were proposed under the New Federalism.

The strategies to reduce inflation with monetary policies, to promote economic growth and to increase income and employment opportunities through the stimulation of economic incentives, and to eliminate the budget deficits by 1987, as was identified in the 1981 pronouncements by the Reagan Administration, have not materialized. Instead, such policies have reversed the federal government's efforts of the past half century to respond to the national, social, and economic needs of vulnerable population groups such as people of color.

Federal withdrawal from policies and financial partnerships with institutions, groups, and individuals has created institutional changes that will complicate further the ability of people of color, who traditionally comprise a disproportionate number of the poor, to access the range of already limited but needed services. The changes in national policies and the philosophy that guides those changes could translate into the perpetuation of the poverty cycle with its negative consequences in practically every aspect of daily living. The failures of the Reagan experiment give United States citizens an excellent opportunity to look back and reassess efforts and strengths, learn from past experiences, regroup, identify commonalities, renew a sense of racial and ethnic pride, and creatively suggest new alternatives for each minority group's determination and self-sufficiency.

Works Cited

Aaron, H. J. *Politics and the Professors: The Great Society Perspective.* Washington, D.C.: The Brookings Institution, 1978.

Billington, R. A. *Westward Expansion.* New York: Macmillan Publishing Co., 1949.

Bloom, L., and R. Riemer. *Removal and Return.* Berkeley: University of California Press, 1949.

Collier, J. *Indians of the Americas.* New York: Mentor Books, The New American Library of World Literature, 1947.

Davie, M. R. *World Immigration.* New York: Macmillan Publishing Co., 1936.

Elazar, D. J. *American Federalism: A View from the States.* New York: Temple University–Thomas Y. Crowell Co., 1972.

Frazier, E. F. *The Negro in the United States* (rev. ed.). New York: Macmillan Publishing Co., 1957.

Guzman, R. *The Political Socialization of the Mexican People.* New York: Arno Press, Inc., 1976.

Hawkins, G. (ed.). *Concepts of Federalism,* proceedings of the 34th Couchicking Conference, Toronto, 1965. Toronto: Canadian Institute on Public Affairs, 1965.

Henry, R. S. *The Story of the Mexican War.* New York: Frederick Ungar Publishing Co., 1950.

Ichihashi, Y. *Japanese in the United States.* Stanford, Calif.: Stanford University Press, 1932.

Lampman, R. J. "What Does it do for the Poor? A New Test for National Policy," *Public Interest,* 34 (Winter 1974), p. 66.

Leighton, A. H. *The Governing of Men.* Princeton, N.J.: Princeton University Press, 1945.

Marden, C. F., and G. Meyer. *Minorities in American Society* (3d ed.). New York: Van Nostrand Reinhold Co., 1968.

McWilliams, C. *Brothers Under the Skin.* Boston: Little, Brown & Co., 1943.

Moquin, W., et al. (eds.). *A Documentary History of the Mexican American.* New York: Praeger Publishers, 1971.

Pattee, R. "The Puerto Ricans," *Annals of the American Academy of Political and Social Sciences,* 223 (September 1942), p. 52.

Pechman, J. A. (ed.). *Setting National Priorities: The 1982 Budget.* Washington, D.C.: The Brookings Institution, 1982.

Perrigo, L. I. *The American Southwest.* New York: Holt, Rinehart & Winston, 1971.

Schey, P. A. "Supply-Side Immigration Theory: Analysis of the Simpson-Mazzoli Legislation." Unpublished manuscript, Washington, D.C., 1983.

Senior, C. *Strangers—Then Neighbors: From Pilgrims to Puerto Ricans.* New York: Freedom Books, 1961.

Shepard, W. "Land Problems of the Expanding Indian Population," in O. La Farge, ed., *The Changing Indian.* Norman: University of Oklahoma Press, 1942.

Swadesh, F. L. *Los Primeros Pobladores: Hispanic Americans of the Ute Frontier.* Notre Dame, Ind.: University of Notre Dame Press, 1974.

Sundquist, J. L. *Politics and Policy: Eisenhower, Kennedy and Johnson Years.* Washington, D.C.: The Brookings Institution, 1968.

U.S. Bureau of Immigration. *Annual Report of the Commissioner General of Immigration to the Secretary of Labor.* Washington, D.C.: U.S. Government Printing Office, 1918.

Wax, M. L., and R. W. Buchanan. *Solving "The Indian Problem": The White Man's Burdensome Business.* New York: New York Times Co., 1975.

Welfare Policy in the United States: A Critique and Some Proposals Derived from the Experience of Former Secretaries of Health, Education and Welfare. Racine, Wisc.: The Johnson Foundation, Inc., 1882.

CHAPTER 2

SOCIAL NETWORKS AND ASIAN INDIAN FAMILIES

PALLASSANA R. BALGOPAL

S ocial networks such as kin, friends, neighbors, and co-workers are supportive environmental resources that function as important instruments of help, especially during times of crisis.[1] Social networks provide emotional resources and strength for meeting the need of human relatedness, recognition, and affirmation. They also serve as mutual aid systems for the exchange of resources such as money, emotional support, housing, and child care. Well-developed social networks often consciously and purposefully serve as helpers to families in crisis, making it unnecessary for these families to resort to institutionalized services through publicly and privately supported health and welfare agencies. The concept of a family's social network emphasizes the idea of the family with multiple affiliations, some of which overlap and some of which do not, as well as the idea of the family as an active selector, manipulator, and creator of its environment (Leichter and Mitchell, 1978).

In this chapter, the role and functions of social networks in helping Asian Indian families cope with and adapt to American society are examined.[2] More specifically, the focus is on understanding the Asian Indians' affinity to traditional norms and their use of social networks after migrating to the United States. In the final section, the implications for social work practice are presented.

---

[1] A family's *social network* is operationally defined as the linkages and interactions among a set of significant others.

[2] The term *Asian Indian* often is used to refer to people from the South Asian countries of Bangladesh, India, Pakistan, and Sri Lanka. However, in this chapter, the term refers only to people from India.

CHAPTER 5

CHICANO SELF-CONCEPT: A PROACTIVE STANCE

MARIA E. ZUNIGA

Negative self-concepts often are viewed as evolving from the rejection and disdain that minorities encounter in the larger society. People holding the psychosocial perspective view minorities as being unable to escape the deleterious effects of societal racism. For instance, Shannon (1973) noted that "there is no way for blacks to escape self-image damage in our society." (P. 521.) Additionally, the human behavior literature is replete with references to the negative self-concepts of minorities (Carter, 1968; Dworkin, 1971; Shannon, 1973; Levine and Padilla, 1980; Logan, 1981; and Mejia, 1983).

Recently, some minority and nonminority theorists have advocated the amelioration of damage to self-concept through the promotion of methods for upgrading and strengthening positive self-concepts among minority children. For example, Powell (1983) discussed processes parents and significant others can use to address the complex issues of self-concept development in minority children. Chicano theorists Ramirez and Castaneda (1974) have delineated the strengths and daily living resources that biculturalism affords the individual. Kendall (1983) stressed multicultural education as a remedying answer. These types of positive perspectives need to be expanded so that Chicano children and all minority children may be provided with adaptive mechanisms for counteracting the effects of racism on their self-concepts.

Social work educative and organizing efforts can be used with Chicano families to promote the positive self-esteem of Chicano children. Three objectives for social work intervention include (1) teaching Chicano families about the political realities of racism, (2) teaching Chicano families how to use the strengths and resources offered by their culture in child rearing, and (3) organizing

Chicano communities to seek cultural democracy from school systems. In this chapter, the effects of individual and institutional racism on Chicano children's self-concepts are detailed. Knowles and Prewitt (1969) define *individual racism* as the acts committed by individual whites to consciously or unconsciously oppress, disadvantage, or dehumanize people of color. They define *institutional racism* as acts or practices used by white-controlled organizations, legitimized through institutions or sanctioned by law, which consciously or unconsciously oppress, disadvantage, or dehumanize people of color. An important element in this form of racism is the effect of the act, practice or policy on the persons of color rather than the intent of the act.

Theoretical Insights into Self-Concept

Self-concept provides an individual with a dual conceptualization: the recognition of one's worth as a good person and as a member of the Mexican American population. Erickson (1966) has emphasized this dual conceptualization in his analysis of the reality of personal and cultural identity that exists for Jews as an oppressed minority group. Like the Jewish illustration, identity for Chicanos also must incorporate the personal as well as the group awareness. Sotomayor (1971) views self-concept as consisting of

> sets of images organized and internalized according to group norms, communicated and reinforced over time through a variety of daily experiences and symbolic interactions. The individual discovers who he [she] is as the self-image becomes affected by relationships, expectations, failures, and by successes in experiences with others. (P. 196.)

Individual Racism

The self-concepts of Chicano children at an early age become susceptible to racism that exists on both individual and institutional levels. For example, Chicano children ages 2½ and 3 years entering preschool are confronted with the individual racism of their white peers. Research has indicated that children as young as age 3 years may be able to differentiate color for self-designation (Kendall, 1983). Goodman's (1964) studies of racial awareness in 103 4-year-old black and white children demonstrated that even at that age, children had a keen sense of race differences—85 percent of the children had a medium to high cognizance of race. One-fourth of the children had strongly ear-marked race-related values. Among the white children, Goodman found evidence of the onset of racial prejudice. Some researchers believe that children's negative racial attitudes are strengthened by the culture in general—the media and adults and children in the child's environment (Kendall, 1983).

Prejudices communicated to Chicano children reflect the norms of the larger society, norms that include a disdain for and rejection of culturally and racially distinct people. These norms usually are coupled with negative stereotypes or

Concept of Social Networks

Since Elizabeth Bott's (1955) pioneering work on the social network among 20 London families, this phenomenon has been studied extensively, especially as its relates to western families. However, it is a relatively new environmental concept for the helping professions of psychiatry, psychology, and social work, and its incorporation into everyday clinical practice has just begun. Collins and Pancoast (1976), in delineating the practice applicability for the helping professions, have indicated that the concept of the social network has distinct advantages over the other ways of describing social collectivities. This approach encourages consideration of the person in his or her setting and the recognition that behavior is a function of both the person and the environment. Whittaker and Garbarino (1983) have provided a clear conception of social networks, including why they are important and how they are maintained. They have suggested ways in which the formal and informal caregivers can come together to develop a partnership and mutual exchanges to respond effectively and compassionately to people in need of help. McIntyre (1986) has proposed that although a social network holds promise for effective social work interventions, practitioners need to be cautious and avoid assuming that individuals' natural networks are uniformally positive.

Speck and Rueveni (1969) hypothesized that the social network of the schizophrenic family is the main mediator between madness in the culture and madness in the nuclear labeled family. Their goal was to increase the communication within the social networks of the family, specifically between individual members of the schizophrenic family and their relatives, friends, and neighbors. This experiment was successful in modifying the relationships among the family members; in strengthening the social network; in providing a viable social structure for continuing encouragement, support, and employment; and in avoiding hospitalization. Horwitz (1977) found that the structure of the networks of kin and friends helped shape the nature or type of psychiatric treatment the patient received. He concluded that schizophrenics accepted advice from other members in their social networks who had psychiatric experience. If the schizophrenics did not have access to these resource people, they relied on professionals. Garrison (1974) studied the successful application of the support system with patients in a psychiatric hospital. The patients' social networks were assembled. Individuals of the networks surrounded the patients, reinforced positive expectations, developed means of handling the crises, and maintained contact with the patients during their hospitalization and return to the community.

Social networks have been studied in different environments. Scheinfeld et al. (1970) reported the successful use of family networks in working with disadvantaged families whose preschool children were showing signs of slow development. Gibson (1972), who based his research on kin networks, reported that the single, divorced, and widowed family members were more integrated into their extended kin network than the married members for whom kin are of relatively low importance. Croog et al. (1972) studied the roles of a kin network, nonfamily resources, and institutions for male patients who had experienced their first heart attack. These researchers discovered that an array of community agencies and such agents as social service professionals, clergy, and public health nurses were relatively unimportant in this crisis situation. Colman and Gatti (1976) reported the results of a three-year experiment in which social networks were used successfully to aid families with troubled children in a public school system. Lopata (1978), in a study of the support systems of metropolitan area widows, reported that children of the widows and surviving parents of the widows were frequent contributors to the support system. Crawley (1987) reported that her study of older blacks revealed that while race and culture may predispose clients to prefer certain resources such as spouses and children, others in the same reference group expected help from their kin and friends. She has suggested that because of the heterogeneous nature of the black elderly group, the caregivers have to be sensitive particularly in assessing the clients' support resources and their attitude in seeking assistance from the caregivers.

The nuclear family theory insists that demands associated with occupational and geographic mobility have resulted in family patterns in urban areas consisting of an isolated family system, which functions without much support from the kinship system. This proposition has been refuted by many researchers, including Sussman and Burchinall (1962), who indicated that the emphasis on the atomistic character of urban families has led to incorrect theories concerning kin networks. These authors suggested that family networks and their patterns of mutual aid are organized into a structure called modified extended family, which has adapted to an industrial society. Litwak and Szelenyi (1969) discussed the significance of technological advancement of society in kin networks. They found that while families were called on for a long-term crisis such as hospitalization, neighborhood groups were used for urgent tasks in crises. Recent studies of kinship in urban, industrial societies have shown that under many circumstances extensive involvement with kin outside the nuclear family continues. For instance, Leichter and Mitchell (1978) reported that extensive ties with kin outside the nuclear family can exist in an urban setting within an industrial society.

Asian Indian Family

Research on Asian Indian families has been extensive. However, in view of regional and cultural variations, research on these families has focused on areas such as the caste system, marriage customs, joint family structure, and social change (Ross, 1961; Kapadia, 1966; Srinivas, 1966; Gore, 1968; and Mandelbaum, 1970, are just a few of the noted scholars who have studied Indian families). Except for the research of Chekki (1974) and Ishwaran (1974), a review of the literature has revealed little material on social networks of Asian Indian families. Even Chekki's research was focused only on the effect of modernization on the extended kin network. In his research conducted from 1962 to 1963 in Dharwar, Karnataka, India, Chekki concluded that

> in an Indian city kinship in the main[stream], far from being atrophied has been resilient. The family without being isolated and atomized is originally fused with the extended kin network, and thereby extrafamilial kin relationships do not tend to be attenuated. Furthermore, modernization patterns and effects have not followed the same lines as in the Western nations and are not likely to do so in the future. (P. 230.)

Ishwaran, in his discussion of the structure of family in India, has warned that "one must not lose sight of the fact that even though nuclear families are on the increase, perhaps because of the greater geographical and social mobility that is found in a society being modernized, these nuclear families cannot live in isolation without active cooperation and contacts with extended kin." (P. 176.) To a great extent, the elementary family still relies on extrafamilial kinship in normal and difficult times, and kinship obligations continue to be fulfilled without the force of the law. Ishwaran has further stated that although the elementary family is perceived as the "model" family, in actuality it is a modified extended family, and this type of family is becoming the viable functional unit in urban India. Ishwaran's ideas are similar to those suggested by Litwak and Szelenyi (1969) regarding American society.

Scholars interested in studying the Asian Indian group have concentrated on the experience of the more numerous overseas groups, especially those in Africa, Great Britain, Canada, Southeast Asia, and Pacific and Caribbean countries. Research on recent Asian Indian immigrants to the United States is minimal. Except for the recent works of Nandi (1980), Fisher (1980), and Saran and Eames (1980), the focus of research on Asian Indians in the United States has been limited to either Indian students (Lambert and Bressler, 1956; Coelho, 1958; and Gupta, 1969) or the early Punjabi settlers in California (Misrow, 1971; Fleuret, 1974; and Hess, 1974).

Migrators

The Asian Indian group in the United States can be classified into five subgroups: (1) Punjabi farmers, (2) scholars, (3) professionals, (4) African refugees, and (5) Caribbeans. The Indian migration to the United States has occurred primarily during the past two decades. Migrators not only are diversified in regard to background, qualifications, and duration of stay in the United States but also have differences in religion, customs, and language.[3]

---

[3] More than two-thirds of the immigrants in 1984 were between the ages of 20 and 59 (*Statistical Yearbook,* 1984).

However, within the context of the American scene, migrants often clustered as a group because of their color and appearance. According to the 1980 census, 361,544 Asian Indians migrated to the United States and 121,000 settled in the northeast, 85,000 in the north-central, 84,000 in the South, and 72,000 on the west coast. Current estimates indicate that more than 600,000 Asian Indians reside in the United States.

Punjabi Farmers. Migration of Indian farmers mainly from the northern Indian state of Punjab began in 1895 and reached its peak of 5,000 immigrants in 1910 (Varma, 1980). The majority of these early immigrants settled in California and began farming.

Scholars. Before 1965, the conservative immigration laws of the United States made migration for the Indians an arduous task. Only 100 immigrant visas were granted per year for Indians. Because of this rigid control, only Asian Indians in pursuit of higher education migrated to the United States. In addition to the rigid American restrictions, India also had stringent foreign exchange regulations, which often prohibited any transfer of money overseas. The result of the restrictions was that those Indians who came to the United States were from an elite group and were recipients of scholarships and fellowships from prestigious American institutions. Soon after the immigration laws were relaxed in 1965, a significant number of Asian Indians who were on student and training visas converted their status to that of immigrants. This group, having lived in the United States for 20 to 25 years and having had educational and social advantages in both countries, is currently socially and economically well placed in the United States. This group includes professionals from virtually every field.

Professionals. Professionals and technical workers along with their families and relatives of already settled immigrants arrive in the tens of thousands (*Statistical Yearbook,* 1984).[4] Members of this group owe their successful migration to the passage of the Immigration Act of 1965, which embodied three major policy changes. The first was the abolition of the national origins quota system. The second embodied the establishment of seven preference categories—four for the purpose of family reunion, two for workers, and one for refugees. This legislation placed greater emphasis on family relationships as a basis for admitting immigrants. Almost 75 percent of all immigrant visas were reserved for family members. This act also introduced distinctions among skill levels, giving preferences to professionals and kindred occupations. The third policy change involved labor certification procedures (Sandis, 1980). The passage of the Immigration Act of 1965 has affected significantly the migration of Asian Indians to the United States.

---

[4] In 1965, 582 immigrants from India were admitted to the United States. In 1984, this figure increased to 24,964. During the 10-year period between 1975 and 1984, a total of 213,252 immigrants from India were admitted to the United States.

African Refugees. Because of the 12-hour eviction notices issued by African countries such as Uganda, a number of Asian Indians whose foreparents had been living in Africa for generations found themselves in a strange land as refugees. This enterprising group was well established in business in Africa. Despite coming to the United States with minimal assets and personal belongings and because of their zeal and courage, they were able to embark on small business ventures.

Caribbeans. During the time of British imperialism, tens of thousands of southern Asians were taken as indentured laborers to work in the sugarcane fields in the Caribbean Islands; their descendants have been living on the islands for more than 150 years. For most of these descendant families, there are virtually no ties with the subcontinent of India, except through religion and cultural heritage. After passage of the Immigration Act of 1965, a number of southern Asian descendants migrated to the United States, and a majority of them were employed in semiskilled and nontechnical jobs, primarily on the eastern seaboard.

Struggles

Coping and adaptation are two important concepts for understanding the struggles of people of color within American society. According to Chestang (1976), *coping* is any strategy used for dealing with threats. *Adaptation* is a dynamic process that includes the entire fabric of life over time and as it applies to the present. Adaptation probably never is complete but represents a series of emergent compromises in day-to-day living within the governing parameters of one's life. Adaptation implies both growth and change as well as stability and maintenance (Balgopal and Vassil, 1983).

Current migration of people between the countries of the free world primarily results from economic incentives; the migration of Asian Indians to the United States is no exception. However, this process of relocating from one's country of origin with traditional cultural norms and mores to the United States, which has different sets of norms and value systems, involves numerous struggles with spiritual and philosophical values, conscience, and dharma systems, parent–child interactions, and cultural barriers.

Spiritual and Philosophical Values. Every culture and civilization is inspired by a philosophy. Historically, Indian culture has not neglected necessarily any of the values of life, but it has concentrated more on some than on others. Politics, economics, art, science, religion, and philosophy have been enriched by Indian contributors, but the greatest contribution of the Indian culture is in the field of philosophy and spirituality. To understand the struggles of this ethnic group, it is essential to be aware of the key philosophical and spiritual dimensions that direct the lives of its members. The Asian Indians are characterized by a tenacious individualism derived from Asian Indian philosophy and religious background. The result is that individuals strongly uphold their right to choose their own way of thinking and acting. In the Hindu religious text the *Bhagavad Gita,* Lord Krishna, having preached a certain outlook and philosophy, advises his disciples: "Thus have I expounded to thee the most mysterious of all knowledge; ponder over it fully, then act as thou wilt" (Desai, 1946). (P. 376.) In this statement, made in the book that all Hindus swear by, the rights of individuals to examine even the words of the gods has been recognized, as well as the right to act as one pleases. In practice, this individualism leads to a precarious reaction—the almost cynical disregard for anything or anybody else outside the narrow interests of one's self and family. Immigrants with this philosophical outlook often perceive the cultural mores of the new host country with reservations and skepticism. Saran and Leonard-Spark (1980), based on their research on attitudes, have suggested that the values of Asian Indian immigrants are more favorable toward India and Indian institutional arrangements than they are toward America and its institutional arrangements, and have a prevailing emphasis on cultural assimilation rather than on the preservation of cultural heritage. The Asian Indian immigrants view the American values, especially those related to parent–child relationships, dating and marriage, and care of the elderly, with considerable internal turmoil and anguish.

Conscience and Dharma Systems. Another important feature of the Indian culture is that it distinguishes between conscience and one's *dharma,* loosely translated as duty. According to Mukundarao (1969), "*Dharma* implies that there is an all-pervading eternal order to which human actions and behavior must conform." (P. 72.) Furthermore, dharma denotes a course of action based on an individual's understanding of his or her duty. This concept is illustrated in the following verse from the *Bhagavad Gita,* as cited in Mukundarao (1969): "Better one's own duty (though) imperfect; than another's duty well performed. Better death in (doing) one's own duty; another's duty brings danger." (P. 73.) A conflict between conscience and dharma is a common struggle for most Asian Indians. They are distressed because they have left their families (especially aged parents) and their homeland. One way they attempt to overcome this conflict and guilt is by their preoccupation with visiting family in India. Even though they now live in the competitive American society, their dharma remains a strong influence and results in trips to India every two or three years. Contacts with the country of origin through such frequent visits is evident in Nandi's (1980) research findings.

Parent–Child Interactions. The philosophical and spiritual beliefs of Asian Indian immigrants often make coping with a different set of values difficult. For instance, the children of Asian Indian immigrants and their parents are caught between two cultures in their attempts to cope with parent–child interactions in the United States. These children live within the Indian cultural environment at home, but they have to interact within the dominant Anglo-American culture at school, in the neighborhood, and at work. Their world is neither the old nor the new, but both. Parents have difficulty completely comprehending their children's attitudes toward interacting with elders (they interact more on equal terms rather than maintaining distance and paying respect); dating and selecting a life companion; choosing their own career goals; and wanting to move out of the parental home. Children also cannot understand fully certain parental behaviors such as why the parents want to cling to their "old country" values. Desai and Coelho (1980) have indicated that adolescents are perhaps the greatest source of anxiety to their immigrant parents. Asian Indian parents who fear that their children may experiment with drugs or sex may wonder whether they should send their children back to India or return themselves.

Cultural Barriers. Unlike other immigrant groups who had formed their own neighborhoods such as Little Italy, Chinatown, and Little Tokyo, Asian Indians have yet to form a clearly visible residential area of their own (Saran and Eames, 1980). Frequently, slumlords take advantage of these new immigrants. A number of the new arrivals live in substandard housing in heavily populated cities such as New York, Chicago, Detroit, Philadelphia, Los Angeles, and Washington. These new arrivals tend to live in larger cities because more opportunities for employment seem to exist and various types of support systems to meet the needs of Asian Indian immigrants are available.

In addition to housing, language is a source of conflict for many Asian Indians. Generally, Asian Indians who have immigrated to the United States spoke English fluently before they immigrated. However, the number of new immigrants who do not demonstrate a proficiency in English is increasing rapidly, especially as dependents and other relatives are sponsored to immigrate by professionals and scholars (*Statistical Yearbook,* 1984).[5] Thus, the language barrier is an added burden for some new immigrants.

Because of their color, Asian Indians have experienced varying degrees of racial discrimination. Many Americans may consider the immigrants as a threat in light of the current economic situation because Asian Indian immigrants tend to be better educated, hardworking, and often willing to work under adverse conditions and at lower wages. The possible end result—overt racist attitudes. Although racial prejudice has not reached levels evident in Britain and Canada, numerous incidents of racial discrimination concerning employment, housing, and other social interactions are reported in different parts of the United States. In recent months, anti-Indian racist organizations called "Dotbusters" have been formed. Dotbusters refers to the *Bindi,* a small cosmetic dot worn for cultural reasons by Indian women on their foreheads. According to the *New York Times* (*Letter,* October 12, 1987), the *Jersey Journal* recently printed a letter signed "The Dotbusters" in which the writers said, "We will go to any extreme to get Indians to move out of Jersey City." Additionally, the *New York Times* reported that the violence against Asian Indians has taken on a new and uglier case. One

---

[5] In fiscal year 1984, 2,431 Asian Indian immigrants over age 60 were admitted to the United States. Most of them entered the United States as dependents.

130,448

Indian resident of Jersey City was beaten to death, and another remains in a coma after being beaten on a busy city corner. According to the mayor of Jersey City, Asian Indians work hard and try to better themselves economically, making the local population act violently in a manner that he describes as "an animalistic approach to territorial domain." (P. B1.)

Because of their backgrounds in higher education and professional training before immigrating, the majority of these immigrants so far have been successful in securing employment. However, despite their training, many of the professionals are underemployed because of their new immigrant status, lack of assertiveness and self-confidence, and ethnic and color differences. For example, a professionally trained and experienced engineer might be hired to perform drafting. A 1985 Equal Employment Opportunity Commission report indicated that Asian Americans constituted 4.1 percent of the professionals and 3.2 percent of the technicians of private companies, but only 1.4 percent of the managers. Discrimination and racism could certainly account for part of this discrepancy (Oxnam, 1986). Recent statistics show that an increasing number of Asian Indian immigrants admitted to the United States lack professional backgrounds. However, this trend is changing rapidly. During fiscal year 1984, 17,116 out of the 24,964 Asian Indian immigrants admitted to the United States did not have any specific occupational background. Of the 24,964 immigrants, only 3,243 had professional specialties (*Statistical Yearbook,* 1984). In the documentary "So Far from India," Nair (1983) has presented the agony and struggles of an Indian immigrant in New York who is not the "typically well-educated professional." The number of immigrants who hold marginal employment in newspaper stands, coffee shops, and convenience stores is increasing rapidly. Fisher (1980), in her study of Indian immigrants residing in New York City, has described graphically the inability of these immigrants to obtain work commensurate with their qualifications. Although lacking the numerical organized strength of other ethnic minorities, Asian Indians have been legally challenging discrimination encountered in employment (*for specific cases, see* Mohan [1980]). Kling (1987), a well-known Indianologist, has suggested that racial discrimination against Asian Indians probably will increase with the arrival of new immigrants who are not as well educated and qualified as their predecessors.

Only recently have Asian Indians had their own places of worship. In the past few years, most major cities have or are in the process of constructing Hindu temples. However, this ethnic group with different religious backgrounds has specific funeral rituals and traditions, which frequently are not understood and sometimes not even supported by local authorities.

Networks and Families

Sixty nuclear families in India who had encountered a health crisis were studied to provide an assessment of the roles and functions of the social networks of Asian Indian families within their cultural and environmental milieu (Balgopal,

1986). Although the sociocultural environments in India and the United States are different, the families studied were similar demographically to those families who have been migrating to the United States since 1965. The families studied shared the following major characteristics: they were nuclear families who were residents of urban areas; spouses in each family were between ages 25 and 60; each family had at least one child under age 18 who lived at home; and each family had at least one spouse who was a professional, such as a physician, attorney, engineer, teacher, accountant, manager/administrator, or scientist. Generalizations drawn from the study are relevant to understanding the social networks of Asian Indian families in the United States.

To determine the support role of the informal social networks of these families, family members were asked to indicate all the nonrelatives whom they and their families considered close, including neighbors, co-workers, and other friends. Data also were collected to understand the formal organizations through which these families received assistance. Data indicated whether the organizations were health, social welfare, religious, government, or private agencies.

Kinship Networks

In modern India, the traditional joint family system is disappearing quickly; however, the nuclear families have not replaced completely this vacuum. Instead, nuclear families greatly depend on their extended kinship networks, a finding of the study that confirmed the findings of Chekki (1974) and Ishwaran (1974). The families studied had a tight and well-integrated kinship network with relatives of both spouses including parents and siblings. Before their encounter with the health crisis, the number of relatives reported close to these families did not increase, but there was a significant increase in the frequency of contacts; for example, the average number of contacts with the relatives before the health crisis was 13.5 per month and after the crisis, 30.5 per month (Balgopal, 1986). It also was found that the families readily sought assistance of every kind from their kinship networks, including emotional support, financial support, household items, service assistance, and child care.

Informal Networks

During formulation of the role of the informal networks of neighbors, friends, and co-workers, it became apparent that religious and linguistic similarities were important determinants. Eighty-nine percent of the neighbors reported as close to the families were of the same religion. Likewise, 78 percent of the co-workers and 87 percent of the friends reported as close to the families were of the same religion. Seventy-eight percent of the neighbors, 69 percent of the co-workers, and 74 percent of the friends had linguistic backgrounds similar to those of the families studied (Balgopal, 1986). On the average, the families took four years to develop informal networks.

Organizational Support

It often is assumed that in urban and industrialized communities formal agencies and organizations have taken over the support functions of the nuclear families. However, this assumption was repudiated by Croog et al. (1972). They reported that 72 percent of the 345 men they studied who had incurred myocardial infarctions did not contact institutions or organizations for help during the 11 months following discharge from the hospital. Similar findings were confirmed in the study by Balgopal (1986), in which only 17.5 percent of the families reported seeking assistance from formal organizations. The number of contacts for those families who had sought assistance from agencies remained the same before and after encountering the health crisis.

In his assessment of preference in seeking assistance from kin, neighbors, friends, co-workers, organizations, and agencies in the areas of emotional support, financial support, household items, service assistance, and child care, Balgopal (1986) noted that the respondents tended to seek help readily from relatives and friends. Additionally, the neighbors were not consulted much for emotional and financial support. However, the respondents depended equally on co-workers, relatives, and friends for service assistance. Significant conclusions concerning preferences in seeking assistance from formal organizations were difficult to make because of insufficient responses.

Implications for Social Work

Asian Indians depend heavily on their kinship networks for emotional, financial, and other assistance. In the absence of such resources, they find themselves in difficult predicaments and often question the decision of having migrated to the United States. According to Nandi (1980), Asian Indians frequently talk about returning home, and, in general, report feeling lonely. Desai and Coelho (1980) also noted that "the most common complaint of Indians, including those who have lived in the United States for many years, is that they have a gnawing sense of being lonely." (P. 368.)

Fortunately, the Simpson–Mazzoli Immigration and Naturalization Reform Bill (1984), which proposed drastic limitations of the family reunification provisions, did not pass. However, in October 1986, after more than a decade of controversy and political turmoil, Congress passed an immigration bill to reform the nation's immigration laws. The bill, which largely addresses the Hispanic interest, was signed into law by President Reagan on November 6, 1986. In a victory for Asian Indians, the Immigration Reform and Control Act of 1986 retains provisions for family reunification that the earlier bills had sought to trade off for the legalization of illegal immigrants. Asian Indians lobbied vigorously for retaining the family reunification provisions (*India Abroad*, 1986). Under the new law, brothers and sisters of American citizens and unmarried adult children of permanent residents continue to be eligible for preferential immigration. Enactment of this law is a relief for many Asian Indians who for the past six years have been concerned about their ability to continue to develop and maintain their family networks.

Despite the advantages the 1986 immigration law provides to Asian Indians, they still face difficulties in adjusting to life in the United States. For instance, this ethnic group has been reluctant to develop close associations with neighbors. In addition, linguistic and religious similarities have been important determinants for them in developing informal networks. Thus, even when Asian Indians find themselves among other Asian Indians, they still experience complete isolation. Reluctance to depend on formal organizations for assistance is further compounded in the United States. To seek assistance from formal human service organizations is an admission of failure for Asian Indian immigrants, adding further agony to the guilt over having left their homeland and having failed to abide by the dharma to be close to their elderly parents. Most Asian Indian immigrants migrate to the United States so they can excel economically, but when they fail in this pursuit, depression, alcohol abuse, psychosomatic problems, and marital conflicts are the major manifestations for their maladaptation to American culture. Even when they encounter severe conflicts, seldom do they seek professional help. Instead, they rely solely on family and friends (Desai and Coelho, 1980).

In addition to their attempts to cope and adapt to American life-styles, these families also face economic hardships; they are at a loss, not knowing where to turn for help. Social service and other human service agencies increasingly are coming in contact with these families—not necessarily through self-referrals, but from diversified sources such as schools and physicians.

As the second generation of Asian Indians increases, the conflicts between the children and parents are becoming more visible through the children's behavior and the confusion and anxiety expressed by the parents. In this context, social workers might organize workshops and seminars for both groups to improve understanding of their respective concerns and dilemmas.

With the changing role of women in America, Asian Indian women also are becoming more assertive. They are unwilling to submit to male dominance and marital conflicts result. Marriage enrichment programs, which are designed specifically for Asian Indians, will be helpful. However, in organizing such services, social workers should remember that specific, goal-oriented groups such as task-centered groups will be more compatible with the cultural norms and expectations of Asian Indians (Ramakrishnan and Balgopal, 1986). Asian Indians generally do not like to engage in confrontation; therefore, they do not participate comfortably in experiential groups.

When family members do not adhere to clearly delineated roles and expectations for the different members, the family experiences conflict. For families where such conflict has been left unresolved for a prolonged period, brief family therapy sessions will be beneficial. In using this intervention strategy, social workers need to be cognizant of the patterns of socialization maintained by the immigrants before their migration to the United States. Also, an understanding of the concept of dharma is essential. Hesitancy to reveal personal difficulties and coping struggles should not be viewed as resistance in the traditional sense. Social workers and all mental health professionals need to be patient in developing a trusting relationship before suggesting options for behavioral change. Clarification and exploration are useful intervention techniques.

Because Asian Indians often are reluctant to seek services readily from any source other than kinship networks, social workers must be creative in developing preventive services. Asian Indian cultural and social organizations, whose numbers are rapidly increasing, are valuable resources, and involving helping professionals belonging to this ethnic group is a viable option.

Finally, social workers must be aware of their own stance on issues such as parent–child relationships, dependency of adult children on their parents, the roles of men and women, arranged marriages, care of the elderly, religion, and diet. The values of Asian Indian immigrants on these issues are different from the norms of American society. For effective interventions, it is imperative that social workers have basic knowledge about this diverse ethnic group, and that they are sensitive to the conflicts and pain these immigrants have experienced in adopting Western life-styles and in giving up some of their cultural identity, heritage, and traditional values.

Works Cited

Balgopal, P. R. "Social Networks in Indian Urban Middle-class Families," *Management and Labour Studies,* 11 (July 1986), pp. 143–150.

Balgopal, P. R., and T. V. Vassil. *Groups in Social Work: An Ecological Perspective.* New York: Macmillan Publishing Co., 1983.

Bott, E. "Urban Families: Conjugal Roles and Social Networks," *Human Relations,* 8 (1955), pp. 345–383.

Chekki, D. A. "Modernization and Social Change," in G. Kurian, ed., *The Family in India: A Regional View.* The Hague: Mouton Press, 1974.

Chestang, L. W. "The Black Family and Black Culture: A Study in Coping," in M. Sotomayer, ed., *Cross-cultural Perspectives in Social Work Practice and Education.* Houston: University of Houston, School of Social Work, 1976.

Coelho, G. *Changing Images of America: A Study of Indian Students' Perceptions.* Glenco, Ill.: Free Press, 1958.

Collins, A. H., and D. L. Pancoast. *Natural Helping Networks.* Washington, D.C.: National Association of Social Workers, Inc., 1976.

Colman, C., and F. Gatti. "Community Network Therapy: An Approach to Aiding Families with Troubled Children," *American Journal of Orthopsychiatry,* 46 (October 1976), pp. 608–617.

Crawley, B. "Older Blacks' Predictions of Their Social Support Networks," *Journal of Sociology and Social Welfare,* 14 (March 1987), pp. 43–54.

Croog, S., et al. "Helping Patterns in Severe Illness: The Roles of Kin Network, Non-family Resources and Institutions," *Journal of Marriage and the Family,* 32 (February 1972), pp. 32–41.

Desai, M. *The Gospel of Selfless Action or the Gita According to Ghandi.* Ahmedabad, India: Navajivan Publishing House, 1946.

Desai, P. N., and G. V. Coelho. "Indian Immigrants in America: Some Cultural Aspects of Psychological Adaptation," in P. Saran and E. Eames, eds., *The New Ethnics.* New York: Praeger Publishers, 1980.

Fisher, M. P. *The Indians of New York City.* Columbia, Missouri: South Asia Books, 1980.

Fleuret, A. K. "Incorporation in Networks Among Sikhs in Los Angeles," *Urban Anthropology,* 3 (Spring 1974), pp. 27–33.

Garrison, J. "Network Techniques: Case Studies in the Screening–Linking–Planning Conference Method," *Family Process,* 13 (September 1974), pp. 327–353.

Gibson, G. "Kin Family Network: Overheralded Structure in Past Conceptualization of Family Functioning," *Journal of Marriage and the Family,* 34 (February 1972), pp. 13–23.

Gore, M. S. *Urbanization and Family Change.* Bombay: Popular Prakashan, 1968.

Gupta, S. "The Acculturation of Asian Indians in Central Pennsylvania." Unpublished doctoral dissertation, Pennsylvania State University, 1969.

Hess, G. R. "The Unforgotten Asian Americans: The East Indian Community in the United States," *Pacific Historical Review,* 43 (November 1974), pp. 576–596.

Horwitz, A. "Social Networks and Pathways to Psychiatric Treatment," *Social Forces,* 56 (1977), pp. 86–105.

India Abroad. 17, October 24, 1986, Vol. 17, No. 17.

Ishwaran, K. "The Interdependence of Elementary and Extended Family," in G. Kurian, ed., *The Family in India: A Regional View.* The Hague: Mouton Press, 1974.

Kapadia, K. *Marriage and Family in India* (rev. ed.). Bombay: Oxford University Press, 1966.

Kling, B. Meeting, August 11, 1987.

Lambert, R., and M. Bressler. *Indian Students on an American Campus.* Minneapolis: University of Minnesota Press, 1956.

Leichter, H. J., and W. E. Mitchell. *Kinship and Casework.* Philadelphia: Teachers College Press, 1978.

Letter, *New York Times,* October 12, 1987, pp. B1–B2.

Litwak, E., and I. Szelenyi. "Primary Group Structures and Their Functions: Kin, Neighbors, and Friends," *American Sociological Review,* 34 (1969), pp. 465–481.

Lopata, H. Z. "Contributions of Extended Families to the Support Systems of Metropolitan Area Widows: Limitations of the Modified Kin Network," *Journal of Marriage and the Family,* 38 (May 1978), pp. 355–364.

Mandelbaum, D. G. *Society in India.* Los Angeles: University of California Press, 1970.

McIntyre, E.L.G. "Social Networks: Potential for Practice," *Social Work,* 31 (November–December 1986), pp. 421–426.

Misrow, J. *East Indian Immigrants on the Pacific Coast.* San Francisco: R. & E. Research Associates, 1971.

Mohan, A. "Acculturation, Assimilation and Political Adaptation," in P. Saran and E. Eames, eds., *The New Ethnics.* New York: Praeger Publishers, 1980.

Mukundarao, K. "Cultural Variants and Social Work Practice in India," *Journal of Education for Social Work,* 5 (Spring 1969), pp. 69–79.

Nandi, P. K. *The Quality of Life of Asian Americans.* Chicago: Pacific/Asian American Mental Health Research Center, 1980.

Nair, M. "So Far From India" (film). New York: Film Makers Library, 1983.

Oxnam, R. B. "Why Asians Succeed Here," *New York Times Magazine* (November 1986).

Ramakrishnan, K. R., and P. R. Balgopal. "Task-Centered Casework: Intervention Strategy for Developing Societies," *Journal of International and Comparative Social Welfare,* 2 (Fall 1985–Spring 1986), pp. 21–28.

Ross, A. D. *The Hindu Family in its Urban Setting.* Toronto: The University of Toronto Press, 1961.

Sandis, E. E. "Ethnic Group Trends in New York," in P. Saran and E. Eames, eds., *The New Ethnics.* New York: Praeger Publishers, 1980.

Saran, P., and E. Eames. (eds.). *The New Ethnics.* New York: Praeger Publishers, 1980.

Saran, P., and P. J. Leonhard-Spark. "Attitudinal and Behavioral Profile," in P. Saran and E. Eames, eds., *The New Ethnics.* New York: Praeger Publishers, 1980.

Scheinfeld, D. R., et al. "Parents' Values, Family Networks and Family Development: Working with Disadvantaged Families," *American Journal of Orthopsychiatry,* 40 (April 1970), pp. 413–425.

Speck, R. V., and U. Rueveni. "Network-Therapy—A Developing Concept," *Family Process,* 8 (1969), pp. 182–191.

Srinivas, M. N. *Social Change in Modern India.* Berkeley: University of California Press, 1966.

Statistical Yearbook for the Immigration and Naturalization Service. Washington, D.C.: U.S. Government Printing Office, 1984.

Sussman, M. B., and L. Burchinall. "Kin Family Network: Unheralded Structure in Current Conceptualizations of Family Functioning," *Marriage and Family Living,* 4 (August 1962), pp. 231–240.

U.S. Congress, Immigration Reform and Control Act of 1986. 99th Congress, P.L. 99–903, 1986.

————. Simpson–Mazzoli Immigration and Naturalization Reform Bill of 1984. H1510 and S529, 97th Cong., 1984.

Varma, B. N. "Indians as New Ethnics: A Theoretical Note," in P. Saran and E. Eames, eds., *The New Ethnics.* New York: Praeger Publishers, 1980.

Whittaker, J. K., and J. Garbarino. *Social Support Networks: Informal Helping in the Human Services.* New York: Aldine De Gruyter, 1983.

CHAPTER 3

GROUPS IN PUERTO RICAN SPIRITISM: IMPLICATIONS FOR CLINICIANS

MELVIN DELGADO

Spiritism is an important component of Puerto Rican culture. The belief and practice of Spiritism among Puerto Ricans emphasizes the importance of groups (Rogler and Hollingshead, 1961; Koss, 1975, 1977b; Delgado, 1977; Garrison, 1977b; Harwood, 1977; Gaviria and Wintrob, 1979; and Comas-Diaz, 1981). Social workers and other mental health practitioners can benefit from learning more about Spiritist group practices and applying key principles to group work with Puerto Rican clients.

Traditionally, the use of group treatment as a means of reaching Hispanics largely was ignored or fraught with limitations (Delgado, 1983). However, within the past decade, group treatment has been accepted more widely by clinicians with large Hispanic caseloads. However, the use of groups to treat Hispanics is not a new phenomenon (Rogler and Hollingshead, 1965; Seda Bonilla, 1969; Halifax-Grof, 1973; and Koss, 1975).

In this chapter, Hispanic folk healing and Puerto Rican Spiritism will be explored. In addition, the similarities between Spiritism and psychodrama will be discussed, as well as methods of adapting Spiritist group practices to group work.

Role of Groups in Hispanic Folk Healing

In examining folk beliefs and healing techniques, it becomes evident that groups play a prominent role in achieving therapeutic change (Frank, 1961; Garrison, 1974, 1977a; Power, 1972; and Sandoval, 1977). The mental health literature on Hispanic folk healing and Puerto Rican Spiritism, in particular, generally has focused on the role of the healer as a psychotherapist using an individual orientation. Delgado (1979/1980), after reviewing the literature on Hispanic folk healing, noted nine major themes: (1) the need for professional awareness and sensitivity to folk healing (2) clinical implications of folk healing, (3) the potential use of folk healers in mental health programs, (4) comparison of healers with "professional" counterparts, (5) delineations of healer therapeutic tools and techniques, (6) examinations of cosmological foundations, (7) descriptions of healer socioeconomic characteristics, (8) descriptions of healer settings, and (9) the impact of healing on the folk healer.

The literature, however, has failed to give sufficient attention to the role of the healer as a group leader. Of the three largest Hispanic groups in the United States (Mexicans, Puerto Ricans, and Cubans), folk healing generally takes place within the Puerto Rican and Cuban groups. Puerto Rican folk healing can encompass a variety of forms, with Spiritism being just one form. Puerto Rican folk healing can consist of herbal medicine and *santiguando*. The *santiguandor* is a folk healer who treats intenstinal disorders, muscle aches, and broken bones (a mixture of internist and chiropractor). Like Cubans, Puerto Ricans may practice *Santerismo,* a mixture of Yoruba (African religious beliefs and Roman Catholicism. The close proximity of Puerto Rico to Cuba and the mass influx of Cubans to Puerto Rico has resulted in greater exposure to this form of folk healing. This synchronism is represented through the manifestations of Yoruba gods in the form of Roman Catholic saints. Therefore, Roman Catholic saints are invested with the supernatural powers of African dieties (Gonzalez-Wippler, 1975). Harwood (1977) noted that

> this incorporation is based on a view of history in which Africans are the chosen people and have been experiencing a prueba [trial] from God through generations of slavery and European dominations. During this Gran Prueba [Great Trial] orichas [African Spirits] are said to have become incarnate in the bodies of Olofi, the highest oricha, while Christian saints and some heroes are lower-order orichas. (P. 46.)

When these spirits are angered, it is believed that ailments and misfortunes can result.

Santerismo healing ceremonies are ritualistic and demand much of the believer's time and energy. The description provided by Borrello and Mathias (1977) highlights this healing process within a group context:

> Latin music, meant to draw spirits, flooded the room. Moving with the music's tempo, the madrina [santera] . . . ignited coconuts doused with Florida water, and using their feet, rolled the flaming spheres around the room to purify it. Members of the congregation then approached the altar one by one, and the madrina assisted each into a trance by passing her flaming hands, which she had lit as she had the coconuts, before the individual's face for a few seconds. She then turned the person around three times, releasing them on the third turn. . . . The trance lasts from a few seconds to several minutes, and may be mild to extremely agitated, depending on the type of spirit entering the person's body. Possessed faithful may fall to the floor in a frenzied state or speak in tongues. (P. 70.)

Borrello and Mathias have delineated just the initial stage in the healing ceremony. After this stage, the santera is able to be possessed by visiting spirits, who in turn can communicate with the congregation (Delgado, 1978).

Puerto Rican Spiritism

It is essential that social workers understand Spiritism to appreciate its value as a therapeutic tool in groups. Puerto Rican Spiritism is the belief that the visible world is surrounded by an invisible world inhabited by good and evil spirits who influence human behavior. According to Fisch (1986),

> in addition to conferring protection and enabling the medium to function, they can both cause and prevent illness. One's spiritual protection acts as a shield, turning away evil spirits and hexes while at the same time bringing one good luck. If one loses spiritual protection . . . one can become ill. The illness may be manifested by such signs as pain, lethargy, nervousness, and bad luck. (P. 378.)

The importance of spirits in helping both to explain and ameliorate a wide range of "earthly" problems is firmly grounded in this belief system, and various manifestations of Spiritism have existed in Puerto Rico since the mid-nineteenth century (Bram, 1958; and Koss, 1978).

Ruiz (1979) comment has commented on the cosmological foundation of Spiritism:

> According to the theory of Spiritism, God is the creator of the universe and all of its worlds. Following the creation of the universe, God created men and later created spirits which are incarnated in men. These spirits are continually reincarnated in order to permit spirit progress. . . . Through the progress made possible by reincarnation, the spirit will have opportunity to get close to God; this is the spirit's ultimate purpose. On this premise all spirits that choose to do evil while reincarnated do so of their own will. . . . While a given spirit cannot be substituted for the original spirit in a person's body, people can assimilate other spirits or be influenced by them. This state is called possession. . . . Spirits can communicate with living persons through people who are capable of detecting the spirits' influence. . . . Those capable of using such faculties effectively are called mediums. (P. 29–30.)

Mediums, as a result of their powers ("faculties"), are the earthly agents entrusted with communicating with the spirit world and, where possible, achieving therapeutic cures through diagnosis and treatment. Earthly problems are believed to result from any one of the following causes: envy; sorcery; an evil influence; having faculties (being a medium and needing to develop one's powers); a trial or test by God; a chain (a spirit of a deceased relative); and punishment by God (Harwood, 1977). If God wills misfortune or an illness as a test or punishment, a medium cannot be of therapeutic help. However, if the cause of the misfortune is the result of any of the other causes, the medium will be able to help (Delgado, 1978).

Characteristics of Spiritists

Puerto Rican Spiritism is practiced in several types of settings by believers who possess certain age and gender characteristics. The study of the characteristics of Spiritists involves limitations, which are evident in the literature on this topic, which has focused almost exclusively on the use of mediums, to the exclusion of other healers. In addition, although research samples have drawn from different populations, most studies have focused on Puerto Ricans who lived in urban areas, lived near Spiritist centers, or used mental health services. Thus, the samples may be subject to bias. Furthermore, studies may have underestimated the impact of Spiritism by focusing specifically on the actual use of mediums—many may believe in Spiritism but not seek the services of mediums. Garrison (1977, 1978) found that among New York City Puerto Ricans, the use of mediums ranged from 36 percent to 68 percent. Harwood (1977) noted in his New York City study that 53 percent of the households sampled had at least one member who practiced Spiritism. Lubchansky, Egri, and Stokes (1970) noted the highest rate—75 percent of the households sampled in New York City indicated that members used mediums. The Rogler and Hollingshead (1965) study in Puerto Rico revealed a 40-percent rate of use.

The studies on use of mediums also have presented a strikingly similar picture concerning gender and age characteristics of those who practice Spiritism. Females far outnumbered males, with a ratio of 3 or 4 to 1 (Koss, 1975, 1977a; Garrison, 1977a; and Harwood, 1977). The ages of the participants usually clustered into two groups—early 20s and 40 to 49 (Morales-Dorta, 1976; and Garrison, 1977b). Harwood (1977) also noted that women over the age of 40 were overrepresented in the population seeking the aid of mediums.

Although little is known about the ages of mediums, usually the sex of the medium when reported is male (Seda Bonilla, 1973; Koss, 1975; Garrison, 1977a; and Harwood, 1977).

Nature of the Setting and Healing Activities

Spiritists and mediums practice healing activities in a variety of settings. The key aspects in the setting and healing activities include the type of setting, the scheduling of group sessions, Spiritist group roles, and the nature of healing paraphernalia.

Type of Setting. Spiritism is practiced in one of three possible settings— (1) healer's home, (2) storefronts, or (3) apartment building basements; the choice of setting is influenced greatly by the popularity of the healer (Harwood, 1977). Mediums who are in the process of establishing their practice invariably hold sessions in their homes in one designated room; there is a limited need for space because the number of clients is small. However, once a medium has established a practice, healing sessions can be conducted in either storefronts or apartment building basements that are used exclusively for Spiritist sessions and can accommodate 20 to 30 individuals. Regardless of the type of setting, the seating arrangements are fairly uniform. Chairs for group members are arranged in rows with a table in front of the first row. The medium sits at the table. Once the healing process commences, individuals sometimes move their chairs to form a semicircle.

Scheduling of Group Sessions. The scheduling of group meetings depends on the level of following a medium enjoys. For mediums with a firmly established center, sessions usually will be held several times each week, Tuesday or Friday nights, or Saturday or Sunday afternoons (Fields, 1976; Morales-Dorta, 1976; and Harwood, 1977). Mediums who are establishing their practices hold sessions less frequently. Sessions may last from two and one-half to three and one-half hours (Morales-Dorta, 1976; Garrison, 1977a; and Harwood, 1977). The length of each session depends on the number of individuals who seek assistance and on the size of the group.

Spiritist Group Roles. Spiritist group sessions generally have a leader, auxiliary mediums or mediums in training, core members, and clients (Fields, 1976; Morales-Dorta, 1976; Harwood, 1977; Ruiz, 1979; and Comas-Diaz, 1981). The head medium, who also is called the president, is the spiritual and administrative leader of a center. The president is acknowledged widely to have perfected his or her spiritual powers. In the course of healing, the head medium often will become possessed with a client's spirit and enter into a trance. Auxiliary mediums or mediums in training are individuals who are progressing to varying degrees in developing their spiritual powers. Consequently, their function within the session is limited compared with that of the head medium. Auxiliary mediums have sensory gifts that make them particularly important—some may have well-developed auditory powers to hear the voices of spirits; others may have well-developed visual powers to see spirits in the room. Nevertheless, they too can become possessed by spirits and fulfill the key role of communicator between the client and the spirit causing the affliction.

Core members (individuals who consistently attend all sessions) may attend sessions for many reasons. Some members enjoy helping others, some may attend to develop further their powers even though they have not entered officially a training role. Other core members may attend to find meaning and direction in life through participation.

Clients experiencing crises seek assistance in Spiritist groups because they feel that in such groups they can confront the spiritual actions that have caused their crises. Clients may attend anywhere from one to several sessions; therefore, Spiritism can best be classified as a short-term intervention (Seda Bonilla, 1969; Garrison, 1977a; Harwood, 1977; and Koss, 1977a). Additionally, Spiritist groups reflect the client pattern of attendance by being open-ended and having a changing membership.

Healing Paraphernalia. Spiritism is a highly ritualized form of helping that relies on an assortment of paraphernalia to develop and maintain an atmosphere conducive to healing (Fisch, 1968; Delgado, 1977; and Sanchez,

1980). Spiritists use any or all of the following: statues and pictures of saints, candles, flowers, cigars, Florida water and other essences, and water (Fields, 1976; Morales-Dorta, 1976; Harwood, 1977; Koss, 1977a; and Delgado, 1979). These healing tools fulfill functions related to goals such as dispelling evil spirits and increasing spiritual protection.

Analysis of Spiritist Group Phases

Spiritist group sessions progress through several phases. Two frameworks reported in the literature describe these phases. Garrison (1977b) notes that Spiritist sessions consist of three segments:

> The first is the "preparation of the atmosphere," of the "development of union or thoughts," during which Spiritist scriptures and prayers are read and all concentrate upon God and call silently upon their protecting spirits. The second is the "working of the causes," during which the spirit mediums as a group define the "causas" or reasons why the people have come, and "mount," "reeducate," or "give light to" troublesome spirits that are discovered. The third segment is "despojos" or cleansing ceremonies in which everyone participates. (P. 398.)

Harwood (1977a), however, divides a Spiritist session into five segments:

> (1) the invocacion or summoning of good spirits to the meeting through prayer, a portion of the santero rite similar to Mesa Blanca practice; (2) despojo or removal of evil spiritual influences from the congregation; (3) preparations for attracting good spirits; (4) buscando la causa or spiritual diagnosis (literally "searching for the cause"); and (5) trabajando la causa ("working the cause") or Spiritist treatment. (P. 58.)

In this chapter, a somewhat different framework was used to analyze the phases of Spiritist sessions and then to draw parallels to traditional clinical group practice. Spiritist sessions were conceptualized as consisting of six phases: (1) introduction, (2) group preparation for healing, (3) healer preparation for healing, (4) healing, (5) termination, and (6) posttermination.

Introduction Phase. This phase can be categorized as comprising three major activities requiring a total of approximately 30 to 45 minutes to complete: (1) Spiritist participants gather first, (2) healer preparation of the setting follows, and (3) *Scriptures According to Spiritism* and passages from the Bible are read, and prayers are said.

Group Preparation Phase. In addition to greeting participants, the head medium sets the stage for healing. Preparation entails lighting candles, cleaning the room, and making sure that each medium has paper and writing tools. These activities serve both to ward off evil spirits and to attract good spirits.

Scripture readings and prayers take approximately 20 to 25 minutes; often everyone in the session is involved in these activities, particularly in the prayers. The readings serve officially to commence the healing process. More important, because the medium reads in a monotone voice, participants relax and enter into a type of trance to create an atmosphere conducive to communicating with the spirit world. This phase allows participants to concentrate on summoning good spirits and dispelling evil ones (Garrison, 1977b; and Harwood, 1977). Morales-Dorta (1976) comments on the importance of this activity:

> These readings may need to be clarified or expounded on by further readings from other Kardec's books or from the Bible. These readings are aimed not only at bringing about concentration and meditation, but about developing a sense of group cohesiveness and feelings of belonging. They are expecting something to happen to all of them, a religious inspiration or cure of their illness. (P. 40.)

This phase of the healing process unifies all participants into a group and sets the stage for the next phase in the group process—healer preparation.

Healer Preparation Phase. This phase puts the mediums and participants in a state of mind that makes them receptive to the healing process that follows and, in contrast to the introduction and group preparation phases, focuses more on the healers than on the entire group. The healer preparation phase, however, overlaps somewhat with the introduction phase in that while one auxiliary medium leads the group in prayers and readings, other auxiliary mediums and the head medium slowly enter trances.

Each medium becomes possessed by a spirit from the membership and carries out one or both of two major activities that draw attention to this possession (Garrison, 1977a; and Harwood, 1977). Possessed mediums may draw figures on paper and then post the paper on a wall. Koss (1979) has suggested that drawing satisfies aesthetic goals of the medium, is an expressive media for observers and mediums, and is a source of entertainment for both observers and mediums. Therefore, some components of Spiritism meet people's needs for self-expression and enjoyment. Possessed mediums also may beat their hands on the table in a rhythmic fashion or move their hands over their heads in a ritualistic manner. These activities often are accompanied by deep breathing, which frequently leads to hyperventilation and its manifestations such as gasping for air. This phase in the healing process varies from approximately 25 to 40 minutes; because attention must be paid to each medium, the number of mediums influences the length of the phase.

Healing Phase. This phase is the most intense and generates the greatest group participation of all the phases because it involves most of the individuals attending the session. It lasts between one and two hours, depending on the size of the group and on the ability of the mediums "to work the spirits," or their efficiency and success rate. This phase is primarily an interpretation of the problem (diagnosis) and the working of the cause (treatment). However, not all of those seeking assistance necessarily receive it because some problems are not considered by the medium to be caused by spirits. Also, a client often must attend Spiritist group sessions several times before he or she is treated because mediums may not be successful immediately in communicating with the spirit afflicting a person, or some problems may require a more lengthy treatment than others (Garrison, 1977a; and Harwood, 1977).

Once either a head or auxiliary medium has achieved a state conducive to communication with the spiritual world, he or she will ask a member of the group (usually self-selecting) to come forward (Koss, 1975). This individual, or client, will engage in a ritual during which the spirit that is possessing him or her will leave and enter the body of the medium. As a result, the medium is able to act as a link between the physical and spiritual world. During this phase, the client, auxiliary mediums, and other members of the group question the spirit through the medium. Questions can cover different topics but generally focus on determining why the spirit is causing the client problems (Harwood, 1977). Morales-Dorta (1976) has commented on the importance of interpretation:

> Contributions by individual members give each one a sense of accomplishment and develop in each person a feeling of belonging to a group. Besides an intellectual exercise, interpretations provide for verbalization and projection of one's own feelings, thoughts, and experiences. The satisfaction gained through interpretations are an incentive for those who want further understanding and to progress in the espiritismo doctrine. (P. 58.)

Interpretation serves as a foundation for working the cause. Working the cause usually involves actual treatment within the group context and postgroup activities. Morales-Dorta (1976), on the first aspect of treatment, describes a typical healing activity:

> Working the causas [cause] brings medium and subject together in a very close relationship. It is not only a mutual exchange of feelings and thoughts, but physical contact as well. This is particularly evident during the despojo period (getting rid of evil spirit). The medium goes around the subject's body and symbolically (for them it is reality) uses her hands to "take away" spiritual vibrations which are harmful to the subject. The effectiveness of the treatment is further strengthened by holding each other's hands and moving them up and around their heads. The circular movement begins slowly, but as the spirit is about to leave both the medium and subject, it gains speed. (When the spirit has left, both persons are exhausted from good physical exercise and release of tension. They seem to have helped each other.) (P. 59.)

This aspect of the healing phase requires the active participation of medium and client. In addition, auxiliary mediums may ask group participants to engage in prayers for the client.

Termination Phase. Near the completion of the session, mediums commence the process of ending communication with the spiritual world; the time required for mediums to reenter the physical world generally is short—about five minutes. Closure is put on the healing process by the head medium who directs all participants to engage in prayer and by the head or an auxiliary medium who spreads Florida water on the participants for the purposes of cleansing them and ensuring their spiritual protection. After closure is completed (it usually lasts approximately 15 minutes), group members exit the meeting place in an orderly fashion. A brief period of socialization follows the session and ranges from an exchange of niceties to intense conversations about local events and the economy.

Posthealing Phase. Postgroup activities constitute an important aspect of Spiritist treatment. These activities generally involve obtaining and using herbs and other healing substances for purposes such as bathing or tea drinking, performing ritualistic activities such as washing floors, carrying out or placing small glasses with Florida water under the bed to capture evil spirits, saying prayers, and making follow-up visits to a medium. However, regardless of the types of activities prescribed in a Spiritist session, they all require active participation by the sufferer to achieve a therapeutic cure; furthermore, these activities usually involve select members of the sufferer's social network—in essence, many individuals are involved in the recovery.

Parallels of Spiritism and Psychodrama

Seda Bonilla (1969) is one of the first social scientists to draw parallels between Spiritism and psychodrama. Other scholars have made similar observations (Garrison, 1978; Koss, 1976; Morales-Dorta, 1976; and Harwood, 1977). According to Seda Bonilla (1973),

> the social organization of psychodrama and that of Spiritism have many points in common. A psychodrama consists . . . of a protagonist or subject, a director or chief therapist, the auxiliary egos, and the group. The Spiritist session consists of a patient or spiritually disturbed person (protagonist or subject), a chairman or president (director or chief therapist), the mediums (auxiliary egos), and the audience or congregation. (P. 116.)

He also has commented on the therapeutic similarities between Spiritism and psychodrama:

> The protagonist in a psychodrama presents a problem, which the auxiliary egos help to translate into a drama, relating the symptoms to the conflicting situation experienced by the patient. . . . In the Spiritist session, role-playing is performed in the name of the spirits that possess the patient and the mediums. These spirits express depressive state of mind, torrents of guilt feelings, symptoms of distrust, and feelings of aggression, fear, and love. Expressions of emotional states and their diagnoses may be represented by the mediums in a way analogous to what has been called "soliloquy-double techniques" in psychodrama. (Pp. 116–117.)

Morales-Dorta (1976) also has noted aspects of the therapeutic process in Spiritism as psychodrama:

> The possessed medium as well as the tormented person both share, on an equal basis, the attention of the audience. Both project their feelings on neutral grounds. Auxiliary egos could be used on both patient and medium. Through projection, externalization, and bodily physical movement, the medium benefits as much as the tormented one. Each one's problems and failures are blamed on the external forces beyond their power and

comprehension. Emotional parts of conflicting internalized objects . . . can be attributed to a spirit, and brings great relief. There is action by both subject and medium. (P. 52.)

Both Seda Bonilla and Morales-Dorta have made strong arguments for viewing Spiritism as a culturally sanctioned form of psychodrama.

As indicated by Fields (1976), everyone in attendance at a Spiritist session is entrusted with the potential to fulfill a helper role.

The categories of healer and sufferer at a centro are not mutually exclusive. All attendees at Spiritist reunions [sessions] are encouraged to use their spiritual faculties [powers] and to volunteer whatever they may see about another person, thus assuming the healer role to varying degrees as their spiritual faculties permit. (P. 6.)

Consequently, as is prevalent in psychodrama, the roles of leader and client become blurred and dynamic; members may engage and disengage themselves as helpers or clients, depending on circumstances and the dynamics of the problems the group is addressing.

Adoption of Spiritist Group Methods

Most Puerto Ricans are much more familiar with Spiritism as a group treatment modality than traditional group psychotherapy, either through direct or indirect contact with Spiritism. It is a culturally acceptable modality to use for help during an emotional or physical crisis. Therefore, if group-work practitioners understand and adopt some of the group methods and principles of Spiritism, they may be more successful in engaging and treating Puerto Rican clients. Practitioners should consider the following six intervention factors that are based on Spiritism as a group modality: (1) composition of the group, (2) location of group sessions, (3) group themes, (4) group activities, (5) group leadership, and (6) language used in the group.

Composition of the Group

Social workers should be flexible in developing Puerto Rican groups. A combination of various age groups, males and females, and levels of acculturation is feasible and desirable (Delgado and Humm-Delgado, 1984). Group themes, however, must appeal to a wide range of individuals.

Location of Group Sessions

The function and location of group sessions play important roles in attracting and maintaining Puerto Rican group members. Mental health settings, in contrast to generic or natural support settings, may have difficulty in reaching Puerto Ricans. Mental health settings often are associated with "mental illness"; a destigmatized setting is crucial in achieving success with this and other Hispanic groups. If the setting for group meetings is not within walking distance or is not accessible via public transportation, geographical barriers may emerge and may hinder participation by Puerto Ricans. Consequently, if the location is not readily accessible, and the setting is a mental health facility, participation may be limited to a small number of individuals.

Group Themes

It is important that social workers understand issues that will attract and maintain a Puerto Rican group. As in Spiritist groups, themes generally should fall into two categories: (1) interpersonal (involving issues of loneliness, unrealistic expectations of self, somatic illnesses, depression, and fatalism) and (2) environmental (involving issues of discrimination, use of human service resources, poor housing, financial worries, and safety). These issues may appeal to a wide sector of the Puerto Rican community and, depending on how the sessions are described, may not stigmatize participants.

Group Activities

Certain activities used at the beginning of sessions may help engage members. A flexible seating arrangement using perhaps a semicircle or tables rather than a traditional circle may help make the activities more successful. To open a session, the social worker should greet group participants to foster a warm and accepting atmosphere. The social worker can develop a ritual to officially start the session. For instance, the social worker simply may ask, "Why don't we start?"

The use of activities, rather than a strict reliance on verbalization, is important to all phases of the group. Activities can be structured during the session. For example, the group can review previous assignments or do exercises such as values clarification (Delgado, 1983). Whenever possible, structured activities should focus on key themes that have immediate implications rather than explore the distant past or look far into the future. Themes such as somatic complaints; interpersonal problems; and mood, thought, and feeling complaints can be expected to elicit intense group participation (Garrison, 1977b; Delgado, 1983; and Delgado and Humm-Delgado, 1984). Activities can take the following forms: members of the group can review key issues raised in the meeting or the group can develop activities for members to do at home. Additionally, social workers should not ignore the parallels between Spiritism and psychodrama. The use of role plays, structured and unstructured, and modeling behavior are means of using important psychodrama principles in group treatment.

Every effort must be made to involve all group members in the treatment process, and the social worker should share his or her opinions or reactions at times. Failure to involve group members may create an atmosphere of distrust of the social worker and members may quit the group. Group sessions, like those in Spiritism, should have an official ending. The social worker should allow time both before and after a meeting for members to socialize. Also, he or she should meet with group members to discuss sensitive issues that the members may have had difficulty bringing before the group.

Posttreatment activities should be an integral and important aspect of group treatment. These activities should require group members to undertake some type of task that will serve as a basis for discussion during the next group meeting. Activities should be related to group themes and are developed during the termination phase of the group session.

Group Leadership

The expectations of the group leader will vary according to the function and nature of the group. However, social workers must be prepared to fulfill authority roles, as well as expect to share a great deal of themselves in the group process (Delgado, 1983). The shift in roles from authority to peer will place great demands on social workers. The group leader should be prepared to be asked to meet the family members of group participants, as well as attend dinner with and celebrations for various members. Consequently, flexibility in meeting member expectations is crucial with Puerto Rican groups.

Language

The group process is facilitated greatly when members and leader can speak and understand both English and Spanish. This particularly is important when members with different levels of acculturation are participants.

Conclusion

The use of groups to provide mental health services to Puerto Ricans in the United States offers great potential for innovation in service delivery. Spiritism and other folk healing beliefs must not be ignored by social workers in seeking out more culture-specific ways of reaching difficult-to-engage populations. What Trottler (1982) has stated about folk healers also applies to social workers:

> One of the primary elements of the healer's role is to translate clinically sound knowledge into culturally appropriate therapy, normally by placing the treatment within a culturally approved symbolic context. . . . Thus, part of the healer's role is to take a technique, a treatment, a therapy, and surround it with the appropriate cultural accoutrements that make it acceptable to the patient. (Pp. 318–319.)

Social workers must endeavor to translate clinical intervention strategies into culturally acceptable methods; failure to do so will result in limited therapeutic results.

Works Cited

Borrello, M. A., and E. Mathias. "Botanicas: Puerto Rican Folk Pharmacies," *Natural History,* 86 (August/September 1977), pp. 64–73.

Bram, J. "Spirits, Mediums and Believers in Contemporary Puerto Rico," *Transactions of the New York Academy of Science,* 20 (February 1958), pp. 340–347.

Comas-Diaz, L. "Puerto Rican Espiritismo and Psychotherapy," *American Journal of Orthopsychiatry,* 51 (October 1981), pp. 636–645.

Delgado, M. "Puerto Rican Spiritualism and the Social Work Profession," *Social Casework,* 58 (October 1977), pp. 451–458.

———. "Folk Medicine in the Puerto Rican Culture," *International Social Work,* 21 (April 1978), pp. 45–54.

———. "Herbal Medicine in the Puerto Rican Community," *Health and Social Work,* 4 (May 1979), pp. 24–40.

———. "Accepting Folk Healers: Problems and Rewards," *Journal of Social Welfare,* 6 (Fall/Winter 1979/1980), pp. 5–16.

———. "Activities and Hispanic Groups: Issues and Recommendations," *Social Work With Groups,* 6 (Spring 1983), pp. 85–96.

———. "Hispanics and Psychotherapeutic Groups," *International Journal of Group Psychotherapy,* 33 (October 1983), pp. 507–520.

Delgado, M., and D. Humm-Delgado. "Hispanics and Group Work: A Review of the Literature," *Social Work With Groups,* 7 (Fall 1984), pp. 85–96.

Fields, S. "Storefront Psychotherapy Through Seance," *Innovations,* 3 (Winter 1976), pp. 3–11.

Fisch, S. "Botanicas and Spiritualism in a Metropolis," *Milbank Memorial Fund,* 41 (July 1968), pp. 377–388.

Frank, J. *Persuasion and Healing: A Comparative Study of Psychotherapy.* Baltimore, Md.: Johns Hopkins University Press, 1961.

Garrison, V. "Doctor, Espiritista, or Psychiatrist?: Help-Seeking Behavior in Puerto Rican Neighborhoods of New York City," *Medical Anthropology,* 1 (Spring 1977a), pp. 65–180.

———. "The 'Puerto Rican Syndrome' in Psychiatry and Espiritismo," in V. Crapanzano and V. Garrison, eds., *Case Studies in Spirit Possession.* New York: John Wiley & Sons, 1977.

———. "Support System of Schizophrenic and Non-schizophrenic Puerto Rican Migrant Women in New York City," *Schizophrenic Bulletin,* 4 (1978), pp. 561–596.

Gaviria, M., and R. Wintrob. "Spiritist or Psychiatrist: Treatment of Mental Illness Among Puerto Ricans in Two Connecticut Towns," *Journal of Operational Psychiatry,* 10 (1979), pp. 40–46.

Gonzalez-Wippler, M. *Santeria.* Garden City, N.Y.: Doubleday & Co., 1975.

Halifaz-Grof, J. *The Role of Ritual in Social and Psychological Adaptation: The Afrocuban Religion.* New York: Wenner-Gren Foundation for Anthropological Research, 1973.

Harwood, A. *Rx: Spiritist as Needed.* New York: John Wiley & Sons, 1977.

Koss, J. D. "Therapeutic Aspects of Puerto Rican Cult Practices," *Psychiatry,* 38 (May 1975), pp. 160–171.

———. "Social Process, Healing, and Self-Defeat Among Puerto Rican Spiritists," *American Ethnologist,* 4 (August 1977), pp. 453–469.

———. "Spirits as Socializing Agents: A Case Study of a Puerto Rican Girl Reared in a Matricentric Family," in V. Crapanzano and V. Garrison, eds., *Case Studies in Spirit Possession.* New York: John Wiley & Sons, 1977b.

———. "Religion and Science Divinely Related: A Case History of Spiritism in Puerto Rico," *Caribbean Studies,* 16 (April 1978), pp. 22–43.

———. "Artistic Expression and Creative Process in Caribbean Possession Cult Rituals," in J. Cordwell, ed., *The Visual Arts: Graphic and Plastic.* The Hague: Mouton Press, 1979.

Lubchansky, I., G. Egri, and J. Stokes. "Puerto Rican Spiritualists View Mental Illness: The Faith Healer as a Paraprofessional," *American Journal of Psychiatry,* 127 (September 1970), pp. 312–321.

Morales-Dorta, J. *Puerto Rican Espiritismo: Religion and Psychotherapy.* New York: Vantage Press, 1976.

Rogler, L. H., and A. Hollingshead. "The Puerto Rican Spiritualist as a Psychiatrist," *American Journal of Sociology,* 67 (July 1961), pp. 17–21.

———. *Trapped: Families and Schizophrenia.* New York: John Wiley & Sons, 1965.

Ruiz, P. "Spiritism, Mental Health, and the Puerto Ricans: An Overview," *Transcultural Psychiatric Research,* 16 (April 1979), pp. 28–43.

Sanchez, F. D. "Puerto Rican Spiritualism: Survival of the Spirit," in C. E. Rodriguez, V. S. Korrol, and J. O. Alers, eds., *The Puerto Rican Struggle.* New York: Puerto Rican Migration Research Consortium, Inc., 1980.

Sandoval, M. C. "Santeria: Afrocuban Concepts of Disease and its Treatment in Miami," *Journal of Operational Psychiatry,* 8 (1977), pp. 52–63.

Seda Bonilla, E. "Spiritualism, Psychoanalysis, and Psychodrama," *American Anthropologist,* 71 (June 1969), pp. 493–497.

———. *Social Change and Personality in a Puerto Rican Agrarian Reform Community.* Evanston, Ill.: Northwestern University Press, 1973.

Trottler II, R. T. "Contrasting Models of the Healer's Role: South Texas Case Examples," *Hispanic Journal of Behavioral Sciences,* 4 (September 1982), pp. 315–327.

CHAPTER 4

HELPING PUERTO RICAN FAMILIES AT RISK: RESPONSIVE USE OF TIME, SPACE, AND RELATIONSHIPS

BRENDA G. McGOWAN

Provision of effective services to families in which children are at risk of placement poses a challenge to all social work practitioners. Given the disproportionate number of ethnic minority children entering and remaining in foster care (Bernstein, Snider, and Meezan, 1975; Children's Defense Fund, 1978; Shyne and Schroeder, 1978; and Gurak, Smith, and Goldson, 1982), a glaring omission in the literature on professional practice with families at risk is the lack of attention paid to ethnic issues. It is common to decry the high proportion of minority families requiring child welfare services, but little consideration is given to how patterns of service delivery can be shaped in ways that are consonant with the cultural traditions of different ethnic groups. This gap is particularly apparent in relation to child welfare practice with Puerto Rican families; the limited available literature on clinical work with Hispanic families focuses almost entirely on mental health and family service agencies (Cohen, 1972; Abad, Ramos, and Boyce, 1974; Ghali, 1977; Mizio, 1979; Garrison, 1978; Delgado and Humm-Delgado, 1982; and Garcia-Preto, 1982). Yet, as Jenkins (1981) has suggested, "[Child welfare] is a service that undertakes primary group functions, and it does so most effectively when it individualizes care and preserves family values. To practice family and child welfare without regard for ethnic variables is to truncate the potential for service." (P. 7.)

It would be naive to suggest that "ethnic-sensitive practice" can have any significant effect on the structural forces contributing to the large numbers of minority children referred for child welfare services (Devore and Schlesinger, 1981). Problems of poverty, racism, sexism and unemployment must be attacked at an institutional level. However, practice that is responsive to the needs

48

of different ethnic groups can contribute to the effectiveness of preventive and protective service programs, thereby reducing the proportion of minority youngsters referred for services who must eventually enter foster care.

This chapter will examine three major variables in clinical social work practice, time, space, and relationships that can be modified to enhance the capacity of an agency to help Puerto Rican families at risk. The discussion is based on the findings of a two-year exploratory study conducted from 1980 to 1982 at the Center for Family Life, a neighborhood-based preventive service program located in the Sunset Park area of Brooklyn, New York.[1] The center was established to provide individualized help to the children, youth, and parents of this neighborhood, many of whom present numerous personal, social, and economic problems; to counter forces contributing to the sense of marginalization and disequilibrium among these families; and to stem influences leading to delinquency, alienation, family disruption, and child placement (Center for Family Life, 1982).

The center's entire service program provides an excellent example of creative implementation of the ecosystem's perspective on practice, but this chapter will emphasize selected aspects of the program model that have evolved to reflect the unique cultural patterns and service needs of low-income Puerto Rican families living in New York City. The variables of time, space, and relationships illustrate how significant components of traditional social work practice can be reshaped to meet the culturally derived expectations of clients separated from their customary sources of support and in need of a modified extended family system to provide a sense of structure, social cohesion, and competency in their daily lives.

Study Design

The objective of the study was to identify promising components of practice at the center and not to evaluate service effectiveness. Essentially, a formulative–descriptive design and several means of data collection were used in the study. The researcher interviewed agency administrators, supervisors, and workers; read a sample of case records; and observed a number of staff and community meetings and client group activities. Afterward, the eight students from The Columbia University School of Social Work placed at the agency from 1980 to 1981 were asked to keep a weekly log of their activities and impressions during the first semester. The logs were analyzed to determine the fit between students' class and field learning and the types of learning obstacles they encountered in attempting to implement the ecosystem's perspective.

---

[1] The research on which this chapter is based was funded in part by a grant from the Foundation for Child Development. The author is indebted to Agnes Rivera-Casiano and Elaine Walsh for their assistance in gathering, translating, and analyzing the data.

Then, a research assistant conducted semistructured telephone interviews with representatives of the 34 community agencies that are the primary source of referrals to the center. She also administered questionnaires in English and Spanish to 31 customers at the agency thrift shop to assess nonclient community residents' view of the center. Data also were collected from an analysis of all intake report forms for February through April 1981 ($n = 107$) and February and April 1982 ($n = 91$). These intake reports were examined to develop a full, descriptive picture of the types of families seeking help from the center and the kinds of services offered during the initial contact.

Finally a client survey was conducted in 1982 to obtain their perceptions of the agency and the specific services offered ($n = 116$). Questionnaires were administered both on a mailed and in-person basis and were available in Spanish and English. The survey form, which was derived in part from instruments developed by Beck and Jones (1973) and Beck (1977) for the Family Service Association of America client surveys, was reviewed by clients in a weekly women's group and by staff at a regular staff meeting. (See appendixes A and B for a fuller description of the client survey methodology and the sample of a survey instrument.)

Limitations of Study

Given the exploratory nature of this research and the difficulties in data collection encountered with the client survey, it must be emphasized that the findings are based on relatively soft, nonrandom data. The fact that the research was conducted at a single study site limits the generalizability of findings. Moreover, the problem of bias inherent in all client surveys was compounded by the author's obvious positive bias regarding the nature of practice in this setting. Hence, the findings can be considered useful only if they lead the reader to reexamine practice variables that often are treated as givens in more traditional clinical settings. Further research is needed to determine the reliability and validity of the findings and the degree to which they can be generalized to other client populations and other agency settings.

Center for Family Life

The Center for Family Life, a division of St. Christopher-Ottilie, was established in 1978 as a comprehensive, community-based preventive service program for families at risk. The program, which is funded primarily by a contract with New York City Special Services for Children, is located in a low-income community of approximately 22,000 families with mutiple indicators of social need. The center serves annually nearly 700 families with about 2,100 children. About 10 to 15 percent are provided brief service and the remainder are seen on a long-term basis. The proportion of monthly cases falling within the "mandated" classification for preventive services according to the New

York State Child Welfare Reform Act is well over 90 percent. This means that one or more children in these families are defined as at imminent risk of placement in foster care.

In addition to offering clients the comprehensive case evaluations and brief and long-term individual, family, and group treatment services traditionally provided in family agencies, the center sponsors a wide range of open group programs and socialization activities designed to expand opportunities for individual and community development. These include planned social activities for parents, teens and children; summer day camp; foster grandparent and big brother/big sister programs; training of volunteer staff for advocacy clinics located in several community facilities; an employment training and job placement service; and projects in some of the local public schools designed to enhance community–school relationships by the provision of family life education, tutoring, recreation, socialization, expressive art, and cultural enrichment programs. Some of the participants in these activities may be former or potential clients; others may never be counted as service applicants. The only intake criteria are that families live in the Sunset Park community and have at least one child under age 18.

The center is situated on a residential street accessible to public transportation and within walking distance of large sectors of the community. It is open seven days a week from 8 A.M. to 11 P.M. Additionally, the directors, two Sisters of the Good Shepherd who reside in the building, are available by telephone for emergencies during other hours. The overall atmosphere, somewhat reminiscent of the old settlement houses, is one of friendliness, informality, and warmth. A welcoming attitude to Hispanics is conveyed by the posting of notices in Spanish and the presence of a bilingual receptionist in the waiting area. The use of homelike furnishings as well as bright, colorful decorations contribute to client perceptions of the center as an accessible, nonstigmatized, comfortable setting where they can feel free to drop in and be themselves. The center offers precisely the type of agency climate that Mizio (1979) and Ghali (1977) have identified as essential for the engagement of Puerto Rican clients.

Population Served

To obtain a picture of the center's client population, the intake sheets for five months in 1981 and 1982 ($n = 198$) were analyzed. Although ethnicity was not recorded on the intake sheet, the information regarding languages spoken, family name, and location of relatives suggested that approximately 85 to 90 percent of the agency's clients are of Hispanic, primarily Puerto Rican, background. Almost 65 (32.8 percent) of the intake cases spoke only Spanish. The intake population comprised largely female-headed households; only 57 (28.8 percent) of the mothers were married or in common law relationships, and fathers or stepfathers were present in the same percentage of homes. Extended family members (grandparents, aunts, uncles, other) were present in only 18 (9.1 percent) of the cases. These figures suggest that a large majority of the parents served by the center are Hispanic women who are raising their children alone without significant immediate or extended family support.

Although intake appointments are arranged when requested, many of the center's applicants prefer to be seen on a walk-in basis; initial contact for 130 (65.7 percent) of the sample cases was made in person. School personnel constituted the primary source of referral (29.0 percent); however, a sizable proportion were referred by self (20.1 percent) or by friends and relatives (18.6 percent); the remainder of the clients were referred by a wide range of community agencies.

Although some of the center's applicants request a single service—such as assistance in applying for public assistance, emergency food, or information regarding procedures for placement in a special education class—most have multiple problems and service needs (Table 1). Note that the highest proportion of applicants requested help related to their children's behavior at home and school. However, the sizable proportion requiring assistance with finances and housing highlight the economic needs of the client population and the apparent failure of responsible public agencies to respond appropriately to these needs.

A more meaningful picture of family problems presented at the center perhaps can be conveyed by a brief description of a few of the intakes recorded during the first week of data collection.

> A remarried mother of three children ages 2 to 8 who had been seen a year earlier requests help for herself and her children. The oldest boy is having behavior and performance difficulties in school and behaves sadistically with his younger sister, a 4-year-old who is very hyperactive. The client has been divorced for two years from the children's father, who was abusive to her and at one point set fire to a room in which the children were locked.

> A single mother who lives with her five daughters and her father, who is alcoholic, seeks placement of the 15-year-old daughter who is not attending school. She explains that she feels overwhelmed by her responsibility for care of her father and the children. The 15-year-old says she thinks her school problems are not that serious and she does not want placement; she believes that she and her mother need help in learning to communicate better.

> A mother with two sons ages 5 and 8 requests help in learning to manage her 8-year-old. He is having difficulty in school and has been shifted between other relatives and the mother. The mother is considering reunion with the father of the 5-year-old. She also is concerned about her current inadequate housing.

> A Spanish-speaking mother of three requests advice regarding housing. She has not paid rent for several months because of her landlord's failure to make building repairs. She also asks for information regarding welfare applications, explaining that she is on the verge of separating from her husband. The social worker provides the information requested and suggests that the woman consider returning for counseling if she decides that she or her children need help in dealing with the separation.

Table 1. Client Problems and Service Needs Indentified at Intake (*n* = 198)

Client Concern	One of Presenting Problems	Problem Mentioned/ No Immediate Help Requested
Child's behavior at home (acting-out, violent, isolated, and suicidal)	91	36
Child's behavior at school (disruptive, truant, and suspended)	86	4
Child's performance at school	74	11
Financial emergency (need for food, clothing, and cash)	60	2
Difficulties with food stamps or income maintenance agency (AFDC or SSI)	48	31
Parent–child conflict and child management concerns	43	7
Housing and relocation problems	28	5
Parental behavior feelings (child and spouse abuse, depression, and substance abuse)	26	25
Marital conflict, disputes about child custody	27	9
Adult role functioning (request for help with employment, job training, adult education, and budgeting)	21	12
Child's medical problem/retardation	18	7
Need for child care, recreation	12	3
Court involvement (arrest, prison record, and probation)	9	5
Child placement in foster care (past or potential)	8	3
Other	21	3
Total	572	163

Total numbers vary because categories are not mutually exclusive; many clients seek help with or mention multiple problems.

Of the cases, 83 (41.9 percent) were termed *reference file,* meaning that they received brief information and referral services, were invited to attend one of the center's open programs, or both, but there was no formal case opening. Thirty-four (17.2 percent) of intakes were families that had been seen previously at the center, often on a reference file basis. Together, these figures suggest the center's readiness to accept the clients' sense of timing and definition of service need. What seems important is that immediate needs are met and clients are encouraged to return when they are ready to deal with other issues.

Actions reported at intake indicate that 88 (44.4 percent) clients were assigned to social workers for full assessment and counseling; 80 (40.4 percent) were provided information and referral; 33 (16.7 percent) were assigned for additional advocacy services and help with relocation; 26 (13.1 percent) were given immediate emergency assistance or cash, clothing, and food vouchers; 26 (13.1 percent) enrolled in one of the center's group programs such as the employment project, tutoring, and mothers' or children's group; and 20 (10.1 percent) were encouraged to attend one of the center's open programs such as teen night or the after school drop-in. The breakdowns refer only to case planning and not to disposition. What is apparent from the data, however, is that despite the large proportion of cases assigned to workers for ongoing individual or family treatment, the intake workers give strong emphasis to meeting immediate needs of clients for information, help in negotiating with other agencies, and concrete assistance; and they make regular use of the center's open group programs as a means of engaging clients. Such an approach, of course, frequently is recommended for the initial phase of work with low-income Hispanic families (Abad, Ramos, and Boyce, 1974; Mizio, 1979; and Garcia-Preto, 1982).

Client Perceptions of Services

One hundred and sixteen clients returned the client survey; 26 surveys were returned by mail and 90 were completed at the center or during social worker home visits and placed in sealed envelopes. Forty of the respondents used the Spanish version of the questionnaire and 76 used the English version. No significant differences were noted between the responses on questionnaires administered in person or by mail or between those on the Spanish and English versions of the questionnaire.

The demographic composition of the population that returned the client survey was similar to the demographic composition of the agency's total client population as well as to that of the intake applicants during the months studied. The referral sources for the two groups also were similar. Additionally, the range and multiple nature of the problems for which these families sought help were similar.

Almost half (47.4 percent) of the survey respondents had been at the center 12 or more times and almost three-fourths (74.1 percent) indicated they had been involved with the center for six months or longer. Three-fourths (75 percent) also said they met regularly with a social worker; and most mentioned that family members had participated in one or more of the center's other programs ($\bar{x} = 2$) (Table 2).

Generally, respondents expressed a high level of satisfaction with the services offered by the center: very satisfied, 93 (80.2 percent); somewhat, 12 (10.3 percent); not at all, 3 (2.6 percent); and not answered/too soon to say, 8 (6.9 percent). However, appropriate distinctions were made by clients regarding the types of help they had received. To illustrate, in response to the question, "Did the staff at the center give you the kind of service or help you were looking for when you *first* went there?" Of the respondents, 81 (69.8 percent) checked

Table 2. Participation by Respondent Families in Center Activities (*n* = 116)

Program	Number	Percent
After school drop-in	28	24.1
Summer camp	27	23.3
Teen nights	24	20.7
Parents' nights	17	14.7
Thrift shop	16	13.8
Latency boys' activity group	14	12.1
Mothers' group	12	10.3
Emergency food center	12	10.3
Advocacy clinic	11	9.5
Employment service	10	8.6
Tutoring	9	7.8
Latency girl's activity group	8	6.9
Foster grandparents program	8	6.9
Big brother/big sister program	3	2.6
Other	2	1.8
Community School Projects at P.S. 94, P.S. 1, P.S. 172	28	24.1
Family Life Education	(7)	(6.0)
After School Program	(13)	(11.2)
Evening Center	(8)	(6.9)

Total number of activities is greater than 116 because categories are not mutually exclusive; family members frequently participate in more than one program.

"yes" and 31 (26.8 percent) checked "somewhat" or "still working on it"; only 4 (3.4 percent) checked "not at all." Yet, in response to a question about whether the staff had given the help needed to deal with *other* difficulties, 19 (16 percent) of those responding checked "no." Similarly, in response to a question regarding how things are now for family members compared with the time when they first started going to the center, client responses demonstrated a realistic range (Table 3).

In response to open-ended questions regarding how clients had been helped and what they liked most about the center, the majority of respondents mentioned their social workers, frequently in combination with one of the nonclinical activities in which they had participated. Sizable numbers identified specific programs—such as tutoring, after school drop-in, summer camp, or teen night—as being most important. This finding suggests that for this population, good clinical services alone are not enough; clinical services must be offered in conjunction especially with programs that meet normal developmental needs.

The clients were positive about the center's staff, with more than eight out of 10 describing them as friendly, concerned, helpful, informative, and available in emergencies. More than 95 percent of those responding said they

Table 3. Client Perceptions of Changes in Family Situation ($n = 116$)

	Number	Percent
"Considering *all* members of your family and *all* the difficulties different members may have had, how would you say things are *now* compared with when you first came to the center?"		
Much better	45	38.1
Somewhat better	31	26.7
Same	14	12.1
Better in some ways, worse in others	6	5.2
Somewhat worse	3	2.6
Much worse	4	3.4
Too soon to say	4	3.4
Not answered	9	7.8
Total	116	100.0

would go to the center if they needed help in an emergency, and more than 70 percent indicated they thought someone else would help them if their own social workers were not available. More than 90 percent also said they would recommend the center to one of their friends, again indicating positive feelings among respondents about the agency.

Determining the precise factors contributing to this favorable sentiment is difficult. Many of the clients have limited writing skills so their responses to the open-ended questions were sparse and simple. What was clearly evident was the view that the center exists for the community and the staff is trustworthy and will try to help with any problem. In response to questions about how they would describe the center to a friend and what they liked most about it, clients said, "It is a place where you feel comfortable, one of the few places where you can really talk and hear"; "The workers of the center are always willing to provide the necessary help in a good disposition"; "As soon as you arrive there, the secretary, who is very friendly, helps you and the workers see you and help you fast"; "The counselors are warm, friendly, understanding people, the rooms very well lit, a bright cozy atmosphere"; "They are friendly, polite, and provide confidence to people"; "You can call whenever you want. You always feel you have someone to talk to"; "There is a lot of help if you need it. There is time to play if you want it"; "They keep in touch and want to know how you are doing"; and "It's a good center, they help you with any problems, they sit down and listen to you."

The comments of the 34 agency representatives who responded to the telephone survey conveyed attitudes similar to those expressed by clients. They were positive about the agency atmosphere and outreach efforts and described the social workers as skilled, caring practitioners who related especially well to the Hispanic community. They noted that the center responded quickly to cases referred and that the staff usually provided excellent feedback. Most also made special mention of the staff's willingness to make home visits, meet the clients at the local public schools, or both, indicating that they find this essential if mental health workers want to reach a population such as the one served by the center. (Almost half [44.5 percent] of the respondents to the client survey said they had met with their social workers at home or in some other location as well as at the center.)

Several of the respondents also commented on the importance of having a facility *not* identified as a mental health clinic but that serves a mental health function in the community. Because the agency services are not labeled, they find that many youths are willing to go to the center and actually find that it is fun. Again, the overall impression was that the center was viewed as a caring, responsive facility that manages to avoid bureaucratic red tape.

Use of Time, Space, and Relationships

The center's overall program illustrates the quality and array of services that Jones, Magura, and Shyne (1981) identified as most promising for the delivery of effective preventive and protective services to families at risk. What may be unique is the style of practice that has evolved at the agency in response to the culture-specific needs and expectations of its client population. The author selected the variables of time, space, and relationships for particular attention because they help elucidate this style, are important to the understanding of primary group behavior, and appear to contribute heavily to the center's serving almost as an extended family for its clients.

As Ghali (1977) noted, "Puerto Ricans will often only make use of social agencies or mental health services as a last resort...." (P. 460.) Instead, they are more likely to seek assistance from family, friends, or people with some special expertise who are known informally through their social networks, not as institutional representatives. Consequently, agencies desiring to serve Hispanic clients on any preventive or early intervention basis must establish themselves as known and trusted in the community. The center appears to have accomplished this in three ways. First, its administrators moved into the area in a careful and planned manner after conducting a relatively extensive assessment of needs and established ongoing linkages with the informal leaders and centers of power within the community. Second, the center defined itself as a facility open to all families in the neighborhood on an informal, nonstigmatized basis. Finally, the center maintains what can perhaps best be described as relatively open boundaries. As Abad, Ramos, and Boyce (1974) and Mizio (1979) have suggested, an agency planning to serve low-income Puerto Rican clients must be flexible, responsive, and adaptive in changing program emphases as client needs shift. This requires the maintenance of organizational boundaries that are open to environmental influences, a difficult charge for any agency concerned about organizational maintenance. Yet, the center has sustained this stance, viewing its program components as in a continual state of development. This openness to change obviously also has its disadvantages because it requires extraordinary staff commitment and effort and means that no one program is ever as carefully planned and executed as it could be. However, the center directors have weighed the trade-offs carefully and believe that the risks of missing opportunities to reach different community residents far outweigh the risks of occasionally moving too hurriedly.

The relationships between staff and clients give the center a quasi-extended family aura because the relationships tend to be diffuse, mutual, personal yet respectful, nonhierarchical, and convey a sense of endurance. To illustrate, the following observations are drawn from notes made during the initial study period:

While reading records in the administrative secretary's office one day, I was startled to find myself surrounded by small groups of elementary school-age children who had dropped by to show off their Halloween costumes to her, the director whose office next to the waiting room is usually open, and any other staff who might be free.

My meetings with the intake supervisor have frequently been interrupted by adult clients who stopped in just to say hello and tell her how things were going or to check on her baby (who was cared for in her office during his first year) and by children who dropped by to show off a report card or to talk about some activity that had just occurred in the after-school program.

The members of the women's group with whom I met to obtain feedback on the data collection instrument for the client survey—many of whom were known to have multiple familial and environmental problems—said immediately that it would be a mistake to ask about the "problem" that brought people to the center. They commented that most people come just to meet with others. They might end up talking about some difficulty they were having but that wasn't their primary or only reason for coming.

Many of the professional staff participate in the center's recreational programs, and the director is as likely as one of the case aides to organize a teen roller-skating party.

Clients are often invited to parties to celebrate some holiday or other special event.

Administration and staff have no hesitancy about asking clients or other members of the community to help in ways that they are able, for example, moving furniture, painting, refereeing a basketball game, watching a younger child, or teaching some special skill.

Sad events experienced by current and former clients, such as an accident, illness, or death of a family member, are shared and truly mourned by staff who know the family involved.

Clients generally feel free to discuss their concerns with staff other than their own caseworkers and to call one of the sisters in an emergency; and staff, although careful to share needed information, feel free to intervene when appropriate with clients of other workers.

Four factors can be identified that contribute to the social workers' capacity to build and sustain client relationships that convey the familial security and intimacy while permitting planned clinical intervention: (1) the center's sensitivity to the traditional Puerto Rican values of *respeto* and *personalismo* (Abad, Ramos, and Boyce, 1974); (2) the strong emphasis on family rather than individual well-being and development (Mizio, 1979); (3) the center's definition of problems in systemic rather than individual pathological terms (Mizio, 1979); and (4) the workers' readiness to meet concrete needs and to act as client advocates in relation to other service institutions (Garcia-Preto, 1982).

Two additional agency characteristics seem to have an impact on the center's acceptance and use by the community. One is its use of time and the other is its use of space. As Germain (1976, 1978) suggested, the two factors frequently are neglected, but are significant, culturally related variables in social work practice. Rather than maintaining the future-oriented, carefully delimited use of time customary in service bureaucracies, the center has adapted to the present-time orientation that characterizes many Puerto Rican families (Cohen, 1972). For example, there is no waiting list; and although many clients request specific appointment times, some simply drop in on perhaps a Monday morning or Tuesday afternoon and wait if their workers are not available immediately. Similarly, group meetings start around rather than at a given time. As a consequence, even the times for team meetings are flexible.

The use of a time frame congruent with client expectations is also apparent in the readiness of social workers to respond immediately to crises, while recognizing that clients may disappear for months at a time and then return when another crisis develops. This results in what is essentially episodic service with large numbers of families. Little effort is made to provide the carefully spaced, time-limited services now being advocated in many mental health and family service settings. Staff realize that this would not mesh with the environmental realities of the lives of many clients and would violate culturally derived expectations of the way to form and sustain relationships. As Mizio (1979) commented, "One does not get immediately down to business. Relationships are expected to be built on a 'familial' basis rather than on a distant professional one; the relationship must become one of *confianza.*" (P. 32.)

The center's use of space reflects a similar sensitivity to cultural norms. The staff do extensive home visiting; and the physical arrangements of the agency, in conjunction with the directors' use of a private apartment on the top floor, function to create a sense that clients are being invited into a home.

The other factor contributing to the center's effective use of space to minimize social distance is its programming in the local public schools. The agency's objective in developing the community school projects is to develop a closer linkage between the schools and the community by providing a focal point for parent and youth activities in the public schools. However, these projects are serving an additional function of providing a natural setting for staff to meet on an equal basis with families who might never go to the center. One of the graduate students placed at the agency wrote the following:

> I am really beginning to see the payoff these school activities have for work with families. All the members of a family I've been trying to engage showed up for various activities tonight; this included the mother who rarely goes out but came to watch a fashion and grooming program! The contact I have with them at the school is so important in seeing them as a family...and the school activities help to normalize problems, adding a positive touch to my involvement. It also makes it possible for me to enter the family in a less threatening manner as they see me in a different context (organizing a basketball game!).

Implications for Practice Teaching

A dilemma inherent in any effort to write or teach about practice with a particular population group is that one inevitably isolates and highlights certain variables while ignoring others. Yet, knowledge about specific ethnic differences is helpful to practitioners if it can be incorporated with other knowledge and used to help clients; effective practice requires understanding of all the factors influencing the transactions between people and their environments. Therefore, although this article focuses on selected ethnic-specific components of practice at the Center for Family Life, it must be stressed that these are meaningful because the social workers at the center view their practice within an ecosystem perspective and have solid clinical knowledge and skills. In other words, ethnic sensitive practice with Puerto Rican families at risk, as with all other client groups, requires what generally is viewed as good practice. This means that any class or field teaching about the culture-specific variables discussed here should take place in the context of teaching about the full range of significant practice variables.

Experience with the students placed at the center over several years suggests some important implications for practice teaching. First, although students were excited about the practice approach used at the center and found it congruent with many of the theoretical concepts learned in the classroom, they sometimes found it difficult to implement. This approach can deprive workers of their customary protections, myths, and sources of individual satisfaction. To illustrate, students commented frequently in their logs on the value of taking people where they are, going at the client pace, engaging parents and children in normalizing activities, and providing extensive outreach. Yet, the students also commented occasionally about their displeasure at having to engage themselves in the very programmatic activities they saw as being so valuable for clients, such as planning a holiday festival, spending a day with a client at a welfare office, or distributing fliers outside of school. They also found it difficult to experience the sense of loss of control that is inevitable when clients are encouraged to drop in and to socialize with other staff, when scheduled student or team meetings may be delayed because of a client crisis, when workers are expected to meet with clients wherever the clients are most comfortable, and when clients have a sense of ownership about the agency and feel free to recommend changes in planned programs.

Student ambivalence can be dealt with by explicit and sustained teaching about what the term *professional* really means. Is it defined by specific activities, roles, and skills, or by purpose, expertise, and task? The experience at the center suggests that students, who usually are struggling with issues of professional identity, must be encouraged to examine such questions thoroughly if they are to learn the practice approach suggested here and to obtain a sense of accomplishment from activities that often are tedious and could easily be carried out by untrained people if they were not part of a carefully formulated, professional plan of intervention.

Another related implication of the student experience at the center is the need for explicit teaching about the professional rationale for adapting traditional practice approaches to meet the culture-specific needs and expectations of different population groups. This is a basic practice tenet for skilled, experienced workers; but students and beginning practitioners who are searching for effective techniques may confuse principles with procedures and attempt to use approaches that work with some clients but not with others, regardless of culture, class, or other differences. For example, students who become enamored of the approach used with many of the center's low-income Hispanic clients occasionally attempted to use the same engagement techniques with other Hispanic and non-Hispanic clients who wanted and could make effective use of more traditional forms of psychotherapy. Such clients could be mystified by the effort to engage them in a range of activities and relationships in which they had no interest. This highlights the importance of carefully examining with students the critical variables in each case and practice setting and why different approaches work with different clients. Students should be asked to differentiate what is culture, person, problem, or situation specific.

The practice approaches discussed in this chapter may be useful with various low-income, Puerto Rican families at risk and they may be applicable to work with other types of Puerto Rican clients or with families of other ethnic backgrounds who are at risk. The major teaching point is that time, space, and relationships are practice variables that can be adapted to client needs, expectations, and patterns of behavior. There is no single, correct way for workers to handle any of these dimensions of practice; what is important is that they be used consciously and responsively and that continued research efforts be directed toward determining the most effective uses of these culturally patterned variables.

Finally, it must be noted that the research reviewed here raises serious questions about some of the emerging practice truisms and research findings. Long-term, psychoanalytically oriented casework treatment is not appropriate for all clients. Similarly, the practice experience at the Center for Family Life suggests that the highly structured, time-limited, goal-oriented services now being advocated widely are not appropriate for all clients. This highly rational, efficient, "quick-fix" approach may be congruent with the values of many middle-class Americans, but it completely violates traditional Puerto Rican cultural values. And, as Jones (1983) suggested, continuity, duration, and a sense of availability may be more important than intensity of service for most families at risk. (P. 17.) Therefore, it would be futile for an agency such as the center to attempt to implement a highly structured, time-limited approach on any widespread basis.

Given the penchant for faddism among social work practitioners and the obvious appeal of time-limited, specific goal-directed services to funding and monitoring agencies, it is imperative for educators in both clinical and administrative courses to help students assess the limits and potential unanticipated consequences, as well as the benefits, of a practice model that quickly is acquiring the label of empirically based practice. Services that are not responsive to the needs of a specific population group, no matter how effective they may be with other client groups, are not "empirically based" for work with that population. The experience of agencies such as the Center for Family Life in working with Puerto Rican families at risk suggests that a rational, time-limited approach is not an efficient or effective means of reaching these families. Therefore, the onus is on those concerned about teaching effective practice with minority populations to identify alternative modes of empirically based practice that take account of and are responsive to ethnic differences.

Specific hypotheses for future study suggested by the research reported are as follows:

■ Use of the practice variables of time, space, and relationships in ways that are congruent with the culturally derived expectations of Puerto Rican families at risk will facilitate client engagement and increase client satisfaction.

■ In work with Puerto Rican families at risk, total agency milieu is as important a determinant of effectiveness as individual clinical skill or specific service provision.

■ Although service delivery patterns may and should be shaped differently to reflect the expectations of different ethnic groups, preventive service programs that serve a modified extended family function for their clients will be more effective in sustaining families at risk than those that provide only specific time-limited, goal-oriented services.

Works Cited

Abad, V., J. Ramos, and E. Boyce. "A Model for Delivery of Mental Health Services to Spanish-Speaking Minorities," *American Journal of Orthopsychiatry,* 44 (July 1974), pp. 594–595.

Beck, D. F. *How to Conduct A Client Follow-Up Study, 1977 Supplement.* New York: Family Service Association of America, 1977.

Beck, D. F., and M. A. Jones. *Progress on Family Problems: A Nationwide Study of Clients' and Counselors' Views on Family Agency Services.* New York: Family Service Association of America, 1973.

Bernstein, B., D. Snider, and W. Meezan. *Foster Care Needs and Alternatives to Placement.* Albany, N.Y.: New York State Board of Social Welfare, 1975.

Center for Family Life. *A Progress Report, April 1, 1982.* Brooklyn, N.Y.: Center for Family Life, 1982.

Children's Defense Fund. *Children Without Homes.* Washington, D.C.: Children's Defense Fund, 1978.

Cohen, R. E. "Principles of Preventive Mental Health Programs for Ethnic Minority Populations: The Acculturation of Puerto Ricans to the United States," *American Journal of Psychiatry,* 128 (June 1972), pp. 79–83.

Delgado, M., and D. Humm-Delgado. "Natural Support Systems: Source of Strength in Hispanic Communities," *Social Work,* 27 (January 1982), pp. 83–90.

Devore, W., and E. G. Schlesinger. *Ethnic-Sensitive Social Work Practice.* St. Louis, Mo.: C. V. Mosby Co., 1981.

Garcia-Preto, N. "Puerto Rican Families," in M. McGoldrick, J. K. Pearce, and J. Giordano, eds., *Ethnicity and Family Therapy.* New York: Guilford Press, 1982.

Garrison, V. "Support Systems of Schizophrenic and Non-schizophrenic Puerto Rican Migrant Women in New York City," *Schizophrenia Bulletin,* 4 (1978), pp. 561–596.

Germain, C. G. "Space: An Ecological Variable in Social Work Practice," *Social Casework,* 59 (November 1978), pp. 515–522.

———. "Time: An Ecological Variable in Social Work Practice." *Social Casework,* 57 (July 1976), pp. 419–426.

Ghali, S. B. "Culture Sensitivity and the Puerto Rican Client," *Social Casework,* 58 (October 1977), pp. 459–468.

———. "Understanding Puerto Rican Traditions." *Social Work,* 27 (January 1982), pp. 98–103.

Gurak, D. T., D. A. Smith, and M. F. Goldson. *The Minority Foster Child: A Comparative Study of Hispanic, Black and White Children,* Monograph No. 9. New York: Hispanic Research Center, Fordham University, 1982.

Jenkins, S. *The Ethnic Dilemma in Social Services.* New York: Free Press, 1981.

Jones, M. A., S. Magura, and A. Shyne. "Effective Practice with Families in Protective and Preventive Services," *Child Welfare,* 60 (February 1981), pp. 67–80.

Jones, M. A. *A Second Chance for Families—Five Years Later: Executive Summary.* Child Welfare League of America, November 1983.

Malucchio, A. *Learning from Clients*. New York: Free Press, 1979.

Mizio, E. (ed.). *Puerto Rican Task Force Report*. New York: Family Service Association of America, 1979.

Shyne A., and A. Schroeder. *National Study of Social Services to Children and Their Families*. Washington, D.C.: U.S. Department of Health, Education, and Welfare, 1978.

Appendix A
A Methodological Note on the Client Survey

Both clients and staff recommended that questions related to nationality or place of birth and income or welfare status be eliminated from the questionnaire because of the numbers of undocumented aliens in the area and the frequent fear among welfare recipients about disclosing any information that might affect eligibility status. This resulted in the loss of some valuable information but was deemed essential to obtain client support for the survey.

The final survey instrument was pretested with 20 clients from whom the response rate after the initial mailing was 60 percent. It was then mailed in May 1982 to 101 of the 107 clients who were listed on the intake sheets from February through April 1981. (The names of six clients were removed from the mailing list at the request of their workers because it was felt the questionnaire would create unnecessary stress. These included clients whose parental rights had been terminated, who were the subjects of a child abuse complaint, and who were severely decompensated.) Both English and Spanish versions of the questionnaire were prepared. The secretary/receptionist who knew most of the clients decided whether to send the English or Spanish version. Bilingual clients were sent the English version to minimize the amount of translating that would be required later.

The response to the initial mailing and a follow-up letter produced only 28 responses (27.8 percent), 26 of which were usable. Almost as many were returned as "Addressee Unknown" ($n = 24$). This figure indicates the degree of mobility and disorganization among this client population; however, this sample loss problem, in conjunction with low response rate, forced a revision in the data collection plan. The original intent had been to survey clients approximately one year after intake, to administer the questionnaire through the mail to preserve anonymity, and to relate the data from the client surveys to the information on the intake report forms. Because this did not yield an adequate response rate, it was decided to administer the questionnaire on an in-person basis after the school year resumed in the fall.

During the last two weeks in September and the first week in October 1982, all clients who came to the center were asked to fill out a questionnaire. These were administered by the secretary/receptionist, who again decided whether to use the English or Spanish version and asked clients to return the questionnaires to a sealed box in her office. In addition, all workers who made home visits during this period were asked to give the questionnaires to their clients and to return them in a sealed envelope. This in-person approach yielded an additional 90 completed survey forms. Agency monthly statistics indicated that this number represented a sizeable proportion of the total number of clients seen in any three-week period. However, it was difficult to determine how many clients were missed through this approach because workers did not always remember to give clients questionnaires during their home visits, some clients took the questionnaires but did not return them, and the receptionist was not certain how reliably the questionnaires were distributed during the evening hours when she was not in the office. Also, despite the use of sealed envelopes, some halo effect must be expected when questionnaires are administered in person, especially because a number of clients with limited literacy skills requested help in writing their responses. No significant differences were noted between the responses given on the questionniares administered by mail or in person.

Telephone follow-up to the mailed questionnaires or in-person interviews as recommended by Beck (1977) would have been a preferable means of data collection. However, a large proportion of the center's client population did not have telephones; and cost factors prohibited in-person interviews.

The survey responses indicated that it tapped a population of what would have to be termed satisfied consumers. This is, of course, one of the drawbacks to any client survey because those who are satisfied are more likely to respond than those who are not. The problem of bias was accentuated in this study because of the need to administer questionnaires in person rather than by mail, a procedure that essentially guaranteed respondents who were sufficiently pleased with the agency's services to remain engaged. Consequently, one could not make any generalizations to the larger population of actual or potential clients seen at the center. The survey results are used here solely to help identify the factors contributing to successful engagement and work with a group of clients traditionally viewed as "hard to reach" and resistant to clinical services of any kind (Ghali, 1977).

The high levels of client satisfaction expressed are consistent with the findings of other consumer surveys and say little about service effectiveness. As Malucchio (1979) has suggested, questions therefore must be raised about the meaningfulness of such findings. However, they have been reported because they do at least substantiate client engagement with the agency, a necessary first—and often overlooked—phase in evaluations of program effectiveness with families at risk.

Appendix B
Center for Family Life Client Survey

The Center for Family Life was established to help meet the needs of families in Sunset Park. You can help us to evaluate and improve our services by taking a little time to answer this questionnaire.

Please feel free to state your opinions honestly. You do not have to sign your name; your answers are confidential and will not affect the services you are now receiving in any way. However, we hope to use the information you give us to improve the services we offer in the future.

Thank you for your help!

:·**********************************

1. Your sex: Female _____   2.   Your age: Under 18_____
                Male   _____   18 to 25_____
                                                       25 to 35_____
                                                       35 to 44_____
                                           45 or older_____

3. What language do you speak at home? Spanish_____
                                       English_____
                                       Other _____

4. How many children do you have living at home?_____

5. When was the first time you came to the Center ?

   Within the last month_____   About 6 to 12 months ago_____
   About 2 to 3 months ago_____   About 1-2 years ago_____

6. How did you first learn about the Center?

   Friend_____   Community Social Agency_____
   Neighbor_____   Legal Aid_____
   Family member_____   Church_____
   Written flier_____   Hospital or Clinic_____
   School_____   Police_____
   Child Welfare Agency_____   Court_____
   Other (Please describe)_____

7. About how many times have you been to the Center?

   1-3_____   4-6_____   7-12_____   More than 12 times_____

8. What was the reason for your going to the Center the first time?

   _____

   _____

   _____

9. Did the staff at the Center give you the kind of service or help you were looking for when you first went there?

   Yes_____   Somewhat_____   Not at all_____   Still working on it_____

Appendix B (Continued)

10. Have you or other members of your family had any <u>other</u> needs or difficulties that you have asked the staff at the Center to help you with?

Problem with welfare department_____

Problem with gas or telephone company_____

Housing problem_____

Medical problem of 1 or more children_____

Own health problem_____

School problem with 1 or more children_____

Behavior problem of 1 or more children_____

Need for day care or child care_____

Looking for recreation program for 1 or more children_____

Help with elderly or sick relative_____

Trouble with the police_____

Trouble with the court_____

Trouble with husband or wife_____

Trouble with the man or woman you're living or involved with_____

Trouble with parent(s) or other relatives_____

Need for tutoring_____

Need for job or work training_____

Need for emergency food, clothing, or money_____

Need for emergency place to stay_____

Trouble with child welfare agency_____

Trouble with other social or community agency_____

Problem with food stamps_____

Other (Please describe)_____

_____

11. Did they give you the help you needed to deal with any of these difficulties or problems?

Yes_____   Didn't ask for any other help_____

No _____   Too soon to say_____

If yes, how did they help you?_____

_____

12. Have you met regularly with a social worker from the Center? Yes_____ No_____

If yes, about how many times have you met?_____

Where do you usually meet? At the Center_____   At home_____
                            Both at the Center and at home_____

13. Please check <u>all</u> the other activities at the Center that you or a member of your family have participated in:

Parent's Night _____   Employment Service _____

Teen Night _____   Thrift Shop _____

Drop-In Program _____   Adolescent Group_____

Advocacy Clinic _____   Summer Day Camp_____

Mothers' Group_____   Tutoring Program _____

Boys' Group_____   Emergency Food Center _____

Girls' Group_____   Big Brother-Big Sister Program_____

Foster Grandparents Program_____

Other (Please describe)_____

_____

Appendix B (Continued)

14. Have you or other members of your family attended any of the programs the Center runs at the local public schools?

No _____   Yes, Program at P.S. 1   Yes, Program at P.S. 172
                 Family Life Education_____   Family Life Education_____
Yes, Program   Afterschool Program _____   Afterschool Program_____
  at P.S. 94___   Evening Center_____   Evening Center_____

15. How many staff at the Center have you met since you first started going there?_____

16. Since you started coming to the Center, has there been any change for the better or worse in the way members of your family get along with each other?   Would you say you now get along:

Much better_____   Somewhat worse_____
Somewhat better_____   Much worse_____
Same_____   Never a problem_____
Better in some ways,   Too soon to say_____
  worse in others_____

17. Considering all members of your family and all the difficulties different members may have had, how would you say things are now compared with when you first came to the Center?

Much better_____   Somewhat worse_____
Somewhat better_____   Much worse_____
Same_____   Too soon to say_____
Better in some ways,
  worse in others_____

18. In general, do you think that the staff at the Center are:

	Very Much	Somewhat	Not at all
Friendly and concerned			
Helpful			
Informative			
Available in emergencies			

19 In general, how satisfied are you with the services offered by the Center?

Very much_____   Not at all_____
Somewhat_____   Too soon to say_____

20. Which of the services or programs offered by the Center do you think have been mose helpful or enjoyable for you and the members of your family? (List as many as you wish)

_____

_____

_____

_____

_____

Appendix B (Continued)

21. If you needed help in an emergency, would you call or go to the Center?

    Yes _____ No _____ If no, where would you go for help?_____

    _____

    If yes, who would you try to talk with?

    Your social worker_____ One of the Sisters?_____

    One of the group leaders_____ Other (Please describe)_____

    If (s)he were not available, do you think someone else would help you? Yes___No___

22. If you wanted to tell someone about the Center, how would you describe it?

    _____

    _____

    _____

23. Have you gone to other social agencies in the past to ask for any type of help or assistance?   Yes_____   No_____

    If yes, how would you compare the Center to other agencies? Is there anything that makes it different?_____

    _____

24. Would you suggest to one of your friends that he or she should go to the Center?

    Yes _____ No _____ If yes, what would you recommend that (s)he go to the Center for?_____

    _____

25. What do you like most about the Center? _____

    _____

    _____

26. What do you like least about the Center?_____

    _____

    _____

27. If you were in charge of the Center, what things would you change?   What suggestions do you have for ways the Center might offer better service?

    _____

    ____ _____

    _____

Thanks very much for your help.

negative expectations of the minority adult or child. From a symbolic interaction perspective, the Chicano child faces the difficult task of creating a self-concept when the child is confronted with two distinct sets of norms, expectations, and interactions that may categorize the child as a certain type of person (Blumer, 1969). One set of norms and expectations is derived from the *sustaining system,* or those institutions and the majority society that typically treat the minority person unjustly by devaluing and disrespecting him or her (Chestang, 1976). The other set of norms and expectations is derived from the minority child's *nurturing system.* The nurturing system includes families and minority communities that generally offer support, nurturance, and buffering from a hostile society.

In *symbolic interaction theory,* an individual's behavior is predicated on the qualities and roles that he or she believes pertain to the self (Blumer, 1969). Blumer has noted that individuals can be objects of their own behavior, defining the kind of people they are and, based on the definition, directing their behavior. For the minority child, the symbolic interaction theory means the child must address the task of formulating an identity and defining qualities and roles, considering the negative societal expectations and negative symbolic interactions that occur particularly in school environments. According to May (1976),

> if we examine the expectations of a racist society about an ethnic group...the expectations, for example, of social incompetence, aggression, or passivity—then that behavior will occur often enough to confirm the substance of the prejudice. It is a monumentous task for a child to overcome the forces of social expectation through the development of his [her] own ethnic identity. (P. 45.)

Institutional Racism

Like individual racism, institutional racism permeates a system to which young Chicano children receive substantive exposure—the school system. Institutional racism within schools contributes to the negative self-identity of Chicano children. The school system that only reflects a white, middle-class orientation jeopardizes Chicano children. Banks (1984) identified the following as adversely affecting minority children: the paucity of ethnic and racial school staff; the lack of multicultural content in the formalized and hidden curricula; the lack of culturally pluralistic teaching strategies and materials; and testing and counseling programs that are culturally biased. Furthermore, the controversy involving the Reagan Administration and the funding of bilingual programs depicts the lack of concern with and awareness of the importance of language to a child's identity. "To the child who speaks a language other than English and whose parents speak another language, language is an important representation of his [her] ethnic identity" (May, 1976). (P. 50.) For the Chicano children who are warned not to speak their native language on school premises, the unequivocal message is that their ethnic heritage is inferior and worthless.

Erickson (1963) has found that school systems may foster negative self-concepts through mechanisms that reinforce the message to the children that skin color and parental background will decide their worth, rather than their will to learn. One mechanism is the kind and quality of interaction between teachers and children. The U.S. Commission on Civil Rights found that disparity in classroom interaction exists as is evident in the findings of the commission's study on the way teachers treated white and Chicano students (*Toward Quality Education,* 1975). In the study, conditions and practices in schools in Arizona, California, Colorado, New Mexico, and Texas were examined. Findings showed that white children received 36 percent more praise than Chicano children; teachers accepted and used the ideas of white children 40 percent more times than the ideas of Chicano children. The white child received 40 percent more positive response (warmth and approval) than the Chicano child. Teachers also spent 23 percent more time talking to white students than to Chicano students.

Other mechanisms that contribute to negative self-concept include ability grouping or tracking, which is decreasing in practice but still evident. Rodriquez (1983) noted that twice as many whites are in high ability classes than are Chicano students and twice as many Chicano students are in low-ability classes than are white students. He maintained that the self-fulfilling prophecy effect of being placed in a slow class can magnify the minority child's sense of worthlessness. He recommended that local school boards place greater attention to how these assignments are made to minimize placements based on inappropriate criteria.

Ramirez and Castaneda (1974) viewed the lack of cultural democracy in school systems as harming minority children. These educators believe that teachers should use teaching styles that fit the learning styles of culturally different students. For instance, although the majority of minority children use a field-sensitive style of learning, they are taught by teachers who typically follow a field-independent approach. This frustrates the learning process and contributes to minority children devaluing the experiences they acquired in their homes and neighborhoods.

These types of behaviors contribute to lower self-esteem for Chicano children, underscoring the unequal educational opportunities of minority children. Therefore, it is not coincidential that Hispanic youngsters have the highest school dropout rate in the nation (U.S. Bureau of the Census, 1983). Various scholars argue that this dropout rate results from insensitivity to the different values and learning styles of minority children that is perpetuated by school policies (Kendall, 1983; Rodriquez, 1983; Rodriguez, 1983; and Banks, 1984).

The examples of individual and institutional racism depict the barriers minority children, and Chicano children, face in their quest for self-identity. Several factors that may contribute to the perpetuation of barriers include parents who are unaware of the identity needs of their children and the problematic aspects of this quest; role models and cultural supports, which are not evident in the school environments; and Chicano children who come from lower class settings where the variable of class and or poverty may contribute additional negative expectations and interactions from peers and teachers.

These realities underscore the need for a proactive disposition toward the rearing and nurturing of positive self-concepts for Chicano children. This proactive stance needs to be instilled within the family system where parents can address this need in a more substantive and consistent fashion. A reactive stance also must be taken by the Chicano community to ameliorate the negative effect of school systems on Chicano children.

Social workers should undertake several intervention schemes in their work with Hispanic families and communities.

Theory and Practice Perspectives

The proactive stance should include the education of families and communities about the strengths their culture offers and the politicalization of families and communities regarding racism.

In work with both families and communities, a politicization process is encouraged whereby Chicano families and their respective communities can comprehend the dynamics of racism and how it functions to limit their access to societal resources. In view of the conservative and possibly defensive stance that some families and communities may express, especially those recently immigrated families who hold high ideals about the United States, it is preferable to enlist a cultural educational stance first, as a lead-in to the politicization process.

Cultural Education

People often may assume that Chicanos recognize the positive aspects of their culture. However, many families require elucidation of the strengths their culture offers so that these families can consciously apply these strengths in child rearing. The use of the notion of social competence, a core principle in human behavior theory, may aid in this cultural comprehension. It also is a pivotal construct in Chicano culture, one that characterizes the interpersonal and humanistic perspectives that describe the Chicano culture.

The idea of social competence is closely tied to the Mexican concept of *una persona bien educada* (an educated person). Una persona bien educada is an individual who has become knowledgeable and skilled in human relationships. Such a person understands the importance of interacting and relating to other humans with respect and dignity. He or she recognizes, believes, and values, that above all else in this life, interactions and involvement with other humans should be the first priority and a major concern (Zuniga, 1987). In U.S. culture, an *educated person* is someone who usually has attained at least a college education, a master's degree, or a doctorate. In Mexican or Chicano culture, a person could be illiterate and still be considered una persona bien educada, or have a PhD and not be in this category. Wahab (1973) found that Chicano families in his research sample viewed people who are educated as those trained in human understanding and interpersonal relationships.

In human behavior theory, the concept of competence is derived from Robert White's (1960) theory of motivation. White asserted that Freud's instinct theory did not explain adequately the curiosity and quest for new experiences that occur in human development. White argued that a human's prowess as a learner does not stem solely from satisfying constantly recurring needs. Instead, this motivation to learn is a desire to become competent, to engage with one's environment through active manipulation and exploration. White explained that *competence* means fitness or ability.

> The concept of competence subsumes the whole realm of learned behavior whereby the child comes to deal effectively with their environment. It includes manipulation, locomotion, the building of cognitive maps and skilled actions and the growth of effective behavior in relation to other people. The directed persistence of such behavior warrants the assumption of a motivation independent of drives, here called effectance motivation, which has its immediate satisfaction in a feeling of efficacy and its adaptive significance in the growth of competence. (P. 137.)

The construct of competence is emphasized in relation to its social dimension. The desired sense of efficacy is derived not only from interaction with the inanimate environment, but from the human environment. As White noted, the sense of social competency may be more important than skills for interacting with the inanimate environment.

The literature on Chicano culture is replete with concepts that undergird the construct of social competence. For example, such ideas as *respecto* (respect) and *personalismo* (personableness) (Aguilar, 1972; and Gomez and Cook, 1978) underscore the importance and value placed on human relationships in terms of the Chicano world view. Pivotal to this orientation is the centrality of the family in each person's life perspective. Social competence is taught mainly through the family medium and strengthened via larger Chicano community circles. The values tend to orient Chicanos to a humanistic view that often clashes with modern and worldly values that emphasize materialism and prestige.

Regarding the literature that addresses the asserted cultural deprivation of minorities and, in this case, of Chicanos, it is critical to recognize the strengths and dimensions of human development that the Chicano culture supports. These dimensions also are recognizable among Chicano children. In their research on Chicano, black, and white children, Goodman and Beman (1971) noted that

> the ideal patterns offered us by the Negro and Anglo children are quite different from those of the Barrio, and it is reasonable to suppose that their behavior patterns differ too. Ideal pattern statements are prime indicators of the standards to which a people aspire and teach their children to accept as proper standards. Without such standard-setting and such teaching children are unlikely even to pay lip service to

values which run counter to ego impulses, immediate gratifications and the gross ac-
quisitiveness which seems to appear in the cultures of all urban industrial societies.
Among Barrio children, though not among Negro and Anglo children, the ideal patterns run strongly counter to these orientations. (P. 116.)

These values included the emphasis on parents and kin in their daily lives and
interactions—affective and friendship feelings. In contrast, white and black
children in the Goodman and Beman (1971) study were more oriented toward
age-mates and friends. Chicano children's respect for and relatedness to their
grandparents exhibited a pronounced caring. The protocol found in these Barrio children was an awareness of and emphasis on people in their environment.
This perspective involved a concern for and sensitivity to the feelings and wishes
of people important to the children. The children were trained early to help,
to be disciplined, and to respect others. The Barrio children valued work as
a way to participate with and contribute to their families—the children valued
social interaction. In addition, concepts of power, wealth, and high prestige
either were valued minimally or were just not considered in the vocational
aspirations offered by the children. Study findings indicated that the Chicano
value of work and training orientation contributed the kinds of skills that nur-
ture and enhance human social interaction or the social competence to which
White (1960) referred.

Chicano families need to know that these kinds of values and training indeed promote competencies in their children that are humanistic and will
facilitate an orientation to people rather than an orientation to objects. Explanation of social competency may result in the strengthening of pride in
Chicano group membership, which would contribute to positive self-esteem.

A variety of other areas within the Chicano culture exist wherein families
can be taught social insights. One critical area involves the viability of being
bicultural. Families must be taught that biculturalism facilitates their children's
participation in two cultural traditions. Mercer (1977) has expressed her view
that the bicultural child demonstrates a more complex level of development
than a monocultural child. Ramirez (1977) has noted that biculturalism provides added resources for solving daily problems. He has classified these
resources as flexibility, synthesis, and expansion. (P. 343.) The expanded
cultural awareness that bicultural persons possess enhances their flexibility in
interpersonal relationships so that they can accept and appreciate cultural differences to a larger extent. As a result of flexibility, they are more receptive
to culturally and racially different people and their world views. As Ramirez
(1979) has indicated,

多multicultural persons can benefit from the life experiences and guiding life
philosophies of people of other cultures. In addition, this ability to relate to others
exposes them to cognitive styles or aspects of cognitive styles with which they are
unfamiliar, thereby stimulating development of bicognitive functioning. These synthesis experiences, and the resultant sociocultural modules, which make it possible

for individuals to function bicognitively and interact meaningfully with people and institutions of other cultures, might result in the creativity and adaptability that Stonequist (1964) and Adler (1974) observed in multicultural people. (P. 350.)

Ramirez also has delineated three important benefits of biculturalism that highlight the social competence principle: (1) a person's life is given meaning, (2) a person's meaningful and effective functioning in different sociocultural settings or in varied situations of the same culture is facilitated, and (3) a person can develop meaningful interpersonal relationships with people of different backgrounds. (P. 353.) Multiculturalism, besides helping to promote social competence, allows for a humanistic orientation. Social workers can teach Chicano families the viability of being bicultural, which will enable the families to take pride in being both Mexican and American, reinforcing their sense of being good persons and belonging to an ethnic group with viable values and customs. This education effort promotes Erickson's dual conceptualization of self-identity as an effective identity framework for minorities.

Political Education

It is critical to the welfare of Chicano families and specifically to the self-esteem of their children that parents understand the dynamics and effects of racism. Ausubel and Ausubel (1963) have indicated that the way in which parents are affected by racism will affect their children. Parents' reaction to racial discrimination determines in part their basic attitudes toward the child, whether they accept or reject them and if they use them for purposes of their own ego enhancement. This same theme can be applied to Chicano families. This author has encountered Chicano parents who are grateful for a child who is born light-skinned rather than dark-skinned. They even use nicknames: *Hueda* (light one) or "Chocolate," "Inky," or *Prieta(o)* (dark one).

The focus on color is an outcome of both U.S. racism and racism inherited from the European colonization of Mexico. For example, in Mexico, racism is directed to the Indian; if one looks and acts European, one is more acceptable. Gibson and Vasquez (1982) have observed this phenomenon among Chicano families:

> One of the first questions usually asked immediately after a child is born is "A quien se parece," whom does he/she resemble or look like? Darker children, those with obvious Negroid or Indian features, often become the scapegoats in the family or the objects of pity. (P. 10.)

Parents need the opportunity to recognize how racism promotes these ideas and reactions. Proshansky and Newton (1967) have identified social insight as the mechanism minorities must be taught to address this phenomenon.

> By this concept, we suggest that the minority group member—child or adult—needs to understand the source of his [her] group dilemma. If he is Negro [Chicano], he needs to view the social system and the white man, not him, as the source of his difficulties. (P. 213.)

Proshansky and Newton's concept of social insight can be called politicization. A central goal of politicization is to integrate affective oppressive experiences with cognitive awareness of racism and its effects. This integration could enable Chicano families and children to recognize racism rather than just experience its negative effects. Additionally, families and children could view racism as a deficiency of the individual or institution supporting that belief, rather than a deficiency of the person who is the object of the racism. Politicization also could involve teaching parents how to prepare their children for racist acts. Parents should be more aware of the self-concept needs of their children and begin early to consciously promote esteem in their child-rearing efforts. Parents need to tell children early about racism—that some people may find the children unacceptable because of their skin color. The children should be taught to never reject others on the basis of color or race. This process could enable children who are confronted with racism to defend themselves or to seek help from their parents. For example,

> a 14-year-old Chicano male was participating in a teen church activity forum where a movie was shown to provoke discussion on moral issues. The film showed the scenario of a poor Chicano family whose son steals a bike. This family was portrayed in a very stereotypical fashion without any redeeming qualities. In this group of 15 teens only two other Chicano or minority youths were present. As the movie progressed the 14-year-old Chicano jumped up and demanded that the movie be discontinued because it was so racist. The other two Chicanos joined him in his protest, the film was stopped, and discussion followed regarding the issues he raised.

The 14-year-old youth in this vignette lived in a female, single-headed household that was struggling economically. However, the ambience in the home fostered social insight. For instance, racism issues and events were discussed as they arose so that the concept would be understood by the children. As a result, the 14-year-old was able to recognize the unhealthy nature of the film and, despite his minority status in the teen group, was able to risk rejection by challenging the film's content. This is the kind of cognitive and affective outcome that politicalization promotes. The youth defended his self-esteem and that of his ethnic group. Additionally, non-Chicano members were exposed to the youth's views, and two other Chicano youths could rally around his leadership.

Introduction of Cultural and Political Education into Communities

Cultural and political education can be introduced into the Chicano community as well as the broader community through community resources, television, formal community services, and school systems.

Community Resources

Social events, including *Cinco de Mayo* (the 5th of May) or *Quince de Septiembre* (the 15th of September), historical dates on which Mexican liberation struggles are celebrated, held in many Chicano communities could foster occasions for the incorporation of cultural content. Educational booths and skits could stimulate discussion of cultural concepts. Chicano drama groups in high schools, community colleges, or universities also could stimulate discussion of cultural concepts following a dramatic presentation of cultural themes. Social workers could provide the cultural and political education using their skills in group work and in community organization.

Television

Another means of culturally and politically educating Chicano families is through television. Most metropolitan areas have one or more television shows that are oriented to Hispanic audiences. Programs often include plays, skits, and educational forums. However, bilingual and bicultural social workers and credible community leaders would be necessary elements in the promotion of discussion about cultural and political concepts. Also, the programs should be accessible to both monolingual and bilingual audiences.

Formal Community Services

Formal social service agencies including Chicano agencies are another conduit for political education through the services they offer.

Mental Health Prevention. Several agencies use an educational format to help parents anticipate the kinds of problems and conflicts their children may face. For instance, the Family Service Agency in Sacramento, California, offers family education groups for those families experiencing separation and or divorce. This prevention effort similarly could be used for minority or Chicano families. Instead of the central theme being the ramifications of divorce, the ramifications of racism would be the central theme. Newspaper and magazine advertisements, and television public service announcements could promote the services of such agencies. A recruitment feature might include a description of educational groups as a means for enhancing the *bien estar* (well-being) of Chicano children.

Direct Interventions. Social workers should include the theme of racism in their assessment of the client system when they provide services to Chicano individuals or families (Zuniga, in press). Evaluation of the self-concept of clients demands that the effects of racism on their personality structure be delineated as part of the psychosocial dimension. Moreover, to the extent client systems are affected by racism, social workers have the responsibility to politicize their clients. Levine and Padilla (1980) have recommended specific roles for the social worker.

An effective therapist for Hispanics will have as a major goal the amelioration of personal distress caused by discrimination and institutional racism. The therapist can help the Hispanic client find appropriate outlets for anger and ways to direct that anger toward effecting social change. When necessary, the therapist will focus on enhancing the client's self-concept and appreciation of his or her cultural roots. In those clients who have dealt with racism by denying their ethnicity, the therapist will attempt to foster pride in Hispanic cultures. (P. 94.)

Cultural and political education should be pursued together. If a family, or client, or community system is defensive about politicalization, cultural education can help facilitate their readiness for politicalization.

School Systems

The realities of institutional racism particularly in school systems demand the pursuit of various avenues for ameliorating its effect on the self-concepts of Chicano children. For example, minorities could be recruited to teach, the curriculum could be revamped so that it would be culturally pluralistic, and the schools could be examined to ensure that they provide courses and experiences that address both racism and cultural differences. Such long-term changes can be effected through political activism by minorities.

A central criticism of U.S. school systems is their promotion of values and learning styles that meet the needs of white, middle-class children but do not acknowledge the needs, values, and learning styles of cultural and racial minorities (Kendall, 1983). Rodriquez (1983) has noted that educators such as Ramirez and Castaneda (1974) have promoted the concept of cultural democracy as an avenue for addressing the unique needs of minority children in educational settings.

The concept of cultural democracy...implies that the individual has a right to maintain a bicultural identity—that is, to retain his identification with his ethnic group while at the same time learning to adopt mainstream American values and life styles. As an educational philosophy, cultural democracy encourages schools to develop curricula, teaching strategies, and instructional methods which are sensitive to the uniqueness which each individual student brings to the classroom. Because cultural democracy focuses on the teacher–pupil relationship, it also suggests a greater emphasis on humanism in the educational process (Martinez, 1970). (P. 503.)

Cultural democracy would benefit not only minority children, but would expose nonminority children to humanistic styles of learning from which they also could benefit. This educational concept also could promote the competencies of personas bien educadas. Although cultural democracy does not characterize educational philosophy and policy as exhibited in American society, it is a goal for which minority communities need to aim. Social workers also can support the efforts toward multicultural education that are occurring in educational institutions. As Banks (1986) has argued, multicultural education helps students become aware of the inconsistencies between democratic ideals and societal practices. They are able to develop skills to promote social reform. As Craft (1982) has noted, school systems themselves can contribute to societal reforms, especially those needed to ensure cultural democracy.

An avenue for achieving cultural democracy is through the election of minorities, sympathetic candidates, or both, to the legislature and to boards of education. Rodriquez (1983) has noted that out of a total of 602 legislators in Arizona, California, Colorado, New Mexico, and Texas, only 62 are Chicanos and 50 percent of the Chicanos are from New Mexico. Without legislators and board members who value cultural democracy in education, policy decisions to support this concept may not be made.

Political education efforts can prepare Chicano families for the broader and active stance they need to take in their communities. Families that are conscious of oppression, their lack of access to societal resources, and particularly the unequal educational opportunities they face, can be recruited more easily to the political arena. They need to become active voters, to participate in voter registration drives, and to provide support for minority or sympathetic candidates. Because Hispanics are the fastest growing minority population in the United States, their potential as voting blocs provides them with increased leverage in their interactions with both national and local political parties. Social workers need to become involved in these efforts by using community organization skills to recruit Chicanos.

Of paramount importance in politicization is the effect it can have on Chicano children. Youths who see their parents, relatives, or members of their communities participating in the political system will be socialized to view the political process in a meaningful way. Such a view will undercut the political passivity that often has characterized Chicano communities (Garcia, 1973). It also will provide the children with role models to emulate. Overall, the view may contribute to a heightened respect these children have for themselves and other Chicanos. In the long run, this political activism will help promote the changes that are needed in societal systems, especially in the educational systems, to make them less racist and unjust.

Professional Mandate

Self-concept is a critical area in the functioning of all persons; for minority children, self-concept is important because of the nature and ubiquity of the racism encountered. If Chicano or minority children do not see themselves positively, their expansion and effective interaction in their social environment will be constrained. A negative view may lessen motivation to seek new experiences, to develop further competencies, and to pursue natural curiosity. Moreover, it may minimize the risks Chicano children would be willing to take in learning about their world and lessen their chances for developing into competent human beings, appreciative of life and learning. Rather, poor self-concept can evolve into neurotic traits or behavior problems that will exacerbate their problems rather than help them realize their potential.

Chicano social workers and social workers who work with Chicanos and other minorities must take responsibility for providing the services to make social change a reality. A critical underpinning to these services must be the incorporation of politicization and cultural education as facilitating mechanisms.

Works Cited

Aguilar, I. "Initial Contacts with Mexican American Families," *Social Casework,* 17 (May 1972), pp. 66–70.

Ausubel, D. P., and P. Ausubel. "Ego Development Among Segregated Negro Children," in A. H. Passow, ed., *Education in Depressed Areas.* New York Teachers College, Columbia University Bureau of Publications, 1963.

Banks, J. "Multiethnic Education in the U.S.A.: Practices and Promises," in T. Corner, ed., *Education in Multi-Cultural Societies.* London: Croom Helm, 1984.

Blumer, H. *Symbolic Interactionism: Perspective and Methods.* Englewood Cliffs, N.J.: Prentice–Hall, 1969.

Carter, T. P. "The Negative Self Concept of Mexican American Students," *School & Society,* 96 (March 1968), pp. 207–209.

Chestang, L. "The Black Experience," in P. Cafferty and L. Chestang, eds., *The Diverse Society.* Washington, D.C.: National Association of Social Workers, Inc., 1976.

Craft, M. "Education for Diversity: The Challenge of Cultural Pluralism." Inaugural lecture presented at the University of Nottingham, February 26, 1982.

Erickson, E. *Childhood and Society.* New York: Norton & Co., 1963.

———. "The Concept of Identity in Race Relations: Notes and Queries," *Daedalus,* 95 (Winter 1966), pp. 145–171.

Dworkin, A. "Stereotypes and Self-Images Held by Native Born and Foreign Born Mexican Americans," in N. Wagner and M. Haug, eds., *Chicanos: Social & Psychological Perspectives.* St. Louis, Mo.: C. V. Mosby Co., 1971.

Garcia, C. *Political Socialization of Chicano Children.* New York: Praeger Publishers, 1973.

Gibson, G., and E. V. Vasquez. "Racism and Its Impact on Hispanics: Cognitive and Affective Teaching and Learning." Paper presented at the Annual Program Meeting, Council on Social Work Education, New York, March 1982.

Gomez E., and K. Cook. *Chicano Culture & Mental Health.* Monograph 1. San Antonio, Tex.: Our Lady of the Lake University, 1978.

Goodman, M. E. *Race Awareness in Young Children.* New York: Collier Books, 1964.

Goodman, M. E., and A. Beman. "Child Eye-Views of Life in an Urban Barrio," in N. Wagner and M. Haug, eds., *Chicanos, Social and Psychological Perspectives*. St. Louis, Mo.: C. V. Mosby Co., 1971.

Kendall, F. E. *Diversity in the Classroom: A Multicultural Approach to the Education of Young Children*. New York: Teachers College, Columbia University, 1983.

Knowles, L., and K. Prewitt. *Institutional Racism in America*. Englewood Cliffs, N.J.: Prentice-Hall, 1969.

Levine, E., and A. Padilla. *Crossing Cultures in Therapy*. Monterey, Calif.: Brooks/Cole Publishing Co., 1980.

Logan, S. "Race, Identity, and Black Children: A Developmental Perspective," *Social Casework,* 62 (January 1981), pp. 47–56.

May, G. J. "Personality Development and Ethnic Identity," in P. Cafferty and L. Chestang, eds., *The Diverse Society*. Washington, D.C.: National Association of Social Workers, Inc., 1976.

Mejia, D. "The Development of Mexican American Children," in G. J. Powell et al., eds., *The Psychosocial Development of Minority Group Children*. New York: Brunner/Mazel, 1983.

Mercer, J. "Identifying the Gifted Chicano Child," in J. L. Martinez, Jr., ed., *Chicano Psychology*. New York: Academic Press, 1977.

Powell, G. "Prologue: America's Minority Group Children: The Underserved," in G. J. Powell, ed., *The Psychosocial Development of Minority Group Children*. New York: Brunner/Mazel, 1983.

Proshansky, H., and P. Newton. "The Nature and Meaning of Negro Self-Identity," in M. Deutsch, I. Katz, and A. Jensen, eds., *Social Class, Race, and Psychological Development*. New York: Holt, Rinehart & Winston, 1967.

Ramirez, M. "Recognizing and Understanding Diversity," in J. L. Martinez, Jr., ed., *Chicano Psychology*. New York: Academic Press, 1977.

Ramirez, M., and A. Castaneda. *Cultural Democracy, Bicognitive Development and Education*. New York: Academic Press, 1974.

Rodriguez, F. *Education in a Multicultural Society*. Washington, D.C.: University Press, 1983.

Rodriquez, A. "An Educational Policy and Cultural Plurality," in A. Powell et al., eds., *The Psychosocial Development of Minority Group Children*. New York: Brunner/Mazel, 1983.

Sotomayor, M. "Mexican American Interaction with Social Systems," *Social Casework,* 5 (May 1971), pp. 316–322.

U.S. Bureau of the Census. *Hispanic Population: A Demographic and Issue Profile, September 1983*. Serial No. 98-10. Washington, D.C.: U.S. Government Printing Office, 1983.

U.S. Commission on Civil Rights. "Toward Quality Education for Mexican Americans." Washington, D.C.: U.S. Government Printing Office, 1975.

Wahab, Z. "Barrio School: White School in a Brown Community." Paper presented at the Annual Convention of the American Anthropological Association, New Orleans, November 1973.

Zuniga, M. "Mexican Immigrant Parents: Educational Interventions." Paper presented at the University of California–Los Angeles First Binational Conference on Mexico–U.S. Migration, Guadalajara, Mexico, November 1987.

———. "Mexican American Clinical Training: A Pilot Project." To be published in a forthcoming issue of *Journal of Social Work Education*.

CHAPTER 6

CULTURAL EVOLUTION OF AMERICAN INDIAN FAMILIES

JOHN RED HORSE

American Indian family systems have drawn considerable attention during the past decade. Researchers during this period encouraged political activism in support of the Indian Child Welfare Act of 1978. They claimed that family systems were fractured by intrusions from child welfare professionals and proposed that due process of law could restore natural strengths of Indian families (Unger, 1977). After passage of the act, jurisdiction for selected child welfare matters was transferred to tribal courts. Red Horse (1982) noted that this transfer of jurisdiction was fraught with problems because of shortages of personnel with appropriate clinical training, and he cited early indicators that suggested that removing American Indian children from their natural families would increase despite the act. Recent data have indicated that "the number of American Indian children in foster care has returned to—or has increased slightly above—the numbers which were cited prior to the passage of the Indian Child Welfare Act" (Sudia, 1986).

Social legislation alone cannot strengthen American Indian families. In addition, professionals armed with knowledge in American Indian family development must implement policies. To help social workers obtain such knowledge, this chapter addresses contemporary variations in American Indian family and individual behavior. The author uses traditional family systems as a benchmark for discussion but does not assume that persistence is preferable to change in traditional beliefs and customs. Adaptive behaviors are common among any cultural group exposed to new life situations; such behaviors among American Indians simply indicate a reframing, and in some cases a revitalization, of cultural beliefs through behaviors that vary from traditional life-styles.

This chapter includes discussion of several aspects of American Indian life-styles. Demographic trends provide a macroscopic view of life circumstances among American Indians. Leading indicators suggest that families and individuals experience life situations that influence rapid change in behaviors and belief systems. Examples of the lives of several individuals capture discrete changes in behavior and aspirations that affect cultural maintenance across three generations and within the same generation. Two representative, existing resource manuals for training professional personnel then examine the art of diagnosis, assessment, and direct service to Indian families and individuals. A discussion of the spectrum of American Indian family systems examines permutations and combinations of behavior that emerge as revitalized cultural systems. A final, summary discussion examines implications for human service education and practice.

Demographic Trends

Most American Indians became urban residents between the 1970 and 1980 census reporting periods (U.S. Department of Commerce, Bureau of the Census, 1983, 1984, and 1985). The 1970 census reported that 45 percent of the American Indian population resided in central cities or in urban areas proximate to central cities, and this group increased to 54 percent by 1980. The data also showed important variations among states. Forty-seven percent of the total American Indian population reside in four states: 201,369 (approximately 15 percent) in California; 169,459 (about 13 percent) in Oklahoma; 152,745 (about 11 percent) in Arizona; and 107,481 (about 8 percent) in New Mexico. Remarkable contrasts appear in residential patterns. California experienced rapid growth, and its American Indian population increased 118 percent between 1970 and 1980. The increase is attributed to migration patterns; 81 percent of California's Indian population resides in urban areas. This migration trend is less demonstrable in Oklahoma, but 59 percent of the American Indian population resides in or proximate to central cities. American Indians in Arizona and New Mexico, however, predominantly reside on reservations; in each state, only 30 percent of the American Indian population lives in urban areas. Eskimos and Aleuts in Alaska appear connected to traditional homelands—less than 30 percent of their in-state population (26 percent of their populations live outside the state) are urban residents.

Nationally, 24 percent of American Indians retain a native language. The 1980 census indicates that 333,000 American Indians ages five years and older speak a native language, and an estimated 15,000 native language speakers do not speak English at all. Native languages are spoken in 125,000 households. Again, state demographics vary dramatically for transmission of language. Forty-three percent of the total native language speakers reside in Arizona and New Mexico, and 33 percent of that group are from school-age populations, compared with only 15 percent from school-age populations in Oklahoma and

25 percent in Alaska. Language transmission across generations exceeded 75 percent in Arizona and New Mexico. In Oklahoma, the rate was 26 percent; in California, 27 percent; in Washington, 18 percent; and in Oregon, 15 percent.

Family structures are losing key members who previously were responsible for passing on traditional matters. Family systems in urban areas usually are nuclear household arrangements that are not influenced by extended kin on a daily basis. Mixed marriages increased 20 percent since 1970, and in 1980, more than 50 percent of all married American Indians had non-Indian spouses. Also, irrespective of urban or reservation residence, a disproportionate number of American Indian families are maintained by single parents (the rate exceeds 20 percent among the total American Indian population).

Demographic trends provide a macroscopic view of life situations. Residential status, language retention or loss, and marriage patterns are three critical variables associated with cultural maintenance. The immersion of families and individuals in urban environments that are distance from native homelands and traditional kin systems requires adaptations in personal life-style, aspirations, and behavior. These adaptive tendencies are not captured by census data, but the following examples of individuals' life choices show contrasting dynamics of cultural persistence and change.

Examples

Ogewabenais and Behmahseis: Across Three Generations

Ogewabenais was born 65 years ago in a remote, traditional village. He was introduced to ritual custom at a naming ceremony seven days after his birth. His American Indian name—Ogewabenais—means *Chief Eagle,* and he assumed a role as a bearer of ritual custom. He learned ritual songs for medicine drum ceremonies and became knowledgeable in medicinal herbs, roots, and tree barks. For most of his life, only the tribal language was spoken in his home.

Ogewabenais was not a cosmopolitan man by American standards. He did not travel much from his village. He did spend several years at a boarding school, which only strengthened his appreciation for traditional ways. Ogewabenais also was drafted into military service during World War II and spent three years in Europe. There, for the first time, he met white people who appreciated Indians, and he was tempted to make the military a career. Despite limited exposure to urban influences, Ogewabenais had an ability for cosmopolitan thinking. However, his skill in ritual healing puzzled medical doctors, and he could trace genealogy better than most professionals.

The path of life that Ogewabenais chose was tantamount to vows of poverty. By most standards in American society, Ogewabenais was a poor man— his lifetime earnings probably did not exceed $75,000, which he earned primarily during the heyday of the Office of Economic Opportunity. His livelihood derived mostly from traditional activities: gathering berries, working in wild rice paddies and cranberry marshes, and making maple syrup. During many summers, he supplemented this income by singing and dancing in a weekly show for tourists. By all standards in traditional American Indian society, however, Ogewabenais was a wealthy man. He knew ritual custom and passed it to namesakes for whom he served as role model and mentor. Ogewabenais died during the summer of 1986. More than 700 people attended his funeral. Most were extended kin and namesakes, who were testimony to his wealth; they were seeds of ritual tradition that he planted.

Behmahseis was born 17 years ago in a metropolitan hospital. He was introduced to ritual custom at a naming ceremony seven days after birth. His American Indian name—Behmahseis—means *child of harmony* and endows him with spirit powers to heal conflicts. Behmahseis spent seven years of childhood on the reservation and in a remote, traditional village. He served as keeper of the medicine drum, participated in ritual ceremonies, and spoke the language fluently. However, when he left the village, he developed other interests.

Behmahseis thrives in an urban life-style and has lived in four metropolitan areas. He comprehends formal science, understands profit margins, and commands Standard English. He aspires to a professional life and plans to become a lawyer or doctor. He was worked in wild rice paddies and cranberry marshes. However, he has decided that menial labor is not his future. Instead, he dreams of money, sports cars, and expensive homes and enjoys rock music and video games.

Behmahseis is preparing for success with meticulous care. He is an honor student in high school and is considering matriculating at Stanford or Harvard, but he has visited more than 30 university campuses in 28 states and Canada. His high school involvements show well-rounded achievement to improve his chances for university admission. He is a four-year letterman, is enrolled in college preparatory courses, is active in student government, and serves as an executive officer in the school's chapter of a national honor society.

By all standards in American society, Behmahseis exhibits attributes common to success; he is bright, motivated, and ambitious. However, he may die in poverty according to the standards of traditional American Indian society. His command of ritual knowledge and language is declining rapidly. He has not planted seeds of ritual tradition. Behmahseis has no namesakes and is too removed from kin to serve as a role model or mentor.

Ogewabenais respected Behmahseis's decision to pursue an individual path of life that departed from tradition. However, Ogewabenais planted tobacco every day while he lived and prayed that Behmahseis would return to traditional ways. This ritual was Ogewabenais' obligation because Behmahseis is his grandson.

This example paints a picture of contrasting persistence and change in behavior and aspirations as life experiences vary over generations. Both environment and personal choice influence patterns of cultural maintenance.

Helen and Marlene: Within a Generation

Helen is 32 years old. She is a traditional American Indian and she lives in a remote but well-developed area of her home reservation. Helen always was an exceptional student. She retained the native language, but acquired an admirable command of English. She graduated from college with a 3.54 undergraduate grade point average and earned a master's degree from a major research university. She experienced some difficulty in graduate school, particularly with theories and concepts in health care. Eventually she mastered health concepts that draw distinctions among primary and secondary institutions, but she no longer uses them, not because of a lack of intelligence but because of immersion in a traditional life-style that does not separate family, religion, and health care.

Helen struggled to retain ritual tradition while she completed her university work. She lived in metropolitan areas for seven years and did not visit a single health clinic, seek out a private doctor, or attend a counseling session to resolve personal stress. Instead, she made 63 trips home to receive health care at ritual ceremonies. Following graduation, she returned home and married a medicine man. They have three children who are becoming fluent in ritual custom and in their native language.

Helen's sister, Marlene, is 33 years old. She lived the first eight years of her childhood in the same traditional home setting. However, she went on educational placement at age nine and was away from family influence for 15 years. She is extremely intelligent and completed undergraduate studies with a grade point average of 3.62. Marlene did not attend graduate school.

Marlene adjusted to American society and lived in a white community. She joined the church that sponsored the educational placement and never went home for ritual ceremonies. She still has an ear for her native language and can understand conversations, but she has little need for the language in daily affairs. Consequently, she speaks it only haltingly and does not dream in it at all.

Marlene married a non-Indian who belongs to the same church, and the couple has four children. English is the language of preference in their home. The children neither speak their mother's native language nor attend ritual ceremonies. They visit grandparents occasionally, but they are not comfortable among extended kin. Also, they enjoy urban life and become bored on the reservation.

The contrasting behaviors of Helen and Marlene reverberate through their entire family of orientation. Their parents had nine children. Four stayed home and retained traditional ways. Five entered educational placement, disconnected from extended kin, and entered the American mainstream. The parents do not make judgments and supported educational placement. The children who stayed home to live according to tradition have mixed opinions about their siblings and find it difficult to reconcile departures from traditional ways.

Two Resource Manuals

Several organizations have developed resource materials that blend discussions of Indian culture with professional concepts of family and individual services. This section examines two representative manuals prepared for distribution to American Indian and non-Indian audiences. One is intended primarily for child welfare professionals and serves a national audience (Anderson et al., 1983). The other is intended primarily for classroom teachers and serves a state audience (Arizona Department of Education, 1986).

Indian Child Welfare Resources and References (Anderson et al., 1983) provides an excellent overview of issues such as tribal sovereignty, intergovermental relations, child welfare law, and program components in child welfare. However, it has limited value as a guide for clinical diagnosis, assessment, and treatment for Indian families and individuals. The manual explains American Indian behavior through a framework of five mutually exclusive life-styles that range from traditional to assimilated, but these five life-style types do not account for many life-style permutations and combinations that lead to behaviors not explained by the model. Such a limited model has serious implications for clinical service. Without some understanding of discrete behaviors that are possible among American Indians adapting to contemporary life stresses, child welfare professionals may reach dubious clinical decisions.

The Arizona Department of Education (1986) manual *A Varied People: Arizona's Indians* is one of the finest documents available. The manual details historical circumstances that shaped tribal diversity (such as custom, language, and life-styles), and it traces historical aspects of family development that link extended kin systems to traditional village organization. Lesson plans with teaching styles that can be adapted to individual children make it an excellent classroom guide for teachers. However, the manual disregards contemporary influences on family and individual development, as if cultural evolution has ceased. Culture systems are not static, however, and departures from traditional value orientations during the twentieth century have reshaped group attitudes among many American Indians. Attcity (1983), noted, for example, that three religious factions among Navajos on the reservation influence behaviors among families and individuals. Families in traditional factions retain a cultural view that one's relation to the physical world is sacred. Another faction modifies this to encourage a utilitarian view of the physical world. One faction retains a sacred view of language; another adopts an instrumental view. Thus, many elders raise concerns about the erosion in traditional understanding of the native language and attribute this erosion to the teaching of language in schools (Zah, 1984).

Both of these resource manuals are important contributions to the literature and serve as laudable efforts that can lead to further refinements. However, teachers and child welfare professionals need more discrete tools to guide their assessments of contemporary American Indian behaviors. Their professional observations in such areas of behavior as potential neglect and abuse, for example, have considerable impact on the lives of American Indian children.

Spectrum of Family Systems

American Indian family systems can be categorized on a continuum that organizes family typology and explicates modal behaviors for individuals and groups within family types (Table 1). The continuum of family typology includes traditional, neotraditional, transitional, bicultural, accultural, and panrenaissance family types. Modal behaviors common within family types include language of preference, religious beliefs, attitudes about land, kin system structure, and health behavior.

The traditional American Indian family is the benchmark for any discussion of American Indian family types. A demonstrable change in at least one modal behavior leads to the emergence of the neotraditional family type. More extreme changes in modal behaviors lead to the subsequent types. The spectrum provides for continuous reclassification during clinical service, so the service provider can update diagnosis and treatment on the basis of specific behavioral tendencies as families and individuals adapt to new life situations. The spectrum of types does not imply a linear phenomenon necessarily. In many instances, modal behaviors change for different situations, and families can move in either direction along the continuum.

Traditional Families

Traditional behavior derives from village structures that were common among tribal groups. Thomas (1982) noted three important attributes of these villages. First, they were extremely small, with a population range of 200 to 350 residents, and contact with outsiders was limited. Ritual events brought several villages together but did not alter social structures in the individual villages. Second, all village residents were members of an extended kin system, so social relations outside of family were limited. This attribute shaped behavior that generally was unobtrusive because maintenance of enduring family relationships was the basis of social control. Third, the villages were considered sacred societies, so life events and kin relationships were interpreted according to sacred law. Elders assumed respected roles because their accumulated wisdom was necessary to interpret lives and relationships according to a sacred context.

The attributes of village and kin structure explain many values that commonly are ascribed to American Indians. Family loyalty was strong, and important roles such as parenting were shared among grandparents, aunts, and uncles. Older children received considerable responsibility for child care. The nature of personal relationships facilitated behaviors that were nonjudgmental and noncompetitive among kin. However, nonjudgmental behavior was not

Table 1. Spectrum of Indian Family Systems with Illustrative Modal Behaviors

Family Type	Modal Behaviors				
	Language	Kin Structure	Religion	Land	Health Behavior
Traditional	Prefers use of native language in home, community relations, and ritual ceremonies. Exhibits homogeneity across generations.	Extended kin system organizes as basic unit of community structure. Kin are dominant in social relations, and community generally is closed to outsiders.	Practices native religion identified with historic custom. Bonds spiritual, human, and universal domains through ritual ceremonies. Retains clans and ritual names if applicable to custom.	Retains sacred view of land. Links to land through ritual ceremonies, including purification rites for residence.	Retains traditional beliefs regarding etiology of disease and seeks care through ritual ceremonies that recapture harmony among mind, body, spirit, and universe, includes use of prescriptive herbal medicines.
Neotraditional	Generally prefers use of native language in home, community, and ritual ceremonies. However, some have adopted second lanaugage, which is preferred and becomes dominant over the native language. Exhibits language homogeneity across generations.	Extended kin system may have been fractured through adoption of new religion, but modified kin system remains extended and community is closed. Kin dominate social relations.	Retains general beliefs associated with historic custom, but adopts new ritual procedures to act out beliefs.	Retains sacred view of land and links to land in a manner similar to traditional groups.	Retains traditional beliefs regarding etiology of disease. Adopts new ritual procedures and spiritual healers.

Table 1 (Continued)

Family Type	Language	Kin Structure	Modal Behaviors		Health Behavior
			Religion	Land	
Transitional	Prefers native language in the home and intimate social relations, but not in community use and other external relations. Language homogeneity across generations declines.	Extended kin system is fractured, but modified system will be available if a colony is organized. Fractured, isolated groups form nuclear households. System opens to outsiders, particularly among children.	Retains beliefs associated with historic custom, but struggles to act it out on a daily basis because of absence of natural system. Travels frequently to homeland to reinforce religion through ritual ceremonies.	Retains sacred view of land and acts this out when visiting homeland. However, begins to acquire utilitarian view of residence and often other land in general.	Retains traditional sense of the etiology of disease and makes frequent trips to homeland for health care. Daily ritual behavior in health matters begins to deteriorate, and American institutional services begin to dominate.
Bicultural	English is preferred language in the home and community. Parents may know native language, but homogeneity across generations declines rapidly.	Nuclear household arrangements predominate, but a strong sense of American Indian identity leads to fictive extended kin structures. Prefers social relations with other American Indians and system is open to them.	Retains a symbolic sense of native religion, but does not practice it on a daily basis. Adopts new religion, but does not adapt it to traditional beliefs; hence, ritual customs are absent.	Aware of the symbolic meaning of the sacredness of land, but adopts utilitarian behaviors with respect to land in general.	Uses American institutional services, but prefers services that involve other American Indians. Has developed extensive parallel network of all-Indian services that mirror systems common to the general population. Prefers non-Indian view on etiology of disease.

Table 1 (Continued)

Family Type	Language	Kin Structure	Modal Behaviors			
			Religion	Land	Health Behavior	
Acculturated	English is preferred language in the home and community. Exhibits total loss of native language.	Nuclear households outside of general parameters of an identifiable American Indian community. Primary social relations are with non-Indians and no fictive system develops. System is open.	Converts to nonnative religion and loses ties to historic religious customs and practices.	Not generally concerned with sacredness of land. Except in narrow terms of secular views on conversation, land view is utilitarian.	Prefers American institutional care without need for all-Indian parallel systems. Adopts non-Indian view on the etiology of disease.	
Panrenaissance	English generally is the primary language in the home and community. Language renewal is emphasized, but homogeneity across generations is low.	Nuclear household arrangements predominate, but a strong effort to reorganize natural extended kin systems prevails. Fictive kin arrangements are common and system is open.	Attempts to revitalize aspects of historic ritual custom. Generally organizes hybrid forms to replicate traditional religious beliefs.	Revitalizes the sacred view of land, but retains utilitarian views with respect to residence and other property in general.	Is extremely critical of American institutional system. Actively pursues expansion of all-Indian parallel networks of care. Attempts to revitalize historic beliefs around the etiology of disease.	

necessarily the norm with people outside the kin systems—which, according to structural limitations common to villages, were organized as closed communities. Harsh opinion toward outsiders still is common today, and social workers familiar with American Indian behavior are aware of intergroup judgments made on the basis of blood quantum, reservation or urban residence, and religious beliefs. Also, value orientations that guided unobtrusive behavior did not allow deviant, irresponsible behaviors that could jeopardize kin. Social control could be exacting, and contemporary discussions on the role of noninterference in family relations often overlooked such control. Pipestem (1980) provides an example:

> Parenting was a sacred obligation in my tribe, and parents could be banished for child abuse and neglect. This was not used often, perhaps only once every generation, because it made a lasting impression. When this occurred, the entire village gathered in a double column as if to watch a parade. The neglectful parent was at the center of the village with a group of elders. They would march out from the heart of the village and move toward the land of strangers. A caller in the group would repeatedly announce the reasons for banishment and explain why the parenting behavior was not good for the village and why the parent must leave forever. This was like a public announcement of the findings of a court in current law. When the group reached the edge of the village, the parent was cast from family membership. No family member who remained in the village could ever again speak to the person that was banished.

Methods of social control among traditional families have changed with contemporary times, but modal behaviors influenced through early village structure remain reasonably constant. Most family households have close ties to extended kin systems, and traditional roles are intact. Grandparents, aunts, and uncles are parent figures who assume primary responsibilities in the lives of children. The families generally live in remote areas, whether on reservations or in rural areas, and the kin system organizes into a closed community. Closed communities are not penetrated easily by strangers; therefore, peer relationships outside of family are limited. Family membership expands through marriage, but spouses are expected to join the new family of orientation in a manner prescribed by custom.

Traditional families interpret life events in sacred terms. Individual behavior reinforces this daily, and traditional values structure sacred relationships among kin and with the universe. These relationships are expressed through ritual ceremonies, and depending upon tribal custom, these families are articulate with sacred bonds such as ritual names, clans, and namesakes. Ritual ceremonies, particularly in health care, generally are family affairs. Other American Indians may be invited as appropriate to custom, but non-Indians rarely are allowed to attend ritual events.

Most traditional American Indians are bilingual, but native language is preferred in the home, in community relations, and at ritual ceremonies. Language maintenance is intended to avoid intrusions from the outside world and is necessary to retain and transmit a precise understanding of a sacred past, present, and future. Ritual names, for example, are important bonds in traditional social structures. They link individuals with a sacred universe, pass spirit powers through the generations during healing ceremonies, and establish personal obligations among kin. As such, ritual names serve as sinews in a social structure that guides individual behavior, and their connotative meaning is lost when they are translated into English.

American Indian health services have introduced modern medicine to remote communities. However, traditional patterns of behavior change slowly, and customary health practices still are used widely among traditional families. Traditional American Indians mirror the general American population by seeking health care through the family system. However, their traditional beliefs concerning somatic and mental health are quite different from those held by the general population. Biological and psychological factors are not considered the only causes of disease, and the concept of health includes a sense of harmony among sociological structures and spiritual forces. Therefore, health care is holistic. Kin, ritual names, and clans play an important part in health care because medical practice includes both using prescriptive medicines and regaining harmonious balance of sociological structures and spiritual forces. Some government programs have acknowledged these important traditional beliefs and have integrated medicine men with doctors to deliver health services. Utilization rates improve among traditional families when such strategies are used (Kniep-Hardy and Burkhardt, 1977).

Neotraditional Families

Neotraditional families emerge most commonly through mass religious conversions. These families organize into closed kin and village structures and simply adopt new ritual procedures for sacred beliefs. Some conversions, such as the Native American Church, occurred with families in tribes from the Southwest to the upper Midwest. In some instances, entire tribes have been converted. The Yaquis, for example, blended native religion with Roman Catholicism. Neotraditional families retain most of the traditional modal behaviors, such as a sacred view of the universe and kinship roles. Yaquis, however, also changed language usage. They retain their native language in limited ways among younger generations, but Spanish is the dominant language in the home and the community.

Transitional Families

Transitional families emerge through geographic relocation away from extended kin systems. They attempt to retain modal behaviors similar to traditional groups, but actual retention varies according to the nature of change and the impact of that change on daily life. Some transitional families relocate as colonies with several members of an extended kin system moving together; they adapt to new living situations with minimal changes in modal behaviors. Other transitional families move as isolated household units, and they experience dilemmas across all modal behaviors. Parents generally retain native language use in the home, but language homogeneity decreases because children adopt English as a primary language. The family retains a sacred view of land, but the urban residence often is treated in a utilitarian manner. The extended kin system begins to fracture. Relationships are maintained through frequent travel to the reservation, but kin have considerably less influence with social roles and behaviors. Social relations in the urban community generally are with other American Indians, but families really do not retain the closed aspect of extended kin systems because urban peers are nonkin.

All transitional families retain traditional health behaviors and maintain frequent contact with their native homelands. A survey on health behavior in the San Francisco Bay area indicated that 28 percent of the sample population used medicine men at their home reservation when treatment was necessary (Kaufman, 1979). Transitional families are underserved by institutional care in urban areas, but certain health care strategies can modify their closed behavior. For example, a family and children's service in Oakland, California, noted that health care utilization rates among transitional families increased dramatically following employment of native language translators (Oakland Indian Child Resource Center, 1982).

Bicultural Families

Bicultural families make important shifts away from traditional modal behaviors. While transitional families reconcile disjunctions between life situations and preferred modal behavior, bicultural families face a dilemma between the symbolism of tradition and actual preferences in life-style. Typically, these families do not transmit specific traditional knowledge across generations. Parents often may understand their native language, but they do not maintain it as the language of preference in the home. Therefore native language use is declining rapidly among younger generations. Parents also are acquainted with ritual custom but have converted to non-Indian religions. Most children in bicultural families do not have ritual names, are not familiar with their clans, and do not have namesakes. This decline in attributes associated with specific ritual custom also leads bicultural families to favor institutional services common to American society. Finally, sacredness of land is acknowledged symbolically, but in actual practice, land is treated in a utilitarian manner.

Although bicultural families have acquired many characteristics of American society, they are not integrated socially. They prefer relationships with other American Indians and have introduced important adaptations that contribute to a construction of generalized American Indian values. Bicultural families often replicate traditional extended kin systems through fictive structures that incorporate nonkin into roles normally found in extended families. They manage geographic isolation by attending pow-wows in urban areas or on nearby reservations. Younger bicultural American Indians elevate pow-wows almost to ritual or ceremonial status, although pow-wows actually are social events that are open to the general public. The behavior, however, is an important form of cultural revitalization that reinforced and maintains a shared American Indian identity.

Acculturated Families

Acculturated families are assimilated and represent the most extreme departure from traditional life-styles. Families in this group differ from bicultural families by enacting social preferences that make them comfortable with non-Indians. They assume modal behavior similar to the American general population without any apparent personal dilemma. The English language is used by both parent and child generations. Acculturated families practice non-Indian religions and do not retain actual or symbolic sacred linkages to land, kin, or health behavior. Health behavior mirrors that of mainstream society. Nuclear households are the preferred family structures, and visits with kin are infrequent. Thus, peer relations generally are with non-Indians for both parents and children.

Panrenaissance Families

Panrenaissance families emerge as important cultural revival responses when external forces place families and individuals in jeopardy, and the emergence of such families and groups is not unique to contemporary American Indians. During the 1800s, for example, the ghost dance society emerged and spread rapidly as an attempt to revitalize American Indian religions that had been banned by the federal government. Contemporary panrenaissance families often exist in militant American Indian groups. Militant groups originally organized out of concern for civil rights, but they have expanded to include treaty rights, tribal sovereignty, and religious freedom, which indicates a shift in emphasis. Originally, the groups stressed cultural awareness, but they gradually included issues concerning language renewal and organized hybrid forms of traditional religion. Support for these activities is mixed. Language renewal generally is supported by traditional groups, but hybrid religions that change ritual custom are not popular.

Modal behaviors among panrenaissance families are similar to bicultural families in many respects. They prefer social relationships with other American Indians and reinforce kinship ties whenever possible, but they also maintain open structures as fictive kin systems. Symbolically, land is viewed with sacred meaning, but panrenaissance families seldom act out that view through daily rituals. The most notable behavior of such families is outspoken criticism of

American Indian services designed by American institutions. Their tactics in areas such as child welfare are controversial, but the issues that they raise apply generally across a broad spectrum of American Indian families. Their efforts have led to the organization of several parallel institutional systems that provide American Indian-controlled services in education, social work, health care, and housing. Their efforts also have heightened awareness among American Indians and non-Indians alike, and they continue to publicize new, alarming matters, such as Indian genocide in Latin America.

Summary and Recommendations

The census data indicated important demographic shifts that affect the degree of cultural persistence and change among American Indian families and individuals. These shifts do not indicate uniform erosion of American Indian culture. However, variations among states and regions suggest that family proximity to native homelands fosters cultural maintenance through frequent contact with extended kin systems and language transmission across the generations. The census data, especially the large proportion of younger people among American Indians, suggest that traditional structures likely will experience rapid modification in years to come.

The spectrum of American Indian family systems describes variations in illustrative modal behaviors among American Indians. Although it is not an exhaustive model, it attributes variations in behavior within and across generations to personal choices that are made in response to external social forces. Thus, modal behavior suggests that personal variations can be situational, that bi-directional movement along with spectrum is common, and that families frequently replicate traditional social organization such as natural kin systems through fictive structures among urban groups. To show the range of the spectrum, accounting for permutations and combinations possible with the family typology and modal behaviors, families and individuals can exhibit 7,776 discrete behavior variations. This range raises implications for professional education, research, and practice that could be implemented through curriculum development, special programs of study, and partnerships between social service agencies and tribal governments.

Curriculum development should support the canons of scholarship. Current strategies in professional schools assume that minority content can be integrated with regular course offerings in human behavior and direct practice. This may be true for subpopulations that speak only one language within the group or have sacred beliefs that mirror organized religion in Western society. However, American Indians depart from the model. Estimates indicate that American Indians, excluding Alaskan natives, speak at least 149 different languages and are organized into several cultural groups with different customs and traditions (Red Horse, 1982). Although American Indians have beliefs about the etiology of health and disease, differences among American Indians affect health behaviors, ritual organization, and leadership in extended kin systems. Many behaviors are retained as American Indians move into the mainstream of American society (Miller, 1975). Integrated curricula simply reduces knowledge to a minimum level. A separate curriculum that provides opportunity for social service practitioners to examine Indian family development, track health behavior, and document effective practice methods is needed.

Special programs of study could be developed at selected professional schools in response to regional variations noted in the demographic trends. Such programs would allow appropriate investigation into American Indian life transitions and facilitate the integration of social service education with networks in health and social services that are common to American Indians. Study programs also would foster the development of research agenda specific to language and cultural groups within a region. The programs could organize independently or through consortia designed to share research and teaching resources among a number of schools. Such programs would provide scholarship opportunities in areas such as native American Indian languages and apply social work content in policy, administration, human behavior, and practice in a manner consistent with the Indian Child Welfare Act of 1978.

Partnerships between social service agencies and tribal governments could benefit both groups. Tribes would gain technical assistance to support the development of clinical programs, and professionals would gain knowledge of practice skills essential for service delivery to Indian families and individuals. Moreover, such structures could provide valuable insights to professional education and could be modeled to track effective practices and inform the profession about teaching models appropriate to American Indian family services.

Works Cited

Anderson, S. C., et al. *Indian Child Welfare Resources and References.* Norman, Okla.: University of Oklahoma, 1983.

Arizona Department of Education. *A Varied People: Arizona's Indians.* Pheonix, Ariz.: Arizona Department of Education, 1986.

Attcity, S. "Navajo Religion and Culture." Symposium conducted during American Indian Week, University of Arizona, Tucson, April 1983.

Kaufman, J. *Patterns of Health Behavior Among Indians in the Bay Area.* Unpublished manuscript, 1979.

Kniep-Hardy, M., and M. Burkhardt. "Nursing the Navajo," *American Journal of Nursing,* 73 (1977).

Miller, D. *Native American Families in the City.* San Francisco: Institute for Scientific Analysis, 1975.

Oakland Indian Child Resource Center. "Toward a Theoretical Model in American Indian Mental Health." Symposium on Indian Child Welfare, Oakland, Calif., 1982.

Passel, J. S. "Provisional Evaluation of the 1970 Census Count of American Indians," *Demography,* 13 (1976).

Pipestem, B. Respondent panel. Colloquium on American Indian Families: Strengths and Stresses, Arizona State University, Tempe, 1980.

Red Horse, J. G. "American Indian Community Mental Health: A Primary Prevention Strategy," in S. M. Manson, ed., *New Directions in Prevention among American Indian and Alaska Native Communities.* Portland, Oreg.: Oregon Health Sciences University, 1982.

——. "Clinical Strategies for American Indian Families in Crisis," *The Urban and Social Change Review,* 15 (1982), pp. 17–19.

Sudia, C. "Analysis Compares Numbers of Indian Foster Children," in *Linkages for Indian Child Welfare Program* (pp. 1, 4), 1986.

Thomas, R. "Mental Health: American Indian Tribal Societies," in W. L. Mitchell, ed., *American Indian Families: Developmental Strategies and Community Health.* . Tempe, Ariz.: Arizona State University, 1982.

Unger, S. *The Destruction of American Indian Families.* New York: Association of American Indian Affairs, 1977.

U.S. Department of Commerce, Bureau of the Census. *1980 Census of Population: Characteristics of the Population, General Population Characteristics, U.S. Summary* (PC 80-1-B1). Washington, D.C.: U.S. Government Printing Office, 1983.

——. *1980 Census of Population, Volume I, Characteristics of the Population, Chapter D, Detailed Population Characteristics.* Parts 3, 4, 6, 7, 11, 14, 15, 17, 18, 24, 25, 26, 28, 29, 30, 32, 33, 34, 35, 36, 37, 38, 39, 43, 45, 46, 49, 51, 52, (PC 80-D3). Washington, D.C.: U.S. Government Printing Office, 1983.

——. *1980 Census of Population, Volume I, Characteristics of the Population, Chapter D, Detailed Population Characteristics, U.S. Summary* (PC 80-1-D1). Washington, D.C.: U.S. Government Printing Office, 1984.

——. *Census Population, Volume 2, Subject Reports, American Indians, Eskimos, Aleuts on Identified Reservations and in the Historic Areas of Oklahoma (Excluding Urbanized Areas)* (PC 80-2-1D). Washington, D.C.: U.S. Government Printing Office, 1985.

——. *General Social and Economic Characteristics, U.S. Summary 1980* (PC 80-1-C1). Washington, D.C.: U.S. Government Printing Office, 1983.

——. *American Indian Areas and Alaskan Native Villages: 1980* (PC 80-51-13). Washington, D.C.: U.S. Government Printing Office, 1984.

——. *Marital Characteristics* (PC 80-2-4C). Washington, D.C.: U.S. Government Printing Office, 1985.

Zah, P. "Mission of the Navajo Trival Government." Symposium conducted during Navajo Divisional Direction Training Workshop, Arizona State University, Tempe, July 1984.

CHAPTER 7

DEVELOPMENT OF AN ETHNIC SELF-CONCEPT AMONG BLACKS

DORCAS D. BOWLES

Three-year-old Jackie's black parents enrolled her in a predominantly white preschool. During the fourth month of Jackie's enrollment, she told her mother that she was white. The shocked mother told her daughter that she was black, to which Jackie responded by running to her room screaming, "I am white! I am white!" When Jackie's father came home he called to Jackie and greeted her warmly. After some of their customary games, he said to her, "You are a black girl, right?" Jackie became negative and angry: "No, I'm not black, I'm white!" Again she rushed to her room screaming and continued repeating "I'm white!" Discussions with Jackie's parents revealed that they had never discussed Jackie's being black with her. They assumed she would know she was black.

In the case study above, Jackie's parents did not understand that part of Jackie's confusion resulted from the absence of an ethnic groundwork—ethnic self-acceptance, awareness, discussions, toys and books that addressed her being black. Faced with a predominantly white preschool without this groundwork, her fragile differentiated sense of self was shattered and unable to incorporate an ethnic sense of self. For minority groups in the United States, culture and ethnicity play important yet poorly understood roles in the formation of self-concept.

Edith Jacobson (1964) has distinguished ego from self-representations and from self. The *ego* represents a structured mental system; *self-representations* are the "unconscious, preconscious, and conscious endopsychic representations of the bodily and mental self in the system ego." (P. 63.) Hence, self-representations as well as object representations develop in response to experiences of pleasurable and unpleasurable sensations and of the perceptions with

103

which these sensations become associated. Jacobson has defined the *self* as the experienced totality of a person that includes body, body parts (including skin color, bodily features, and hair texture), and psychic organization.

Eisnitz (1973) has noted the potential for destructiveness if fundamental problems arise as self-representation develops:

> Units within the self-representation provide the quality for ego activity. The ego selects and cathects the appropriate unit of the self-representation. Conflict can promote instability within the self-representation (and within the experienced self) requiring special defenses to deal with the narcissistic stress. Such narcissistic conflict can arise at all levels of maturity. (P. 400.)

A basic function of the ego and, to a somewhat lesser degree, of the superego, is the development and maintenance of cohesive constellations of self-representation. An individual must maintain a stable sense of self while functioning simultaneously in a range of situations, with a range of demands, and influenced by a range of self-representations (Blanck and Blanck, 1979).

Significant among the units within the self-representation is that related to ethnicity. Each culture fashions an ethnic group members' manner of experiencing, perceiving, and behaving in subtle, almost indiscernible ways that are not always conscious even to its members. The cultural ethos is taken in, internalized, assimilated, and processed by the individual so that it becomes part of the ethnic self-representation unit which is passed from one generation to the next. Individual ethnic experiences will determine the private way in which the ethnic self-representation unit (that is, the functional organizing unit within the self-representation) is shaped; the individual ethnic self does not always match the group's experience if that individual is not affiliated or connected with the ethnic group. Therefore, there is a distinction between that which is universal within the culture and that which holds particular meaning for the ethnic individual. The strength of an individual's ethnic self-representation unit is determined by the child's family and later the larger environment affirms and accepts a given ethnicity and the subsequent internalization of this by the child. The ethnic self-representation unit can be traced back to the infantile objects, and it continues to be shaped and influenced via transmuting internalizations (Tolpin, 1972) and selective identification throughout a child's development.

The ethnic self-representation unit is one's inner ethnic identity. This differs from the personal ethnic identity, which is based on one's external sense of self. As we know, internal perceptions are more fundamental than external ones; though external perceptions shape and influence internal cognizance. Inasmuch as the ethnic self-representation unit defines, for example, a black person, it is the core and major organizer of the self-representation and must develop cohesion and solidity. Cohesion of the ethnic self-representation unit is possible when the child has been made to feel special in his or her early environment and this sense of specialness has continued to be externally affirmed and supported, for example, from the extended family, peers, church, school, and community. Although the ethnic self-representation unit can develop as a structured functional unit, lack of external affirmation and support coupled with continual assault will undermine the self's ability to maintain cohesion and remain intact.

While the ethnic representation functional unit is individually unique and autonomous, it is interrelated to and has influence on all the other self-representation units. The ethnic self-representation unit sends and receives messages from the other parts of the ego for maintenance of the self. When there is a threat to the ethnic self-representation unit, conflict ensues. The conflict shakes or jolts the self and the individual uses defense mechanisms to protect, support, and maintain self-cohesion, stability, and hence, self-esteem.

Social conditions modify an ethnic cultural character. Ethnic individuals from each generation must struggle, therefore, with what is to be passed on to the next generation. This must allow for growth and for what needs to be altered to avert dysfunctional behavior. Ethnic group and individual change is not always possible because there is both historical and individual transmittal of culture. Also, what is transferred is not always conscious and deliberate, but unconscious. While individuals are free to affiliate and identify with their ethnic group to the extent that they feel comfortable, the basis for this comfort is rooted in life experiences shaped by the family, the unconscious, and the environment.

Blacks, as a subcultural and ethnic group, share in and are influenced by the experience of the dominant culture through, for example, speech, politics, religion, economic conditions, and education. Values, beliefs, and behaviors of the dominant culture are translated through an ethnic vision whose meaning is individually determined based on one's family and life experiences. For blacks, it has been important to assimilate the dominant culture to allow for the preservation of subcultural values, while at the same time creatively adapting to the dominant culture for survival. While creative adaptations have been identified in the social sciences as examples of how ethnicity affects psychic development, thereby shaping individual and group development, they are poorly understood in psychiatry, psychology, child development, and clinical social work.

The literature indicates that the ability to discriminate physical differences based on race and color develops rapidly during preschool years. McDonald (1971) postulated that the earliest meaningful perception of a child's color difference would occur at about age eight months, during the period of stranger anxiety when the child becomes capable of discriminating his or her first love object. Children as young as three years are capable of distinguishing races based on color. According to Harrison-Ross and Wyden (1973), the skin "is not just wrapping paper around a person package." (P. 11.) Instead, it is the earliest physical determinant in the development of a psychological sense of identity (Greenacre, 1958; and McDonald, 1971). These early interactions serve as prototypes for later social and problem-solving skills and for the beginning development of a sense of self as well as an "observing ego," where the infant begins to sense how his or her behavior results in certain responses from adults and to pay attention to adult behaviors as a basis for his or her own behaviors. For example, the black parent has found ways to keep a child feeling special and has provided ways for the child to respond to subtle racism. In addition, the extended family, the black community, and the black church serve as "refueling stations" where the black child's sense of self is reaffirmed. These exchanges are ongoing and prepare the child for self-definition, which will undergird the seeming dual existence with which he or she will be faced. Modell (1968) has stated that

> the cohesive sense of identity in the adult is a sign that there has been a "good enough" object relationship in the earliest period of life. Something has been taken in from the environment that has led to the core of the earliest sense of identity, a core which permits further ego maturation. (P. 59.)

The roots of the ethnic sense of self are laid in the early mother–child interaction, heightened by the child's locomotion.

A number of theorists (Blos, 1962; Giovacchnini, 1963; Jacobson, 1964; and Erikson, 1968) have contributed to an understanding of identity formation. Their works, however, do not address how ethnic identity is formed and shaped.[1] How then does the black infant, for example, originally unaware of self and other and of ethnicity and color, come to develop the ethnic self-representation unit? The black infant's sense of ethnicity or color is not present at birth. Mahler's (1975) work had explicated carefully how the infant differentiates self from other, yet it does not speak to the development of a black ethnic sense of self, but rather to the issue of object development and differentiation from an individual other. Such theories, while informative of how one develops a sense of self, have not articulated how an ethnic sense of self for blacks is shaped. It is as if the experiences for blacks were the same as the experiences for members of the dominant society, although experts assert that this is not the case. For every child there is a style of maternal–child interaction that reflects culture. A black ethnic self-representation unit must entail not only the usual phases that are necessary for the development of an inner

---

[1] Jacobson's contributions are extraordinarily valuable to an understanding of identity formation. While a brief overview of the process of identity as set forth by Jacobson (1964) may be simplistic, it may be useful to us in our understanding of how the stages of ethnic identity develop. Jacobson describes the gradual unfolding of object relations, beginning with the symbiotic mother–infant dyad, in which fusion of object representations and self-representations exist, resulting in a blurring of ego boundaries. At about three months, there is beginning differentiation, which extends through the second year of life and results in a stage of individuation and the beginning of secondary ego autonomy. In this unfolding process, the infant shifts from the wish to merge with the primary love object to a wish to be like the primary love object.

sense of self, but additional steps that incorporate one's sense of being black. The following discussion on this dimension identifies its connection with experiences within one's family and the larger societal system in an attempt to broaden our understanding of the developmental process that shapes the formation of the black ethnic self-representation unit. The discussion resulted from interviews with 21 black mothers and upon the author's personal and professional experience.

The ethnic self-representation unit for the black child begins prenatally with the parents' feelings about themselves as black people and their hopes and ambitions for their child's future. Where either or both parents are black, the child is considered by this society to be black. The black mother's positive feelings about herself as a black woman, her confidence, security, self-esteem, and joy and delight in her infant are transmitted to the dependent, helpless, insecure child and are the beginning affirmation of the child's worth and specialness as a person of color. Anxiety and unhappiness, whether these be intrapsychically caused or socially caused, are conveyed to the infant and experienced as a sense of worthlessness.

The undifferentiated phase described by Hartmann (1946), which correlates with Freud's (1950) stage of autoeroticism, Kohut's (1977) stage of the fragmented self, and Mahler, Pine, and Bergman's (1975) autistic phase, is characterized by two features: (1) the infant's mind functions by *sensing* rather than by perceptual cognition, and (2) the mother–infant dyad acts as a unit. The mother–infant union includes both the biological and psychic realm; the infant takes in the mother's touch, body movements, voice tonality, and perhaps, if the infant breast-feeds, the taste of the mother's milk. The black mother's feelings about herself and her infant, with which her feelings of blackness are inextricably tied, are experienced by the infant. Hence, what will influence the child's sense of self is in existence prenatally and is continued during the phase of autism and within the symbiotic mother–child matrix so that there is some correspondence between the black mother's sense of self and the child's later capacity to see himself or herself as a black person. These feelings become the basis for memory traces and perceptions, which are the precursors of the black ethnic self-representation unit. If the black mother and father accept their being black, the infant will have a beginning acceptance of herself as a black.

During the later phase of the fifth month, psychic differentiation begins. Voluntary use of hands in coordination with eyes and mouth at about six months represents the infant's beginning awareness of body image and a beginning awareness of the mother as a separate object. The practicing phase, roughly spanning the tenth to the sixteenth month, highlights locomotive skills for the toddler. Physical separation is a reality and the child's joy in her motor skills creates a period of elation, a "love affair with the world" (Mahler, Pine, and Bergman, 1975). It is at this time that the parents begin the process of helping the child to verbalize and to identify body parts. This is the time that black parents include in this listing the child's color so that the child takes joy in his or her body, including its color.

During the practicing phase, black parents should demonstrate acceptance of and delight in the child's achievements and display of his or her body (Mahler, Pine, and Bergman, 1975). Although the concept of color is not present for the child at this age, its inclusion lays the groundwork for positive ethnic affirmation. It is during the practicing phase that black parents develop a protective stance toward their child and become attuned to the child's movement into the environment and to the reactions of others to the child (Bowles, 1983). With rapprochement at 18 months, the child becomes increasingly aware of separateness from the mother. Increased verbal skills allow the child to understand and absorb stories. The child can identify himself or herself and members of her family from photographs. It is important that black parents offer books that have black children in them. Also, black dolls and other toys should be provided for the child because social and cultural attitudes about race are now available to the child.

Jacobson (1964) elaborated that the child's entry into the second year results in the development of a definitive capacity for observation of his or her own body and of the bodies of others with perception of similarities and differences between the self and others. As differentiation proceeds, the black parents' positive ethnic expressions and acceptance lay the groundwork for the child's acceptance of being a black person. During this period, the child learns to use words to label people and things. Development of a sense of self requires that parents be attuned to the child's basic psychological needs, including the child's need for protection from a hostile environment, and will respond to them. The infant needs the parents' availability as a calm, reassuring force during the time that the immature ego is unable to mobilize personal resources for self-soothing. The parents' availability and their buffering from external assault of the child's emerging sense of self as a person, as well as a black, are necessary prerequisites for the child's being able to take inside, in small doses, those maternal functions that bring relief.

At about age three, the child, having barely negotiated differentiation from the parents, is able both to note and comment on differences in people that include color, bodily features, and hair texture. The awareness of differences based on color can become embedded in the matrix of the already developing sense of self, acquiring additional meaning from the messages the child receives and will continue to receive from his or her family of origin and from external sources. The child's beginning and fluid structural personality development, including the emerging sense of self, takes on an increased capacity for differentiation and individuation and further individuation must now include an ethnic sense of self. This occurs when the child is able to internalize an ethnic sense of self derived from the sense of ethnicity of the parents. This level of individuation allows for integration and synthesis of a sense of self that includes an ethnic sense of self. Social and cultural attitudes about race are screened through the beginning ethnic sense of self matrix and require buttress-ing by the parents, family, community, and other external sources.

Facility with language, which began in the midst of the separation and in-dividuation stages, now assists this process. As the child begins to master language, he or she begins to discern subtle differences in the meanings and usage of words. Previously, feelings and moods were the medium of com-munication between the child and the mother and words had an external mean-ing, whereas the tone of the expressions carried the internal meaning. The child experiences words as being internal and affective, based on the manner in which they convey thoughts and feelings. Hence, both words and feelings are per-ceived by the child as having external and internal meaning. The word "black," used during this time to refer to the child and her parents, becomes laden with a variety of meanings, some of which are positive, negative, ambivalent, or contradictory. With mastery of separation and individuation, the child is ready to add to his or her already budding sense of self a sense of ethnicity based on experiences with family and beginning socialization with the external world. Hence, the ethnic self-representation unit is given shape between ages three and five and becomes a part of the child's sense of self.

From the initial, exclusive relationship between parents and child, the child is introduced to an array of socializing experiences and contacts with other adults. The child is able to receive new information about himself or herself. The child watches television, travels with parents, and is involved in a general expansion of his or her environment. Messages received from ex-ternal sources that affirm or negate the sense of self based on color become important. White parents at this time can be sensitively attuned to their child's growing curiosity and exploratory behavior, which facilitates the child's ability to question and internalize the environment. With the attain-ment of object constancy the white child is able to sustain good feelings about the self from inner resources as well as from continual external af-firmation. Black parents carry an additional responsibility. Good self-feelings from inner resources as a result of the taking inside of the maternal func-tions are insufficient to protect the child from external assault on his or her sense of self. Black parents also must be attuned to their child's exploratory behavior, but in addition, they consciously and actively must begin to buf-fer and specialize the child's sense of self as a black child. The evolving body ego now must incorporate a concept of color into the physical and psychic definition of one's sense of self. This ethnic dimension to one's sense of self forms an overlay to the beginning cohesive sense of self and shapes the ethnic self-representation unit.

The second phase, which is the development of the ethnic self and is shaped between ages three and five, gets firmly grounded between ages 6 and 12 although it continues to be shaped over the course of a life. With separation and individuation fragilely negotiated at age three, the black child needs con-tinued affirmation of himself or herself as black and special so that a positive ethnic sense of self is consolidated. The sequential unfolding and timing of the negotiation of separation and individuation and the beginning sense of self with the further development of the ethnic sense of self necessitates sensitive attunement from parents and others. This second step allows the child to accept himself or herself positively as a person of color. Negative parental and societal responses to the child's black features, color, or hair can lead to the internalization of a negative ethnic self-representation unit and can become the seed of future self-pathology.

The black mother must make peace with her shortcomings as any mother does: she has to acknowledge her limitations, accept both her imperfections and her potential to make innocent mistakes that can cause pain to her child. With "good enough mothering" the mother's love and caring for the child is conveyed in immeasurable ways and will far outweigh any errors that occur. For the black mother, however, there is yet an additional message. That message is that no matter how much she loves her child, or attempts to protect and care for her, the child can be deeply hurt by racism in our society. Hence the parents' communication of a sense of ambivalence about their capacity to protect translates into the child's feeling that her parents can protect her in certain situations, but not in others. The black mothers I spoke with often made statements like "I love my child, but I can't totally protect him from the world he has to live in. I hope he will survive." This ambivalence becomes part of the ethnic self-representation unit and gives the black child a defensive, affect-laden, questioning attitude about living in the world. It is what many authors refer to as healthy ethnic paranoia. While a white parent as well might make this statement, it means something different for blacks given the devaluation of blacks in our society.

Tolpin (1972) has used the term "transmuting internalization" to describe the process by which the beginnings of a cohesive self during the separation and individuation phase evolve (Kohut, 1977). When phase-appropriate frustrations and disappointments are gradually experienced by the child, the mother's availability, presence, and actions toward the child serve to calm, soothe, and regulate the child's anxiety to tolerable dimensions. The external, self-soothing, anxiety-relieving capacities of the mother are gradually internalized by the child, making the child less dependent on the mother to perform these functions. These mothering capacities have been variously referred to as "physical relation" (Freud, 1926), "symbiotic relationship" (Mahler, Pine, and Bergman, 1975), and "auxiliary ego" (Freud, 1965). The child's capacity to provide self-soothing becomes more and more self-regulated and maintained as the separation and individuation occurs. The child is still sensitive to the mother's feelings during this time and is able to sense her moods and attitudes quickly and rather spontaneously. This sensitivity or empathic ability in the child is a continuation of that which bonded the infant to the mother during the early weeks of life. The nurturing, attuned, holding environment provides the matrix for the gradual development of a beginning sense of self.

When the black child first confronts the issues of his or her race as being different from others in the environment, the parents serve as external buffers by continually clarifying to the child that he or she is black and special and loved. "Good enough parenting" means that black parents provide a positive ethnic groundwork and an attunement to the child's experiences so that they can assist the child in dealing with and responding to situations that reflect on her being black.

The need for black parents to serve as an auxiliary ego for the growing child about issues of race continues through adolescence, when issues of identity are reawakened. External assault on the ethnic self-representation unit can be pervasive through adolescence, necessitating ongoing parental auxiliary ego support. The black child and later the adolescent will continue to internalize the parents' capacities to tolerate anxiety. The parents' words and actions become restorative. Gradually, the words and actions are included in the child's own mental activity. (Some may wish to equate this with transitional object phenomena.) The slow internalization by the black child of the parents' availability is soothing and is not a transient or temporary state, but is, of necessity, extended through adolescence. With young adulthood, the child is able to use his or her internal ethnic sense of self as a primary base for effectively dealing with racism. The family and other network and support systems continue to serve as important and valuable resources that provide clarity, help process information, and aid in reality testing. Hence, for the black child there are two phases during which maternal regulations are taken inside. During the separation and individuation phase, many maternal regulatory functions undergo the process of transmuting internalization. For the black child, this represents the first self-soothing phase. Another phase extending from age 3 to age 12 is necessary and requires the black child to take in another set of maternal functions that relate to ethnic sense of self. The second set of maternal regulations must also be processed by the black child via a sort of second transmuting internalization process. This second phase of transmuting internalization is an active process that continues in diminishing form for the black child throughout adolescence.

While the black mother–father–child triangle is the primary dynamic by which development of the ethnic self-representation unit is nurtured, the external society becomes the "testing ground." The black parent recognizes that the black child must learn early to defend himself or herself in the external society and so the parent may push the child's early development, sense of autonomy, and independence, gauging permissiveness versus setting limits, because he or she cannot afford to have the child vulnerable. This requires the maintenance of a delicate balance between pushing the child toward early independence and allowing the child to bathe in the comfort of their support. When there is a good balance it can be utilized by the ego in the service of strengthening and aiding in the development of an independent, self-reliant ego that is not overburdened by premature responsibility and autonomy. The black mother and father will have consciously and unconsciously learned how to provide this parenting from their parents and their exposure to and observation of other blacks.

If the parents' self-acceptance and acceptance of the child within the family environment is positive and strong, the ethnic self-representation unit will be positive and strong. When the child as an adult is faced with a situation in which he or she is the only black or one of a few blacks among many with the dominant group, the child might experience a brief period of culture shock but will be able to extract from the early positive experiences received from his or her family and supportive networks. If the child's experiences with his or her family of origin have been less than satisfying in terms of the family's acceptance of their and the child's ethnicity, the child will falter miserably—either by feeling overwhelmed by insecure, negative feelings or by needing to deny his or her ethnic self and wishing to become part of the dominant group.

The black parent–child interaction must from the start be an interaction where there is recognition of differences between needs of the parents and needs of the child. This places a special demand on black parents in that they must prepare the child to live not in their world of the past or even the world of the present insofar as race relations are concerned, but in the world of the future where it is not clear what will be the nature of race relationships. Mastery of this task is ongoing, necessitating constant assessment and dialog among members of the ethnic group to determine alternative choices that are in their children's best interests.

Mahler, Pine, and Bergman (1975) and others have articulated the development of the sense of self for the child as encompassing the following tasks: the establishment of object constancy and self-constancy, the establishment of an individuated self, and the establishment of a gender-defined self-identity. To this process is added a fourth task for the black youngster: the establishment of an ethnic-defined self-representation. The development of theory about the development of an ethnic sense of self will enhance our understanding of the process by which the black family and other community support systems have historically shaped black children's attitudes about themselves despite societal oppression. An appreciation of how a positive ethnic sense of self unfolds will aid practitioners, educators, and mental health professionals in a better assessment of the internal resources available to blacks.

Works Cited

Blanck, G. and R. Blanck. *Ego Psychology Two: Developmental Psychology.* New York: Columbia University Press, 1979.

Blos, P. *On Adolescence: A Psychoanalytic Interpretation.* New York: Free Press, 1962.

Bowles, D. D. "The Impact of Ethnicity on Africa-American Mothering During the Separation Individuation Phase of Development." Unpublished PhD dissertation, Graduate School of the University of Massachusetts, September 1983.

Eisnitz, H. "On Selfhood and the Development of Ego Structures in Infancy," *The Psychoanalytic Review,* 59 (1972–1973), pp. 389–416.

Erikson, E. H. *Identity: Youth and Crisis.* New York: W. W. Norton & Co., 1968.

———. "The Problem of Ego Identity," in *Psychological Issues I.* New York: International Universities Press, 1969.

Freud, A., H. Nagera, and W. E. Freud. "Metapsychological Assessment of the Adult Personality: The Adult People," in R. Eissler et al., eds., *The Psychoanalytic Study of the Child* (vol. 20) (pp. 9–41). New York: International Universities Press, 1965.

Freud, S. As cited in J. Strachey (ed.). *Inhibitious, Symptoms and Anxiety* (vol. 10). London: Hogarth Press, 1926.

———. As cited in J. Strachey (ed.). *Collected Papers* (vol. V). London: Hogarth Press, London, 1950.

Giovacchini, P. L. "Integrative Aspects of Object Relationships," *Psychoanalytic Quarterly,* 32 (1963), pp. 393–407.

Greenacre, P. "Early Physical Determinants in the Development of the Sense of Identity," *Journal of the American Psychoanalytic Association,* 6 (1958), pp. 612–627.

Harrison-Ross, P., and B. Wyden. *The Black Child: A Parent's Guide.* New York: Peter H. Wyden, Inc., 1973.

Hartmann, K. E., and R. M. Loewenstern. "Comments on the Formation of Psychic Structure," in R. Eissler et al., eds., *The Psychoanalytic Study of the Child* (vol. 2) (pp. 11–38). New York: International Universities Press, 1946.

Jacobson, E. *The Self and the Object World.* New York: International Universities Press, 1964.

Kohut, H. *The Restoration of the Self.* New York: International Universities Press, 1977.

Mahler, M., F. Pine, and A. Bergman. *The Psychological Birth of the Human Infant.* New York: Basic Books, 1975, pp. 52–64.

McDonald, M. *Not by the Color of Their Skin.* New York: International Universities Press, 1971.

Modell, A. *Object Love and Reality.* New York: International Universities Press, 1968.

Tolpin, M. "On the Beginning of a Cohesive Self," in R. Eissler et al., eds., *The Psychoanalytic Study of the Child* (vol. 26) (pp. 316–354). New York: Quadrangle Books, 1972.

CHAPTER 8

ADVOCACY RESEARCH: SOCIAL CONTEXT OF SOCIAL RESEARCH

MARY E. DAVIDSON

he danger of social research is that it often creates mythical "truths" about the phenomenon under study. Because these truths emanate from a scientific process, they are transformed into facts and become a part of the conceptual universe of society. As such, they provide information for policies and guidance for programs whose goal is to solve important social problems. However, determining which research findings should be promoted as facts is a matter of choice. This choice is influenced by values, ethics, and by who stands to lose or gain. Even the original questions to be researched are subject to choice.

These choices are of particular concern when the subjects of research are members of a disadvantaged group—disadvantaged in that historically they have not had an opportunity to select or even influence the research questions, methodologies, or interpretations of findings concerning their lives. This opportunity is denied even when the members are subjects of study, and when they have to live with policies and programs resulting from such research.

Empowerment as a goal of social work practice subsumes that the knowledge and skills the professional social worker places at the service of the client will be useful in the problem-solving process (Solomon, 1976). Here, the social worker defines his or her role as assisting individuals in conducting their own research, or working with professionals in solving problems the clients help define. In advocacy research, the professional assumes major accountability to the subjects of study. As in other aspects of social work practice, this stance is complicated by the fact that, in addition to clients, professionals are accountable to funding sources, other agencies, and their peers. Often, the interests of these different groups conflict.

114

This chapter is an argument for the promotion and practice of advocacy research by social workers. Two case studies illustrate the effectiveness of such research. The main difference between advocacy research and other research is its emphasis on the researcher's responsibility to the client or the client group being studied. This entails

■ involving the client in the research process from start to finish;

■ lending support to the worldview of the client or client-group, including cultural, ethnic, linguistic, religious, socioeconomic, or other minority orientation; and

■ devising a research method and issue implications for practice that stand to improve the quality of life of the client group.

The discussion begins with definitions and assumptions about advocacy research. Then, the discussion turns to a brief overview of how the cognitive and interactional tasks of social research are modified in an advocacy research study. The two examples of advocacy research in local communities are discussed in light of their potential significance for assisting disadvantaged groups.

Description and Assumptions

Advocacy research is social research carried out with the sanction and participation of the individuals under study. In an advocacy research process, researchers are accountable not only to peers and funding sources, but also to the subjects whom they investigate. This accountability, however, does not mean subject control of the research process. Rather, it suggests that the researcher is sensitive to the worldview of the population throughout the research process; that is, from the formulation of the problem to interpretation and dissemination of findings. The purpose of advocacy research is sometimes stated as the provision of scientific information to community organizations for planning, evaluation, and decision making (Davidson, 1981). Advocacy research, like all other social research, is a social process and involves cognitive and interactional tasks. The *cognitive tasks* are the definitional, methodological, and technical aspects of the research. The *interactional* tasks involve the relationship between investigator and the people, place, and system under study.

In advocacy research, it is assumed that the investigator bias intrudes on the cognitive and interactional tasks. This is so because social research, however objective it may appear, is a process that cannot evade the influence of human values. The researcher is a product of a particular background and thus brings certain values and assumptions that guide the design and implementation of his or her work. Thus, according to Boykin (1979), "wittingly or unwittingly, the researcher is an advocate." (P. 97.) The greatest sin of any researcher, in this view, is to assume that scholarship and expertise inexorably lead to objectivity, and that bias is likely to surface only when the subjects under study are from a different racial, ethnic, cultural, or socioeconomic background than the researcher. Boykin (1979) noted:

> Although the realization that the research process is influenced by our initial assumptions might seem disappointing, let me emphasize that this is not inherently unfortunate. What is unfortunate, however, is a conscious or unconscious choice to ignore the "unscientific nature of the scientific enterprise" and to operate as though one were in a value-free vacuum with the resulting implications having deleterious effects on a group of people. Furthermore, this lack of understanding of the nature of scientific endeavors makes even the well-meaning researcher vulnerable to the prevailing political, institutional, and social positions and to the practices of the status quo, which may themselves need to be examined. (P. 100.)

Solomon (1976) went a step further and suggested that science is a tool of the oppressor, used often to justify oppression. Advocacy researchers acknowledge the bias and inherent political nature of the research process: It is one group posing a set of questions about another. In advocacy research, the we–they relationship blurs and questions are posed, lines of inquiry drawn, and data collected as a joint enterprise between researchers and research subjects.

Not only does this process protect against the abuses of research alluded to by Solomon, it helps ensure the use of research results. Indeed, many studies of blacks and other minority communities have not yielded findings useful to local policymakers, community organizations, social agencies, and the people studied. When the subjects have a major investment in the research process, it is likely that the community members will heed the findings and that fewer research reports will be shelved as dust collectors.

Advocacy research likely will be controversial for it may appear to attack and question many of the assumptions of traditional academic research. It does not. Advocacy research espouses scientific rigor and systematic principles of problem solving. However, similar to advocacy planning, it proceeds from a philosophical assumption of the existence of competing worldviews, and correspondingly competing or complementary conceptions of the public interest. This is a concern usually not considered by the traditional researcher (Table 1).

Table 1. Assumptions of Advocacy Research and Traditional Research

Assumption	Advocacy Research	Traditional Research
Conception of public interest	Multiple publics and competing interests	Single public interest
Accountability	To subjects and community of study	To peers and funding sources
Participation of subjects	Maximized in all phases of research process	Limited in scope and importance
Investigator–subject relationship	Equals; subjects as partners	Unequal; subjects only as target of study

Also, advocacy researchers do not question the integrity of traditional social research, but question whether integrity and pursuance of scientific rigor guarantee useful findings. Indeed, advocacy research is social research done in a traditionally rigorous scientific manner with one important addition—the researcher–subject relationship is an integral part of the research effort. Developing ways of employing the scientific method while directly involving in the research a neighborhood, a community, or its representatives is one expectation proponents of advocacy research have, essentially, ensuring that the findings are sensitive and useful to those affected by the problem under study.

Researchers must be aware of personal biases as well as the advocacy stance they represent—implicitly or explicitly—through their funding source and other agencies whose cooperation is sought. The recognition and respect of biases may enable the researcher to accommodate the unique perspective of advocacy research. In other words, the researcher is responsible for entering the world of the subjects of the study, and seeing it as they do.

Implications for Cognitive Tasks

Paradigm Construction

Too often research on social problems begins with an abstract point of view of a group of professionals or agency officials about what should be studied and how. Problems rarely are seen in context of the structures and processes of the particular community or from the perspectives of the subjects. As noted previously, all research brings to the scientific process a set of biases that shape how the inquiry is framed and conducted. If a researcher is not cognizant of this and has not made conscious choices about the set of biases he or she brings to a particular research, an "investigator paradigm effect" exists. That is, the researcher brings a *paradigm*—a conceptual framework and a body of assumptions and beliefs—to the task of research that is ignored by the researcher or treated as unimportant and unrelated to the process of scientific inquiry.

In reality, paradigms and their implied methods and techniques govern the choice of problems to be studied, appropriateness of methods, and the criteria for evaluating suggested solutions to the preselected problems. Paradigms define what is normal, accepted, and natural, but in so doing, act as a blinder to other points of view (Barber, 1976). Thus, a social scientist's paradigm determines what questions are asked; the kinds of data considered relevant; and how the data will be gathered, analyzed, interpreted, and related to theoretical concepts. Consider, for example, research on minority unemployment. Much, if not most of this research begins with assumptions based on a paradigm of "individual deficiency." This leads to research questions and intervention strategies derived from "person-centered" causal attribution schemes (Warren, 1971; Solomon, 1976; and Boykin, 1979). An alternative paradigm might indicate research from the perspective of institutional patterns of discrimination leading over time to patterns of unemployment or underemployment. A shift in paradigm has moved cause to effect and pointed to other foci of study. The shift in framework may challenge the fundamental assumption (individual responsibility) to the point where it is discredited and a new one put in its place (institutional discrimination), or the new theory may incorporate some sizeable bits of the old (Warren, 1971).

Hypothesis Formation and Variable Operationalization

A critical part of research is the development of hypotheses. Even in exploratory research, there are hunches that guide the beginning of the inquiry. In most research, identification of variables and variable relationships is necessary to delimit the data to be studied. The choice of variables leads a researcher to ask certain questions and not to ask others.

In advocacy research, development and operationalization of the variables of study occurs in collaboration with the people, place, or system being studied. If the research is to be relevant to the needs of the study population, researchers must involve the study population in the decisions about the dependent and independent variables. First, the dependent variable and its operational indicators must be conceptualized in a way that is understandable to the study population. Do all agree that this is the important question they want answered? Second, independent variables should be identified and refined in collaboration with representatives of the study population. For example, it is not helpful for a poor community to have its delinquency rate "explained" by the variable of income. This does not mean an abrogation of the responsibility of the investigator; rather it encourages the investigator to be sensitive to the worldview and economic and political vulnerabilities of the persons studied.

Research Strategy

In developing an overall research strategy, two things should be considered: (1) maximizing subject participation in all phases of the research process and (2) maximizing the social usefulness of the findings. The latter is particularly important for the population of study. Are the problem and possible solutions that emerge from a research process meaningful to the population? In addition, the researcher has to decide whether findings should be descriptive, associative or causal, and if appropriate data are available. In most cases, the topic determines what kind of data should be collected. For example, with inner-city residents who often lack basic information about their own neighborhoods, efforts should be made to include descriptive data. The Logan Square and Avondale study in Chicago is an example of such use. In addition, even though most research designs are not stringent enough to allow for causal analysis, researchers should at least strive for associational findings in which policymakers and community advocates can place some degree of confidence. The associations may prove useful in understanding a problem and therefore lead to more appropriate programs in the local community to address the problems or needs.

Data Collection

Many community studies have found it useful to recruit, screen, train, and supervise local residents in the collection of data. In the following advocacy research case studies, local residents from the study populations carried out face-to-face, in-home interviews and telephone interviews (Davidson, Chase, and Johnson, 1971; Davidson, Burrows, and Broughton, 1979). Researchers in a range of settings effectively have selected field interviews from the study population (Weinberg, 1971; and Myers, 1977). Using local residents as interviewers has benefited the researchers and the residents. It placed dollars in the pockets of often poor and disadvantaged inner-city residents, some of whom had no previous work experience. Some residents were later hired as interviewers by research organizations because of the experience they obtained. Many community organizations have limited funds to support research; therefore, resident volunteers serving as interviewers significantly decreases the cost of the research. Finally, the use of local interviewers expands the number of community residents directly involved in the research, increasing the likelihood that the effort will leave the community more familiar with research as a process and more likely to apply the findings of the research.

Data Analysis

Data analysis increasingly is equated with statistical analysis and the accepting or rejecting of hypotheses. In advocacy research, statistical analysis should be concerned with the importance of a relationship as well as its statistical significance. Too often, trivial results are interpreted and reported as "significant." This occurs when a small relationship between variables becomes observable because of the large size of a study sample. While the findings may be statistically significant they also may be unimportant in terms of their social usefulness. Unfortunately, statistical significance testing lends an air of objectivity because of the mathematical procedures involved. Rather than presenting data solely in terms of tests of statistical significance, data also might be presented to estimate the strength of the association (Carver, 1978). Finally, the researcher should explain the findings in clear terms, free of jargon. He or she also should indicate the implications of the findings for possible action.

Dissemination and Use of Findings

A basic tenet of science is public verifiability and the inclusion of sufficient information to allow for replication of any work that has been done. Only in this way can findings be challenged. A problem that is faced by most researchers—

minority or nonminority, in or out of academia—is pressure to publish positive results (Barber, 1976). There are subtle private judgments made by researchers about what data to declare in a report. This area of the research enterprise needs strong safeguards. Completeness in reporting negative as well as positive findings allows reinterpretations by other researchers and contributes to creative dissent.

Because accountability to community residents is a norm in advocacy research, final reports must be prepared with and made available to the residents, their organizations, and policymakers concerned about the residents' welfare, in addition to any funding sources outside of the community. The completion of the research and publication of a report sets in motion another process with the community of study—that of sharing the study findings and examining options implied for action. This is another way that advocacy research is different from more traditional research, which does not emphasize this kind of dissemination process with the study subjects.

Results can be shared through community meetings, publication of part of the findings in community newsletters, brochures, articles in local papers, as well as through delivering a full research report to community representatives. In addition, the researcher should be on call to assist the community in understanding and intepreting the findings. The sharing and interpretation of research findings with the community can provide information to identify needed services or to plan and organize community development strategies aimed at improving the quality of life for residents.

Implications for Interactional Tasks

Social research is a social process. It has an interactional dimension—the relationship of the investigator to the people, place, and system under study. The researcher is involved in a process of questioning, both of himself or herself and of the community residents being studied. The ongoing communication between researcher and researched, from beginning to end of the research effort, is as important as the methodological and technical aspects of the research. That relationship can help correct any of the investigator's erroneous assumptions and presuppositions that could limit the value of the overall research effort.

Two central issues for the researcher concerned about the interactional dimension of social research in minority communities exist: (1) accountability and (2) the enduring debate over who should do research in minority communities or on minority populations. To whom is the researcher accountable? As mentioned previously, advocacy research assumes that investigators should be accountable to the subjects of research in addition to peers and funding sources. This especially is crucial for the poor, because some academic researchers share neither their values nor backgrounds. The poor have a personal interest in the research conducted in areas that affect their lives; they must live with the outcomes. Such accountability is vital because of the pervasive input of researchers into governmental policymaking and the lack of input by the poor (Moore, 1973; and Western, 1975). The poor and other deprived groups in this society lack resources to fund their own research and generally must accept the research findings—all too often resulting from processes in which they have not been a part.

The so-called alien researcher is a concern of many. Who should or can do research on a minority community? Does a researcher have to have the same racial or ethnic background as the population under study? Does the minority researcher relate to minority respondents more appropriately? Merton (1972), Smith (1973), Baca-Zinn (1979), Boykin (1979), and others have addressed directly or indirectly the question of "Who should do research on minority communities?" Some have supported the position that valid research into ethnic minority concerns only can be done by minority researchers. Others have suggested it is an "argument absurdum" to say that only minorities can study minorities. Such a posture leads to the ultimate conclusion that only women can study women, only the aged can study the aged, and ultimately that only children can study children. Smith constructively bypassed this argument and suggested that it might be possible to develop procedures to ensure the protection and advancement of minority community interests without compromising the scientific integrity of research efforts. This is the hope of advocacy research, regardless of the background of the researcher. Experience with the advocacy research model suggests that insider researchers (the researcher demographically related to the subjects under study) are not necessarily more sensitive to value and normative differences between themselves and their subjects. However, many still assume that shared characteristics between researcher and subjects somehow enhances the value and normative convergence between them. Too often, race or ethnicity is viewed as the critical variable. Instead, the heightened sensitivity of the researcher to his or her own values and the extent to which he or she is aware of how those values may or may not converge with those of the study subjects is critical. (It may be that the sensitive researcher is as close as we can come to the mythical objective researcher.)

Whether a researcher is a member of the study population may not be the primary issue. Indeed, the "alien" researcher may elicit more reliable and complete data, once trust is established. Yet, prior familiarity with the worldview of the respondent population facilitates the research task. Here, however, it is important to distinguish between sensitivity to the norms and values of the subject population and the assumption that the researcher can adopt the perspective of the subjects. What is important for the researcher without experiential familiarity is the need to be sensitive to the norms and values of the study population.

The extent to which issues of entry, legitimacy, sponsorship, and trust are addressed early in the research process was found to be important for both researchers and the persons studied (Adams, 1979). The importance of these issues varies depending on whether the impetus for the research originated within or outside the community being studied. When the research initiative comes from outside the community being studied, the researchers will have to place special emphasis on the process of entry into the community and on building of trust. Even when the need for research has been identified by the community, the researcher may encounter difficulties. For example, competing community groups may seek the assistance of researchers to enhance their own status. These conflicts of interest must be negotiated carefully by the researcher to achieve a workable consensus. The researcher needs to be sensitive, therefore, not just to entry and legitimacy but also to sponsorship. He or she needs to ask, "Under whose auspices will I carry out the research?" and "How will the research process and its product alter the community's organization, ecology, and balance of power?" It is this type of sensitivity and skill that will generate trust on the part of the community and the subjects of study. This is necessary to develop the advocacy research partnership between researcher and subject. To illustrate how these concerns in studying a minority community were addressed, two case examples from Boston and Chicago follow. These cases represent two different examples of advocacy research.

The first case is a description of the Public Welfare Revision Study, one of the fourteen projects funded by the U.S. Department of Housing and Urban Development Model Cities Administration in Boston, Massachusetts (Davidson, Chase, and Johnson, 1971). The research study was a community survey of Boston's Model Neighborhood. The study population was primarily black, low-income, and in neighborhoods characterized by blight and problems associated with poverty and urban decay. Most of the researchers were black, but culturally and socioeconomically different from the study population. One black researcher was from the far west and another team member was white and from what is known as west Texas. Another black researcher was a first-generation American from Panama and the fourth team member was a black resident of Roxbury. With the exception of the latter, the researchers were in a cultural sense outsiders to the study community.

The second case centers on two near northwest-side Chicago communities—Logan Square and Avondale (Davidson, Burrows, and Broughton, 1979). This study was sponsored by the Logan Square and Avondale Community Foundation with support of a cross section of community organizations, churches, and local leaders. The neighborhoods were 98 percent white, reflecting the ethnic diversity of Chicago. The majority were Polish. The research team's principal investigator and project director were black. Other members of the research team were white graduate students at a local university, and forty additional community residents who contributed in some phase of the research project. Most of the volunteers were white, from Polish, French, and Russian backgrounds. Some Cubans and Puerto Ricans participated as well.

These case studies differ in several ways:

■ locale—one in Boston, one in Chicago;

■ auspices—one public (Boston), one private (Chicago);

■ impetus for research—one outside of the community (Boston), one community initiated (Chicago);

■ racial-ethnic-cultural matching—one partially matched (Boston), one not (Chicago).

A common factor the two projects shared, and one critical to the concept of advocacy research, was that community residents participated at every stage of the research process.

The case descriptions provide background on the studies as well as an overview of the methodology that emphasized the process of engaging in advocacy research. The role of community residents is detailed.The ideological, intellectual, and personal commitments that influenced the research process and its outcomes are described also.

Case Study 1:
Boston's Public Welfare Revision Study

Background

In 1968, residents of Boston's Model Cities area, assisted by Michael Piore and graduate students from the Massachusetts Institute of Technology (MIT), Department of Urban Planning, began planning an Income Maintenance Demonstration project for the Model Neighborhood, which included parts of the Roxbury/North Dorchester communities. The original funding request submitted to the city council included an Income Maintenance Demonstration Project as one of its 14 components. The project, if funded, would have given a sample of families from the Model Neighborhood an opportunity to participate in a research demonstration project similar to the New Jersey Income Maintenance Experiment. It would have provided funds to residents—both families and single individuals. The city council, however, rejected the demonstration project and instead proposed a research feasibility study on the impact of the welfare system on the day-to-day life of Model Neighborhood residents.

The residents—many not knowing what had occurred at the city council months earlier—thought that funding of the research study meant they were going to have the Income Maintenance Demonstration Project. The researchers informed the community that they were not going to have a demonstration project; that needed dollars would not come to the community (Davidson, 1975). Entry and legitimacy under these conditions were a challenge. The faculty-student research team from MIT served as a bridge to the community, having established a long-standing relationship of trust with them. The MIT team lent their support to the research team at a community forum and helped ease these entry and legitimacy problems.

The principal investigator's first step was to develop a consensus on a working philosophy to guide the research. Consensus was needed on several assumptions guiding the approach to the research task and to the Model Neighborhood residents. These assumptions related to the function of research as well as to the causes of poverty. The team agreed on the following (Davidson, 1972):

> that social research has the latent, if not manifest function of legitimating the status quo, of maintaining the present distribution of power and privilege in society;
> that research is often used as a political strategy to legitimate already agreed-upon policy decisions;
> this being so, those without power to fund their own research, or those without power to resist having research studies imposed upon them, needed advocates who were accountable to them; and
> many blacks and the poor have not had access to this source of legitimacy and that most research done about poor people is done by nonpoor people as is most research on blacks by nonblacks. (P. 4.)

The researchers also believed that research done on the poor and black populations usually was done by people whose primary accountability was to their funding sources and not to their research subjects. Therefore, it was decided that as researchers the primary accountability should be to the residents of the Model Neighborhood, then to the City Demonstration Agency, the city council, and the Department of Housing and Urban Development.

The researchers also sought a common definition of poverty. Notions of a culture of poverty or inherent individual dysfunction or deviance were rejected. Instead, researchers and subjects assumed that the causes of poverty can be traced to structural arrangements of this society and the functioning of its institutions. In this latter paradigm, poverty and any associated symptoms witnessed as individual dysfunction result from the thwarting of individual drive and the systematic deprivation of opportunity. In this view, poverty and dysfunction were effects, not causes.

Social Process

Those representatives of the groups studied are selected to be a part of an advisory council to serve as partners in the research effort. The resident committee members contributed by identifying areas in which field interviewers could gather information.

Research Design

The researchers, residents, and the Income Maintenance Advisory Committee developed the survey instrument. Researchers and residents engaged in a series of discussions that led to the specific questions asked of respondents in a stratified random sample of Model Neighborhood heads of households. The residents suggested the areas in which they wanted more information. For example, some members of the committee were concerned about documenting the extent of need for day-care facilities. Others were concerned about assessing the desire for subsidized housing. Still other committee members were troubled that residents were moving out of the neighborhood and they wanted to know why. Some wanted to know the extent to which recipients of welfare endured excessive rent and heating costs. The questionnaire that finally was developed reflected resident concerns as well as questions to obtain the data requested by the Boston City Council. Frequent discussions with the resident committee contributed to a questionnaire that captured a broad picture of the functioning of a variety of institutions in the lives of community residents.

Data Collection

The residents also participated in designing methods for and implementing data collection. Only residents of the Model Neighborhood could be hired as field interviewers (Davidson, Chase, and Johnson, 1971).

All field interviewers were required to complete successfully a week-long training program. Training was in English and Spanish. Interviewers were supervised closely during the actual data collection process as well as during the training period. The use of alternative screening and training procedures to hire local residents as interviewers, together with consistent supervision, proved quite effective in this study. The same procedures were followed to select interviewers in the Chicago neighborhood study (Case 2).

Dissemination of Findings

Once the data were collected and analyzed, the resident advisory committee, along with other leaders from the community, participated in disseminating the report. They joined the research team in interpreting the findings for community groups and the general public. The study received widespread publicity both within and outside New England once it was officially released by the Mayor of Boston and the director of Model Cities Administration in Boston (Davidson, Chase, and Johnson, 1971).

The findings challenged some of the myths and misconceptions about the day-to-day lives of both black and white welfare recipients and of the working poor living in the Model Neighborhood (Davidson, Chase, and Johnson, 1971; and Davidson, 1972). Moreover, it did so using a methodology that involved active participation of the subjects of study. This gave legitimacy to their concerns, norms, and values.

Case Study 2:
Chicago's Study of Community Satisfaction

The following section presents the background of the Chicago case. Additionally, the research process is described primarily as it differed from the Boston example.

Background

Historically, Logan Square and Avondale have been populated largely by middle- and working-class white families. Avondale has been noted for its stable Polish population. Access to public transportation; closeness to Chicago's Loop (the downtown shopping and business district); and the physical beauty of the neighborhoods made them attractive to the relatively affluent. In the past few years, many of these people have moved away from the community. Remaining and new residents include middle- and working-class whites, more minorities—particularly Hispanic—and young white, middle-class couples who are buying and renovating old buildings.

The research on community satisfaction in the Logan Square and Avondale neighborhoods of Chicago was sponsored by the Logan Square and Avondale Community Foundation. The foundation is a neighborhood association of representatives of churches and social agencies formed in 1975 in cooperation with the Logan Square Neighborhood Association to sponsor projects that contribute to the betterment of the community.

The executive committee of the foundation was concerned with the problems of delinquent youth, crime, and housing. The committee also lacked up-to-date data about population characteristics and resident views on the community, its institutions, and its problems. The foundation decided to initiate its own research study. This research project came about as a result of that decision.

Faculty and students in a University of Chicago Advocacy Research seminar responded to the community's request for a research study in its neighborhoods. Entry and legitimacy into the community was, in contrast to the Boston case, formally negotiated with the community of study in response to their initiative. In 1978 the research process began in these northwestern Chicago communities.

Social Process

Similarly to the Boston example, the original approach to the research and methodological strategies were agreed on by the research team and the Executive Board of the Logan Square and Avondale Foundation. This sponsor was a part of the community, unlike the Boston example where the sponsor was the city government.

Research Design

The focus of the research was to be community satisfaction with the quality of life. It involved looking at the relationships of various social factors in the neighborhood with levels of resident satisfaction. As the study developed, it became clear that a major percentage of the new residents to the community were Hispanic. The old-time white residents were curious about their new

Hispanic neighbors. The white residents feared the influx of minorities into Logan Square and Avondale would cause the deterioration of the neighborhood. The white residents believed this happened in Westtown and Humboldt Park in Chicago.

And so, a second focus of research developed—a comparative analysis of Hispanic and non-Hispanic households (Davidson, 1980). A full secondary analysis was conducted based on the original telephone survey concerning characteristics of the residents regarding education levels, economic status, household composition, values, and attitudes toward the community. Specific questions in the study centered on how the Logan Square and Avondale community compared with the Hispanic neighbors' previous residence and how residents perceived the functioning of social resources in the neighborhoods. Also, information was collected on residents' views on social issues and social problems affecting neighbors at that time.

In this case study, the community sponsored the research and through the process of their continued participation the focus of the research and analysis broadened to meet their emerging needs for information. Also, the research was designed for multivariate analysis of the data and for causal inferences to be made about the findings. The Boston research sponsored by the city was more descriptive in scope.

Data Collection

Fewer resources were available on this project than in Boston ($2,000 plus labor versus $100,000) and nearly twice the number of respondents were sought (410 versus 296). To minimize costs, instead of an in-person interview as in Boston, random digit dialing was used to generate the sample and data were collected by phone interviews. It was determined that more than 95 percent of hoped for respondents had phones, so this would not distort the randomness of the sample.

As in Boston, only residents of the community were screened and trained to do the interviewing. In Chicago, training was in Polish in addition to English and Spanish. Forty Logan Square and Avondale residents were selected and trained as interviewers, this time on a volunteer basis. They were supervised by the University of Chicago research team.

Here, the community offered work space to the research team; the community volunteers, and other community members, including priests from the local churches, proofread documents and report drafts.

Data Analysis

In Chicago, the local community members played a more active role in data analysis and interpretation of findings than was the case in Boston. This was so for both the demographic assessment and analysis of the relationship of the demographics to satisfaction with the quality of life and concern for the problems in neighborhoods today.

It was extremely useful for the transition process of long-term residents to interpret data they had themselves collected. The data indicated that most of the
new Hispanic neighbors, although different demographically than the white ethnic
residents, shared many of their views on community institutions, social problems,
and quality of life in Logan Square and Avondale. To have been told this by an
outside-community (here culturally and racially different) team of researchers
would not have been as effective. The residents saw the results themselves.

Dissemination of Findings

This part of the process was similar to that in Boston. The community in
Chicago was as much involved as they were a part of the earlier phases of the
research. Community meetings were held in different languages and over 10,000
summaries of the findings were distributed throughout the community in several
different languages by the community foundation and by the Logan Square
Neighborhood Association. Findings also were published in local newsletters
as well as covered by the major press.

Other Effects of the Research Process

The Logan Square and Avondale research project represents a model of
research in the service of community development. As a result of this research
project, the Logan Square Neighborhood Association obtained money from two
Chicago foundations to hire Spanish-speaking organizers. Knowing more about
their new Hispanic neighbors—in particular that there were so many and that
their values and concerns were similar to the white residents—the white residents
were receptive to the idea of helping their new neighbors adjust to the community.

The effectiveness of this research and the publicity it received generated interest
in understanding other Chicago neighborhoods undergoing racial or ethnic transition. It challenged misconceptions—that the immigration of Hispanic or other
minorities was responsible for the deterioration of the neighborhood. Hispanics
were just as concerned about crime and good schools, and about keeping up their
neighborhood.

The process in Logan Square and Avondale seemed to have a more fruitful outcome and was an impetus for other community action than in Boston. This is likely
because of the way in which the research project was undertaken.

Conclusion

Advocacy research represents a strategy for achieving the results discussed in
the two case examples in Boston and Chicago. Information presented in a meaningful context and form to members of a local community and a commitment
to local participation allowed residents to work with professionals to better understand themselves, others, and institutions and problems in their neighborhoods.

In Boston, information was obtained on the working poor and welfare recipients, their demographic profile and the day-to-day problems they faced. In Chicago, community members had a better understanding of their perception of quality of life in their community. In addition, residents gained objective understanding of their new neighbors and found that they shared many values. This helped in the acceptance of the new minority and eased the process of community change.

Advocacy research, in emphasizing the involvement of the subjects of research, shows the need to conduct research from the point of view of those with the problems and those who must organize to do something *of their choosing* about it. Only through an advocacy research process will the poor, uneducated, and deprived gain an appreciation for the value of social research and scientific methods. If research does not account for the everyday world of the researched, its findings—however scientific—will be ignored.

Indeed, most social research has been accountable only to peers and funding sources. Low income individuals, racial minorities, and other disadvantaged groups rarely have had the resources to do their own research or challenge others' findings. In many cases, they have not appreciated research as a process of value to them. Advocacy research is both an opportunity and a challenge. On the one hand the active participation of community residents means cost savings and greater research relevancy. On the other it means heightened vulnerability of the researcher to scrutiny. Social work's contribution to the research enterprise need not be with advocacy of one or another worldview but with promoting and practicing advocacy research. This will help ensure that all relevant views, concerns, and facts will be represented in societal decision making, not only a few.

Works Cited

Adams, A. "An Open Letter to a Young Researcher," *Royal Journal of African Affairs,* 28 (October 1979), pp. 451–479.

Baca-Zinn, M. "Field Research in Minority Communities: Ethical Methodological and Political Observations by an Outsider," *Social Problems,* 27 (December 1979), pp. 209–219.

Barber, T. X. *Pitfalls in Human Research: Ten Pivotal Points.* Elmsford, N.Y.: Pergamon Press, 1976.

Boykin, A. W. "Black Psychology and the Research Process: Keeping the Baby but Throwing out the Bath Water," in A. W. Boykin, J. Franklin, and J. Yaters, eds., *Research Directions of Black Psychologists.* New York: Russell Sage, 1979.

Carver, R. P. "The Case Against Statistical Significance Testing," *Harvard Educational Review,* 48 (August 1978), pp. 378–399.

Davidson, M. "The Process of Welfare Research in a Model Neighborhood." Unpublished manuscript, Boston, 1972.

————. "Alternative Planning Models and the Boston Model Cities Planning Experience." Unpublished PhD dissertation, Brandeis University, 1975.

————. *Unity in Diversity: Differences and Similarities Between Hispanics and Non-Hispanics in Neighborhoods in Transition.* Chicago: The Logan Square and Avondale Community Foundation, 1980.

————. "Advocacy Research: Implications for Research on Mental Health Services in Black Communities," in G. G. Wade, ed., *Development of Research Priorities for Blacks in Mental Health Service Delivery.* Washington, D.C.: National Institute of Mental Health, 1981.

Davidson, M., D. M. Burrows, and W. D. Broughton. *Unraveling Community Satisfaction.* Chicago: The Logan Square and Avondale Community Foundation, 1979.

Davidson, M., J. Chase, and H. Johnson. *The Impact of Social Irresponsibility: An Example of Advocacy Research in a Model Neighborhood Area.* Final Report of the Public Welfare Revision Study (vols. 1 and 2). Boston: Model Cities Administration, Office of the Mayor, 1971.

Merton, R. K. "Insiders and Outsiders: A Chapter in the Sociology of Knowledge," *American Journal of Sociology,* 78 (July 1972), pp. 9–47.

Moore, J. "Social Constraints on Sociological Knowledge: Academic and Research Concerning Minority Communities," *Social Problems,* 21 (Summer 1973), pp. 65–77.

Myers, V. "Toward a Synthesis of Ethnographic and Survey Methods," *Human Organizations,* 36 (Fall 1977), pp. 244–251.

Smith, N. F. "Who Should Do Minority Research?" *Social Casework,* 54 (July 1973), pp. 393–397.

Solomon, B. *Black Empowerment: Social Work in Oppressed Communities.* New York: Columbia University Press, 1976.

Warren, R. L. "The Sociology of Knowledge and the Problem of the Inner Cities," *Social Science Quarterly,* 52 (December 1971), pp. 469–491.

Weinberg, E. *Community Surveys with Local Talent.* Chicago: National Opinion Research Center, 1971.

Western, J. S. "Investigators, Subjects and Social Research," *The Australian and New Zealand Journal of Sociology,* 11 (October 1975), pp. 2–9.

Part 2
CURRICULUM ISSUES

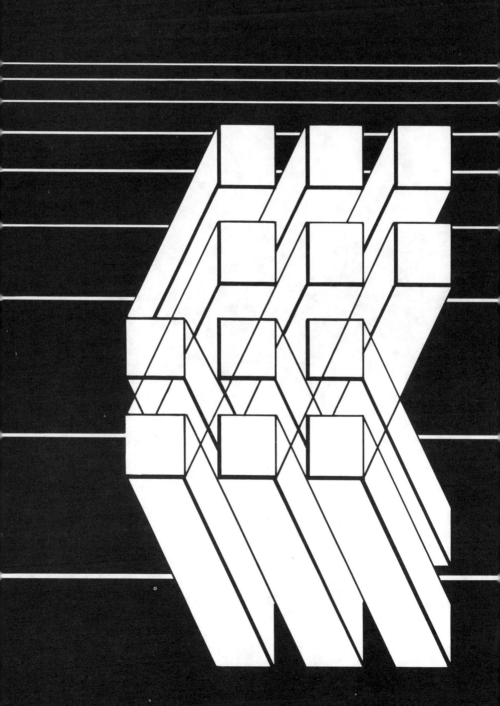

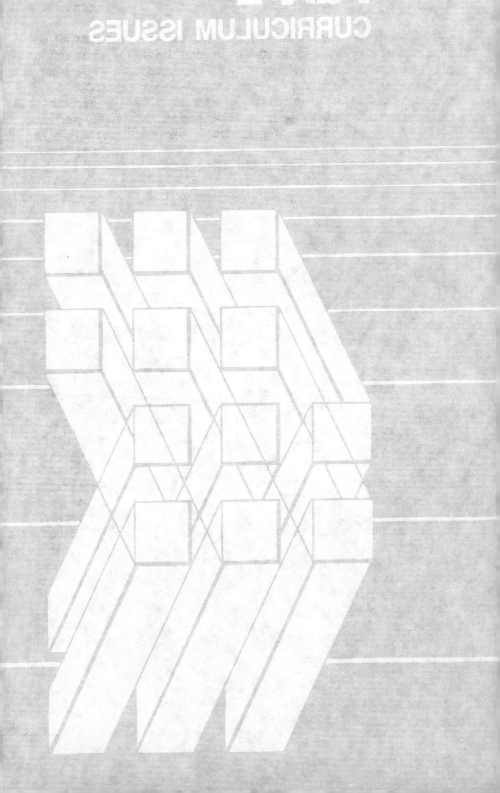

Part 2
CURRICULUM ISSUES

INTRODUCTION TO PART 2
Curriculum Issues

CAROLYN JACOBS

It is imperative that the social work curricula address the changing demographics of the twenty-first century. The gradual but dramatic growth of ethnic minorities in America indicates that by 1990 minorities of all ages will constitute 20 to 25 percent of the total population. Their percentage among youth cohorts will be over 30 percent. In some states, particularly Texas and California, minorities will compose over 45 percent of the birth cohorts in the states. By 2000, California will have a "minority-majority" (Hodgkinson, 1983). Or rather, the majority will be people of color—Mexican Americans, African Americans, Asian Americans, and native Americans. The influx of immigrants of color from Southeast Asia, Central and South America, and the Caribbean will contribute to the increasing ethnic minority populations. In light of the changing demographics, it behooves social workers in education to consider curriculum needs and their transformation to meet the future.

Transforming social work curricula to reflect theoretical and practice content of importance to ethnic minorities is a major challenge for educators. Part 2 offers those persons committed to and charged with such a task a series of articles presenting current knowledge, dilemmas, and pathways for the future of curriculum development. The need for such formulations has been substantiated in numerous places. The publication *Mental Health and People of Color: Curriculum Development and Change* (Chunn, Dunston, and Ross-Sheriff, 1983) is an exploration and detailed discussion of the sparsity of overall integrative approaches to including ethnic minority content in mental health curricula. As well, that publication sets forth a series of six guiding principles for integrating content. These principles include: (1) the involvement of ethnic minorities in leadership roles and as sources of information for relevant content; (2) well-defined curriculum and policy statements regarding the content's significance, purpose, and thrust; (3) the individualization of content by relevant groups linked, when possible, by overarching frameworks protecting the viability of the groups; (4) the placing of responsibility for ethnic minority content under an ongoing school committee designated for that purpose to ensure continuity, viability, and priority; (5) insistence that ethnic minority content be part of the core curriculum, rather than elective or peripheral; and, (6) that ethnic minority curriculum content should focus on normative behaviors and wellness, rather than on abnormal and illness reactions.

These principles and the challenges surrounding their implementation are important objectives and concerns for social workers in education. The principles have evolved from the pressures and commitment of minority groups and coalitions within the social work profession; professional organizations such as the National Association of Social Workers, the Council on Social Work Education (CSWE), and the National Conference on Social Welfare; the President's Commission on Mental Health; the National Institute of Mental Health and other funding sources that have supported projects to assist in attaining the many goals set by the schools of social work to meet the challenges of integrating ethnic minority content (Chunn, Dunston, and Ross-Sheriff, 1983).

In 1983, Smith College School for Social Work conducted a survey of 90 graduate schools of social work. The survey sought to examine the process graduate schools of social work used for integrating and supporting ethnic minority content within the curriculum. Forty of the 90 schools (44 percent) completed the questionnaire, which consisted of a series of open-ended questions designed to explore the planning, implementation and monitoring processes for the inclusion of ethnic minority content. An analysis of the data led to the following conclusions. For the 40 schools responding, the four-phase planning process was as follows: (1) schools began offering isolated electives from the mid-1960s through the early 1970s; (2) special faculty committees for general planning appeared; (3) individual faculty members assumed responsibility for course development; and (4) faculty curriculum committees were responsible for including ethnic minority content in core course offerings. Of the schools responding, 57.5 percent of the schools viewed the position of CSWE on standards for the inclusion of ethnic minority content in required courses as the major impetus in shifting the focus from isolated electives toward the goal of full curriculum integration.

Despite this thrust, ethnic minority content was not infused throughout the curriculum. Evaluation and assessment of integration efforts remained the focus of special committees and individual faculty members who are committed to ensuring the inclusion of ethnic minority content. Integration did not permeate the entire curriculum process. Each school noted fiscal and attitudinal deterrents to full integration. Loss of funding and faculty for curriculum development; the limitations of the existing knowledge base; a trend toward integrating other oppressed groups and diluting the content on specific ethnic minorities; and increased resistance of administrators, field and classroom faculty, and students all serve to heighten the difficulty of proceeding toward full integration of ethnic minority content. These schools were concerned with how to continue intensive efforts given the constraints. The articles in this section focus on the work ahead. They invite the reader to move toward thinking creatively about the issues of curriculum development and pedagogy in light of the concerns expressed by those educators responding to the Smith survey of graduate social work in education.

Critics of social work education, and the various knowledge bases from which it draws, have brought to light the many ways in which blindness about the cultural heritage and history of ethnic minorities has compromised some of the most cherished values of the profession—the ability to understand and respect diversity in ethnic background, race, class and culture in a pluralistic society; a commitment to value clients' interests as primary in designing and implementing intervention strategies; and a willingness to engage in practice from a value base that will reduce inequalities in the allocation of societal resources and enhance social functioning. These values permeate the educational experience in various ways. They suggest the redefinition and selection of content to be taught and the exclusion of disruptive language and observations that are laden with cultural bias. Social work values require that the bias about race and class, which is carried into the classroom and field practicum, be examined, and that the interactions between teacher and students and among colleagues be informed by the issues of diversity in a pluralistic society. All of these are issues having major consequences for moving the solitary educator from the simple addition of a unit, text, or case illustration to the successful collaborative transformation of the curriculum.

Transforming the curriculum involves analyses of how the professional values, sequence organization, course syllabi, teaching styles, and faculty resources intersect with students to achieve the educational goals. Theories of curriculum development and phases of curriculum transformation have been developed (Posner and Rudnitsky, 1982; McIntosh, 1983; and Schuster and Van Dyne, 1985). Their various phase formulations acknowledge that educators, curricula and students are not static but dynamic forces in the learning environment. Movement through phases of transformation depends on the state of the art in the knowledge and practice bases and in the resources of the specific school. However, an interactive phase formulation allows social work educators to push beyond the limitations of their current curricula to a more inclusive one.

The following interactive phases are designed to determine the inclusiveness of a curriculum. Phase 1 is the colorless curriculum. In this phase, there is a prevailing belief and practice that theory is color blind; race, ethnicity, oppression do not matter; and no ethnic minority content is taught. Given the current CSWE standards, this phase should not exist. In phase 2, ethnic minorities are in the curriculum. Here, racial and ethnic minorities are added as variables or factors to be controlled. The paradigms are not changed but applied indiscriminately to all ethnic groups. There is a search for an exotic exception to the norms for illustrative use. This phase characterized most social work curricula prior to the 1960s. In phase 3, the ethnic minority is deviant. In this phase, minorities are seen as a problem or anomaly. Paradigms of deviancy and victimization prevail. Phase 4 includes the ethnic minorities in the context of their own culture. In this phase, culture is taken into account and attempts are made consciously to include writings and frameworks developed by individuals in the respective groups. An analysis of the appropriateness of the existing paradigms occurs. Phase 5 is an inclusive curriculum. The curriculum in phase 5 combines the double vision of phase 1 and phase 4. A healthy dialectic occurs as the patterns of life in a multicultural, inclusive, pluralistic society are presented. The inclusive curriculum requires reconstruction and redefinition that reflects all perspectives and people. The transformation occurs and leads to a more accurate reflection of the cultural, ethnic, and philosophical diversity in the world.

The movement toward transforming a social work curriculum in preparation for the year 2000 can be undertaken with the beginning step of critiquing one's syllabus. The following structure adapted from Van Dyne and Schuster (1985) and Posner and Rudnitsky (1983) can be applied to any syllabus. A series of questions is organized around components of the syllabus such as goals, content, organization, and method. For each component, convention or accepted wisdom is identified and the transformation questions are asked to move the educator beyond the limitations of the existing design components and perspectives to more accurately represent diversity.

The goals of a syllabus describe those desirable attributes that are expected to result from the educational process. They are drawn from professional values, and conceptions of society, the learner, and of the subject matter and its importance. Convention or accepted wisdom would lead a student to ask: What is the purpose of this course? What is its function in the sequence, school, and profession? The questions asked to transform the course are: How would the goals of the course change if the course included a critique of the knowledge or intervention strategies that reflect the ethnic minority experience in its categories of analyses? How would the goals change if more conscious attention was paid to the choice of case materials, examples, and the uses to which the examples and research are put? Who is served politically, socially, and economically by the particular perspective?

Content is the set of intended learning objectives presumed to lead to the achievement of educational goals that specify knowledge, skills, and attitudinal outcomes. The conventional questions are: What areas of research and theory are privileged and considered most important to the sequence? Where do those values come from? Who benefits from that value system? What areas or researchers are dismissed as less important? What groups are devalued or considered deviant or marginal by the normative descriptions or generalizations about human behavior or capability? Questions of transformation might be: Are the descriptions of representative human behavior derived from a sample limited by race or class? How would these descriptions change if minority issues were considered of primary importance to the majority of researchers in social work education? Who are the major sources for understanding ethnic minorities in the field? How are their writings used in curricula?

Organization is the structured and sequential delivery of content to and with students. The conventional questions are: When is ethnic minority content relevant in social work? In the design of the curriculum and of individual courses? Is it studied primarily in reference to the larger society or in interaction with other systems and the society? Transformation questions are: How could the ethnic minority perspective be taken into account beyond the study of racism or special problems? What new courses, content, or research questions become possible when the interests and needs of ethnic minorities are addressed?

Method addresses general teaching strategies or pedagogical issues ranging from didactic to experiential that include evaluative components. Conventional questions are concerned with: How does the educator's ethnic background, values and level of comfort in teaching ethnic minority content affect the design of teaching and evaluation strategies? Questions related to transformation are: Is any research design or paradigm ever free of social context? Should it be? What social or cultural biases and expectations are carried into the classroom or field that affect the learners' practice with ethnic minorities differently than with nonminorities? What pedagogical strategies could be devised to recognize and correct social and cultural biases? As these questions are asked of courses in social work education, educators must think about the value and inclusiveness of the questions.

Several may provide useful content and pedagogical strategies. Chapter 9 is a study of ethnic theory and its role in social work education. The problems of definitions and isolating relevant variables are explored. Major trends and content in ethnic studies presented for inclusion in the social work curriculum include ideologies of assimilation, pluralism, and conflict; prejudice, racism, and ethnocentrism. Pedagogical issues, including the role of consciousness raising, also are discussed. The desired link with practice in the core curriculum and specialized courses is highlighted. Chapter 10 is a discussion of the significance of culture and power relationships in understanding and treating ethnic minorities. A course design for including these interactive variables is presented after a detailed discussion of theories of power and culture. The purpose of the article is to demonstrate the development of curricula that provided students with a strong theoretical framework and clear self-awareness regarding ethnic minority issues. Chapter 11 is a description of the efforts of one school to introduce content on racial and ethnic minorities such that it is integrated into the core curriculum. As well, students are required to take an intensive course that focuses clearly on conceptual and affective content. Basic knowledge of racism and discrimination is integral to understanding social processes from individual identity development to policy formulation and is presented to enhance student learning at all levels.

In chapter 12, an approach to the inclusion of ethnic minority content in the teaching of social work research is described and illustrated. The approach is based on the premise that the sequence of research courses in a school of social work should have, as one of its components, the opportunity for students to learn skills in the assessment and utilization of research knowledge for practice purposes. Ethnic minority content can be incorporated into the teaching of these skills.

In chapter 13, a pedagogical model for incorporating conceptual frameworks is presented. The model is focused on the dual perspective and the ethnic reality with a teaching and learning approach that draws on the students' life experiences both from the past and the present. The learning environment is structured to provide a setting for moving beyond stereotypes. The culturally aware educator as teacher and group leader is critical in creating a learning environment conducive to exploring and modifying biased attitudes and discriminatory practice through the use of techniques that focus on conflict, controversy, and mutual aid. A second pedagogical approach using a group experience as the primary method to explore the complicated intersection of racism and sexism for black, Puerto Rican and white women in three independent study courses is presented in chapter 14. The structure of the courses is discussed in the context of the overall curriculum. The format challenges the traditional teaching methods by creating an environment where all are adult learners.

In chapter 15, a strategy to facilitate the infusion of content on racial and ethnic minorities is presented. The strategy relates the content to the purposes of the field of social work, proposes a structure by which this content can be infused and integrated throughout the curriculum, and provides examples of learning experiences. A framework is provided that promises to facilitate or transform the inclusion of ethnic minority content in social work courses whatever their central objectives or themes.

Works Cited

Chunn, J. C., P. J. Dunston, and F. Ross-Sheriff (eds.). *Mental Health and People of Color: Curriculum Development and Change.* Washington, D.C.: Howard University Press, 1983.

Hodgkinson, H. L. "Guess Who's Coming to College," *ACADEME Bulletin of the American Association of University Professors* (March-April 1983), pp. 13–20.

McIntosh, P. *Interactive Phases of Curricular Re-vision: A Feminist Perspective,* Working Paper No. 124. Wellesley College Center for Research on Women: Wellesley, Mass., 1983.

Posner, G. J., and A. N. Rudnitsky. *Course Design: A Guide to Curriculum Development for Teachers.* New York: Longman, 1982.

Schuster, M., and S. Van Dyne. *Women's Place in The Academy: Transforming the Liberal Arts Curriculum.* Totowa, N.J.: Rowman & Allanheld, 1985.

Posner, G. J., and A. N. Rudnitsky. Course Design: A Guide to Curriculum Development for Teachers. New York: Longman, 1982.
Schuster, M., and S. Van Dyne. Women's Place in the Academy: Transforming the Liberal Arts Curriculum. Totowa, N.J.: Rowman & Allanheld, 1985.

CHAPTER 9

ETHNICITY: THEORY BASE AND PRACTICE LINK

SHIRLEY JENKINS

To establish ethnic studies in the social work curriculum, it is necessary to link both theory and practice. Without a theoretical foundation, the current interest in ethnicity can dissipate into anecdote and folklore. Without implying a practice outcome, the subject may be abandoned as superfluous, with no utility for the field. But with both theory and practice connections, ethnic studies can be a force in deepening our understanding of client behavior, facilitating treatment, and reconceptualizing many aspects of service delivery. Additional components in teaching ethnicity to social workers include self-examination by students and faculty and the heightened consciousness of one's own attitudes, beliefs, and behavior on issues of race and ethnic differences. Unless theoretical learning is filtered through such a screen of consciousness, it is doubtful that social workers will achieve appropriate practice outcomes. This chapter on theoretical focus includes a discussion of how students and faculty can integrate content and how to process content in practice.

Comparative Approach

Introductory ethnic studies, for reasons of both practice and theory, are best undertaken in a comparative context. Social work students are a mixed group, from a range of cultures and backgrounds. Clients also are varied, and disproportionately from black and Hispanic groups. A substantial number of social work transactions are intergroup, and it is within the comparative context that they are best appreciated. The preference of many parents that children marry "one of their own kind" is not unique to any one group, nor is the desire of mothers that their children eat, nor is the invocation of tradition, myth, or special pleading with the "powers-that-be." The forms may differ, but the phenomena persist. As medical students must learn not to confuse symptoms with disease, social work students should not confuse culture with "crazy." Furthermore, the comparative approach works in all directions. For example, a black woman student social worker said in a class, "My placement is in a Jewish agency and my clients are all Jewish. I need to know more about their background and culture."

In support of the comparative approach, Schermerhorn (1970) has suggested that the main task of social science is "the discovery of generalizations that transcend the boundaries of single societies." (P. 4.) This is a move beyond the case study to look at the social context of ethnic relations. Are the same phenomena operating in black–white relations as in black–Puerto Rican relations? In Italian–Polish relations as in Sephardic Jewish–Ashkenazi Jewish relations? What differences can be attributed to class? To national origins? To time of migration? The goal is not to build an encyclopedia of customs and habits, but to study ethnic issues to differentiate similarities from differences. As Schermerhorn (1970) has stated, "If research has confirmed anything in this area, it is that prejudice is a product of situations, historical situations, economic situations, political situations; it is not a little demon that emerges in people simply because they are depraved." (P. 6.)

Putting the issue another way, Steinberg (1982) has said, "Without doubt, ethnicity informs consciousness and influences behavior. But . . . what informs ethnicity and influences its character? (P. ix.) Ethnic differences are not etched in stone, but are themselves the product of history, class, place, and time. Thus, the comparative approach involves more than a study of the interaction among groups; the comparative approach sets that interaction within its social context. To know the etiology of a phenomenon is the first step in a strategy for social change.

Ethnicity Defined

In a sense, the comparative approach grows from the nature of the concept itself. Ethnicity has many definitions. Weber (1961) has defined an *ethnic group* as "a collectivity based on an assumption of common origin, real or imaginary." (P. 305.) Schermerhorn (1970) has defined it as a "collectivity within a larger society having real or putative common ancestry, memories of a shared historical past, and a cultural focus on one or more symbolic elements. . . . A necessary accompaniment is some consciousness of kind among members of the group." (P. 12.) Among the symbolic elements are physical contiguity, language or dialect, religion, features, kinship patterns, and nationality, or any combination of these. According to Merton (1972), the identity of a group may be apparent more to "insiders" than to "outsiders."

Some social scientists resist using ethnic group as a descriptive variable on the grounds that it is imprecise, subjective, and hard to validate historically. Many sociologists, in Great Britain in particular, are more comfortable with the concepts of class and race. But in moving from theory to practice, and from abstractions to people in need of services, both race and class have substantial limitations as referents to describe the content of services. A poor black family in New York City, for example, may need either a Spanish-, French-, or English-speaking social worker, depending on former residence, and may show striking differences among themselves in foods eaten, child-rearing patterns, and kin relationships. Adoption of unrelated children may be a desirable program for one group, unacceptable for another. Hysterical outbursts may be frequent and tolerated in some cultures; silence and withdrawal may be typical reaction patterns in others. Many behaviors need more than race, class, and individual differences as explanatory variables. Although race and class are powerful concepts and are essential for social analysis, they must be buttressed by other components of the variable ethnicity when the issue is the delivery of social services.

In a society that is socially mobile with few legal barriers to interracial marriage, the task of drawing ethnic boundaries around groups is difficult. Sometimes differences and allegiances only become apparent at points of conflict. One British sociologist, Parkin (1974), goes so far as to have defined ethnicity as the articulation of cultural distinctiveness in situations of political conflict or competition. Does this definition stand the test of reversal? If political conflicts were not present, would ethnic distinctiveness and differences disappear?

This comingling of the two phenomena of conflict and ethnicity in American history and social awareness of it may be one reason why ethnic characteristics and differences rarely are presented in a positive or constructive light. An alternative thesis is that each group brings rich and positive cultural contributions and that ethnicity offers a base to establish group identity, which can be supportive to individual and familial functioning.

Racism: A Separate Issue

Ethnicity has been discussed as a significant and useful variable. But there also are important limitations. If the curriculum includes ethnicity as course content, then what happens to black studies and to Puerto Rican studies? If the ethnic group is stressed, what happens to the study of race and racism?

Conflicts exist between ethnicity and black and Puerto Rican studies in the struggle for curriculum space. Black and Puerto Rican studies came on campus after the turbulence of the sixties and the demands of minority students for equal time. Following the initial political pull of these subjects, however, the courses frequently faltered in registration for several reasons. One of the main problems was the uncertainty about the constituency. Was the course in black studies, for example, primarily for the white student, as an introduction to black family life and culture, or was it for the black student, to develop identity, race consciousness, and pride? The black student did not need the introduction; the white student could not use the identity.

There should be a place in the curriculum for the study of specific group cultures, life-styles, history, and social problems, including black, Hispanic, and Jewish studies. But these appear to have most utility as electives and advanced work, with the comparative ethnicity course orienting the entire student body to theory, consciousness, and practice in intergroup relations.

Asking what happens to the study of racism if ethnic groups rather than race is the unit of attention is related to the issue of color, which cannot be ignored. Hopps (1982), in an editorial for a special issue of *Social Work* titled "Social Work and People of Color," said: "To deny that color is the basis for much of today's oppression only continues to avoid confronting the problem that has existed throughout America's history and further delays its remediation." (P. 4.) Color surfaces as one variable among others in the ethnic definition, but it needs separate attention in relation to the racism issue. This can be done in one or more sessions of an ethnic studies course, with attention to the special problems of blacks in a white-controlled society. The use of the comparative approach should not be used to avoid this issue.

Theoretical Content

The development of a general theory of ethnicity is a complex task, exacerbated by the imprecise definition of the variable under study. Women's studies over time, for example, deal with changing economic, political, and psychological circumstances. But, these all impact on a defined group. In the case of ethnic studies, the dependent variable has several definitions depending on time and place; so the cause-and-effect equation is never static. There are no elegant mathematical solutions for such a shifting phenomenon. Theories of ethnicity, therefore, tend to be eclectic and subject to interaction with related but separate phenomena such as class and social stratification.

A problem in evaluating the utility of any theory is the extent to which it is "partialized" or concerned with only one set of relationships, one combination of groups, or one time in history. In the United States this problem is relevant because theories of assimilation, which appeared to have universal application, are more relevant for ethnic whites than blacks, and light-skinned rather than dark-skinned Hispanics. Similarly, loss of native language over generations has been shown to occur under one set of political circumstances, but not another. The movement back and forth from Puerto Rico to the continent, for example, and across the Mexican border, means that the retention of Spanish and issues of bilingualism assume a different form than in the case of the turn-of-the-century immigrants from eastern and southern Europe.

The issue of "partializing" is not raised with the assumption that a general all-encompassing theory is needed before ethnic studies can be learned or taught. But the literature on ethnicity too often reads as if only issues of whites are relevant, and too little attention is paid to the groups referred to by Bryce-LaPorte (1977) as the "visible ethnics"—the blacks, Hispanics, Asians, and native Americans.

A second issue in the development of a viable theory of ethnicity is the interrelationship of the variables of class and group. Most people, excluding the total bigot, believe there are individual differences and that people can be outstandingly able or deficient in all groups. The problem is dealing with group norms. When 90 percent of a group is disadvantaged, how do you "control" for racism? Rather than separate genetic factors of a group or persons, it is more useful to move to a multivariate analysis and deal with more than one variable. An example is the work of Gordon (1964), who postulated an intersection of ethnic subsocieties (basically blacks, Roman Catholics, Jews, and white Protestants) and social classes, resulting in what he labels "ethclass." These units mostly circumscribe the primary relationships, such as family and friends, rather than the broader structural aspects of functioning, such as jobs and political behavior. The concept of ethclass is introduced to illustrate the need to consider the relationship of class and ethnic group, as well as the implications for ethnic stratification arising from that interaction.

Given the problems of definition, and of isolating the relevant variables, the study of ethnic theory tends to be exploratory rather than explanatory. However, it is still possible to suggest curriculum themes. Social work students should be familiar with the main trends in ethnic ideology, the main theorists of each school of thought, and the current issues. Some of the suggested content is discussed in the following material.

Three Ideologies: A Historical Perspective

Three ideological positions have dominated the literature: assimilation, cultural pluralism, and conflict theory. Following an early thrust to Anglo-Saxon conformity, the emerging United States, with its burgeoning immigrant population, tended to adopt an assimilationist ideology. The slogan of the "melting pot," after a popular play by Zangwill in 1908, was cited widely. Assimilationist ideology proposed that diverse ethnic groups would come to share a common culture and have equal access to the opportunity structure. Underlying the assimilationist theory is the evolutionary concept that modernization would result in the eclipse of the folk community. Industrialization would put people to work on factory assembly lines, public school education would "Americanize" the next generation and provide a trained and literate labor force, and old ways would recede as the new American ethos took hold. Intermarriage could provide the final blow to ethnic differences.

Among the theorists who supported the early assimilationist theory were Robert Park and Louis Wirth. Park (1950) developed the concept of a "race relations cycle," which involved contact, then competition, then accommodation, then assimilation in intergroup relations. (Later in his life, after a visit to Hawaii,

Park changed his position after recognizing the sharp racial differences that existed on the islands, and he questioned the inevitability of assimilation for all groups.) Wirth (1956) wrote on Jewish immigrants to Chicago from the perspective of an observer of generational change. He saw the move from inner-city ghetto to suburban homeowner, with attendant dimunition of ethnic behavior.

In an influential study, Myrdal (1944), the Swedish economist, suggested that there was a contradiction between the discrimination against blacks and the professed American creed of equality. Myrdal was optimistic that forces of industrialization, urbanization, and mass education would move society toward the eradication of irrational prejudices. The focus on white society and white morality, however, ignored black consciousness and black identity—and assimilation was seen only in the image of white America.

Not all assimilationist theory predicted smooth accommodation. Marxist theory suggested that class, rather than ethnic group, would claim the allegiance of workers, and as capitalist crises deepened, workers would unite, regardless of national and racial differences. Thus, conflict would be intensified, but on class rather than ethnic lines.

An important contribution to the consideration of assimilation was made by W. Lloyd Warner, who studied social stratification in small communities. The description of ethnic occupational and social status led to Warner and his collaborator, Leo Srole (1945), developing certain hypotheses about the process of assimilation and the time element involved in assimilation in terms of differences between the host and immigrant groups. Whether the assimilation of blacks was different in degree or in kind was one question raised in the literature. This question was argued in two main formulations, the caste hypothesis and the contact hypothesis. The former held that differences between blacks and whites were institutionalized in the society, whereas the latter held that intimacy between groups would link accommodation to assimilation.

As successive waves of immigrants settled in the United States, and earlier arrivals experienced social as well as geographic mobility, ethnic differences were persisting beyond expectations, although in new forms and patterns. The concept of ethnic pluralism developed, based on the view that American society was composed of ethnic subsocieties, each with a distinct subculture. Related to this was the important differentiation between cultural and structural pluralism. For example, a factory worker on an assembly line with others from a dozen different nationalities and from different races, and paid at the same scale outside of work may associate almost exclusively with members of his or her own group. This situation can be explained in terms of the pluralist ideology in which modernization affects the structure of society but primary group relationships retain the ethnic group base. Supporting this thesis is the work of Bogardus (1928), who developed the social distance scale. The scale measures attitudes toward assimilation and defines the levels of acceptance. Other writers, such as Glazer and Moynihan (1970), called attention to the persistence of ethnic groups and to the important political roles ethnicity plays in modern society. Writing primarily about white ethnics, Gans (1979) has questioned the hypothesis that ethnic differences are persisting as before. He has suggested that "symbolic ethnicity," or ritual following of form, is replacing major ethnic group commitment.

Attention to political factors related to ethnic behavior raises new issues and accelerates the application of a conflict model to ethnic issues. Conflict theory, however, tends to have an economic base. Conflict theory suggests that the modernization of society will affect different ethnic groups differently, thereby increasing intergroup competition and conflict and exacerbating existing ethnic stratification and exploitation of weaker groups by a powerful elite. Two other concepts of importance are issues of racism, in which racial attitudes are institutionalized and become part of the structure of society, and ethnocentrism, in which there is a tendency of members of a particular group to see their lifestyle and customs as superior to others. Ethnocentrism can be expressed as a separatist position. Theorists in the Marxist tradition such as Cox (1948) place both racism and ethnocentrism in the broader analysis of class struggle. Other writers who follow a function theory see conflict as necessary for realignment of social forces and resolving differences to improve social functioning as a whole.

Gordon (1975), who contributed to the pluralist ideology, has sought to develop a general theory of racial and ethnic group relations that also would encompass psychological variables—an approach of particular relevance to the field of social work. In developing the dependent variable (outcome) for his causal theory, he has suggested that it be a construct of four subvariables: (1) type of assimilation (cultural versus structural); (2) degree of total assimilation (scores for subtypes); (3) degree of conflict (both intergroup and majority-minority); and (4) degree of access to societal rewards (an equality variable). The operationalizing of this concept could result in looking at a society and evaluating ethnic positions with regard to high, moderate, or low assimilation in a construct that includes information on a series of variables, including structural and cultural factors, conflict and power.

On the other side of the equation, Gordon classifies relevant independent variables in biosocial development, interaction process, and societal categories. Each of these is a complex concept, and actual operationalizing of the proposed equation to predict assimilation would be difficult. But the essential point is that Gordon's work is designed to encompass both psychological and societal factors as causative of assimilation processes. This is a different method than approaches that tend either to "over psychologize" ethnic factors or to look only at race and class.

For at least three reasons, social work students review literature on prejudice: (1) it comprises an important part of the history of the field of intergroup relations, (2) it has clear implications for practice, and (3) classroom discussion can lead to the students' self-awareness and self-examination. Hraba (1979) has organized the prejudice and discrimination literature according to the psychoanalytical, the cognitive, and the behaviorist schools of thought. An example of the psychoanalytic theory is the work of Adorno (1950) and associates, whose book *The Authoritarian Personality* suggests that a prejudiced person, as a result of early suppression of aggression and submission to authority, may later in life displace aggressive feelings onto others, typically scapegoats and members of outgroups. A high correlation was found to exist between authoritarianism and ethnocentrism. This work related primarily to anti-Semitism, and it contained some useful insights into that phenomenon. It is less useful, however, in explaining the social correlates of discrimination, or the variety of personality types who hold prejudiced positions.

The cognitive school of thought disagrees with the psychoanalytic approach, believing that prejudice follows belief, and thus represents a rational consequence of assumed belief dissimilarity. The behaviorists, representing a third approach, postulate that prejudice is learned through conditioning because of association or reinforcement. Theorists help illuminate the complexities of this issue: Katz (1960) called attention to the functions of prejudice; Merton (1949) developed a typology showing the relationship between prejudice and discrimination; and Festinger (1964), in his discussion of cognitive dissonance, has shown how, after making a decision, people will try to bring their attitudes in line with their actions. This last contribution has important implications for the possible consequences of structural change on attitudinal change.

Screen of Consciousness

Discussion of theories of prejudice is a natural route to self-awareness for students and to examination of their cultural biases. Incorporation of such a goal in the curriculum, however, must be undertaken with extreme caution. A classroom is not a treatment group, and the structure, basic goals, timing, and relationships for each are essentially different. Students can be helped to gain insights into their attitudes and behavior through the instructional process, but the boundary lines that circumscribe classroom education need to be respected, or the impact on the total educational process could be dysfunctional. In particular, good peer relationships need to be maintained for student functioning so that students of all groups can continue to interact as classmates. Issues of race and groups should be ongoing subjects of concern and discussion, not of bitterness and anger. Too often instructors avoid raising issues of race because they fear that intense feelings and intergroup hostility will be aroused. Raising issues, allowing for differences, and providing a climate for self-examination in an atmosphere of constructive discussion is not an easy process.

An oblique approach to the issues of examination of prejudice, which often leads to substantive discussion, is through use of films, tapes, and case presentations. With materials to discuss, students can move naturally from looking at others to sharing their experiences and biases. Prejudicial attitudes should not pass without examination, but students who share their own prejudices should be helped, particularly by peers, to recognize the need for change, rather than be judged, sentenced, and proclaimed guilty, thereby arousing defenses and more hostility. One question on a take-home examination in an ethnicity class will be noted because it has had a payoff in self-awareness. Students were asked to report an ethnic joke and analyze it in terms of two theories of prejudice. By the time this assignment was completed, many students had undergone a profound conversion in their use of ethnic stereotypes.

Litwak and Dono (1976) suggested that ethnicity is an intervening variable that can be useful in bridging the gap between bureaucratic organizations and primary groups. Ethnic factors relate with special force to families, and for social workers this is particularly meaningful. With a grasp of major ethnic theories, and heightened self-awareness, students can examine family patterns of their ethnic groups as well as their clients. In the ethnicity class, students study a particular group in depth, and class reports, readings, research materials, and the sharing of personal experiences give depth and meaning to this unit of work.

Reports on family life help students to relate themselves to their groups, to examine their ignorance on the customs and cultures of others, and to appreciate some of the commonalities. Anecdotes are plentiful here; just a few illustrations will be cited from classroom experience.

■ An Irish student said, after doing some recommended reading, "I didn't know Andrew Greeley knew my mother."

■ An Italian student who amused half the class while the other half sat silent said, "I hadn't been to church in seven years, and then I agreed to be a bridesmaid at my sister's wedding. I didn't know it was High Mass." (She would have to go to confession first.)

■ A discussion about whether clients who have experienced confession are more or less amenable to psychotherapy.

■ A Chicano student said, "Obviously I am a Mestizo," with the class asking "Why is it obvious?" (His bone structure was indicative.)

■ The black and Hispanic students listening in amazement to a lively argument between Orthodox and Reform Jewish students on what was appropriate Jewish religious observance.

Discussion of immigration policy and the history of the settlement of the United States is buttressed in class by a student census of from where and when their families came. The roster of dates and places is like a microcosm of the settlement of the United States, and this provides another opportunity to link personal identity with ethnic history.

■ A Polish student brought the framed citizenship papers of her father.

■ A Jewish student, the daughter of survivors, brought a book of photographs of Holocaust victims.

■ Puerto Rican students in class explored their ambivalence about their "nationhood."

■ Blacks and white Anglo-Saxon Protestants recognized that their groups were the early arrivals on the continent and that the conditions of arrival rather than the date of arrival affected their group's history.

Link with Practice

In a professional school, the theory base and consciousness raising must be goal directed, and the goal is the training for practice. Use of ethnic background as one more variable in service delivery makes good sense and follows sound theories on the role of identity and the positive function of group support. The theory rarely has been empirically tested, however, to obtain proof of outcome.

Although there are few carefully designed research studies, there are dozens of examples in the literature of practice experience in service delivery where special attention has been paid to ethnic factors. An important effort to develop effective practice with black clients was discussed by Solomon (1976), in her book *Black Empowerment: Social Work in Oppressed Communities.* The concept of empowerment was an attempt to strengthen problem solving on the part of members of a stigmatized group, and the involvement of the black church in the service program reflected traditional cultural patterns.

The link between ethnicity and practice does not relate to case services only, but encompasses policy, programming, and planning. Social work students should be challenged to think about the ethnic dilemma defined by Jenkins (1981) and the questions of how, where, and when ethnicity should be a factor in service delivery. In a research study of social workers, services to minority groups, and parental attitudes, Jenkins (1981) identified some guidelines to decision making. She documented a dual approach to many issues on the part of white and minority workers and found that agencies could be evaluated on the dimensions of ethnic culture, ethnic consciousness, and policy on mixing and matching along ethnic lines. Furthermore, on the international scene, programs on ethnic issues were found to reflect national social policy.

Having discussed the ethnic content that should be in the social work curriculum, it is only fair to ask whether this content needs to be in a special course or dispersed among the several practice, policy, and background courses. Essentially, this is not an either–or issue, and no ethnic blueprint is appropriate for all schools. Ideally, ethnicity as a variable should be integrated throughout the course of study and should be included appropriately in the various courses, depending on specific content. If this occurs, an elective on ethnicity could be an advanced course that stresses theory and research. In those schools where the desirable level of ethnic content is not diffused throughout the curriculum, the ethnicity course can be a required introduction, offering some exposure to all students. In a basic course, the practice implications should be stressed. Whether as a single course or as integrated content, ethnic studies in social work will give visibility, credibility, and a knowledge base to the premise that ethnic content is needed for appropriate service delivery and policy development.

Works Cited

Adorno, T.W.E., et al. *The Authoritarian Personality*. New York: Harper & Row, 1950.

Bogardus, E. S. *Immigration and Race Attitudes*. Boston: D. C. Heath & Co., 1928.

Bryce-LaPorte, R. S. "Visibility of the New Immigrants," *Society,* 14 (September–October 1977), pp. 18–22.

Cox, O. C. *Caste, Class, and Race*. Garden City, N.Y.: Doubleday & Co., 1948.

Festinger, L. *Conflict, Decision, and Dissonance*. Stanford, Calif.: University Press, 1964.

Gans, H. J. "Symbolic Ethnicity: The Future of Ethnic Groups and Cultures in America," *Ethnic and Racial Studies,* 27 (January 1979), pp. 1–20.

Glazer, N., and D. P. Moynihan. *Beyond the Melting Pot: The Negroes, Puerto Ricans, Jews, Italians, and Irish of New York City*. Cambridge, Mass.: M.I.T. Press, 1970.

Gordon, M. *Assimilation in American Life*. New York: Oxford University Press, 1964.

———. "Toward a General Theory of Racial and Ethnic Group Relations," in N. Glazer and D. P. Moynihan, eds., *Ethnicity, Theory and Experience*. Cambridge, Mass.: Harvard University Press, 1975.

Hopps, J. G. "Oppression Based on Color," Editorial, *Social Work,* 27 (January 1982), pp. 3–6.

Hraba, J. *American Ethnicity*. Itasca, Ill.: F. E. Peacock Publishers, 1979.

Jenkins, S. *The Ethnic Dilemma in Social Services*. New York: Free Press, 1981.

Katz, D. "The Functional Approach to the Study of Attitudes," *Public Opinion Quarterly,* 24 (Summer 1960), pp. 163–204.

Litwak, E., and J. Dono. "Forms of Ethnic Relations, Organizational Theory, and Social Policy in Modern Industrial Society." Unpublished manuscript, Columbia University, December 21, 1976.

Merton, R. K. "Discrimination and the American Creed," in R. MacIver, ed., *Discrimination and National Welfare*. New York: Harper & Row, 1949.

———. "Insiders and Outsiders: A Chapter in the Sociology of Knowledge," *American Journal of Sociology,* 78 (July 1972), pp. 9–47.

Myrdal, G. *An American Dilemma: The Negro Problem and Modern Democracy*. New York: Harper & Bros., 1944.

Park, R. E. *Race and Culture*. Glencoe, Ill.: Free Press, 1950.

Parkin, D. "Congregational and Interpersonal Ideologies in Political Ethnicity," in A. Cohen, ed., *Urban Ethnicity U.S.A.* Monograph 12. London: Travistock, 1974.

Schermerhorn, R. A. *Comparative Ethnic Relations: A Framework for Theory and Research*. New York: Random House, 1970.

Solomon, B. *Black Empowerment: Social Work in Oppressed Communities.* New York: Columbia University Press, 1976.

Steinberg, S. *The Ethnic Myth: Race, Ethnicity, and Class in America.* Boston: Beacon Press, 1982.

Warner, W. L., and L. Srole. *The Social Systems of American Ethnic Groups.* New Haven, Conn.: Yale University Press, 1945.

Weber, M. "The Ethnic Group," in T. Parsons et al., *Theories of Society* (vol. 1). New York: Free Press of Glencoe, 1961.

Wirth, L. *The Ghetto.* Chicago: University of Chicago Press, 1956.

Zangwill, I. *The Melting Pot.* New York: Macmillan Publishing Co., 1910.

CHAPTER 10

SIGNIFICANCE OF CULTURE AND POWER IN THE HUMAN BEHAVIOR CURRICULUM

ELAINE B. PINDERHUGHES

In July 1983, the Board of Directors of the Council on Social Work Education adopted a curriculum policy in which all schools of social work were mandated to include in the curriculum content on

> the relationships among biological, social, psychological and cultural systems as they affect and are affected by human behavior, and of the consequences of diversity in ethnic background, race, class, sexual orientation, and culture in a pluralistic society (Council on Social Work Education, 1982). (P. 10.)

Ethnic minorities usually has referred to people of color in the United States, including Afro-Americans, Asian Americans, Mexican Americans, native Americans, and Puerto Ricans. The influx of new groups of immigrants who are people of color may expand this definition to include them as well. In the conceptualization of course content, their inclusion as ethnic minorities would constitute a logical addition. Such ethnic minority content that is added to the human behavior curriculum could provide students with a strong conceptual base and clear self-awareness of ethnic minority isses so that the students could better understand minority clients and could engage in actual problem solving with them. This necessary conceptual base and self-awareness would involve comprehension of the culture of ethnic minorities, one's own culture and its meaning, and the effect of one's own culture at the interface with ethnic minorities. The curriculum also would need to address the dynamics of power, which offer a perspective too little understood and frequently omitted as a factor in human behavior. Knowledge of the use of power in interpersonal, group, and social system levels has increased and has been characterized by fragmentation, overlap, and paradox. Thus, its usefulness has been limited. In this chapter, culture and power, which are transitional phenomena whose dynamics exist at all levels of human functioning, are defined and described as they relate to traditional human behavior content. Additionally, the transactional nature of culture, the role's culture and power play in the systemic process, power and powerlessness in families and in individual functioning, and the relevance of the dynamics of power to social work students and their mastery of ethnic minority content are discussed.

Transactional Nature of Culture

Culture generally refers to the ways of living that characterize larger social segments, whereas *subculture* generally signifies the ethnic background, race, religion, and status of groups within the larger society. Culture, in this chapter, is used interchangeably with subculture and refers to commonalities around which a group of people have developed values, norms, and behavior practices.

Culture too often has been considered to be a static phenomenon wherein unique characteristics of a given group are identified and seen as unchanging. Recently, attention has been focused on the *transactional nature of culture*—the way in which it evolves and changes as people interact with the various systems, such as families, schools, social groups, health care agencies, and judicial and welfare systems, that constitute their environment (DeVor and Schlesinger, 1981; and Green, 1982). This perspective on culture merely does not involve labeling traits and other symbols of cultural belonging, but involves attending to the ways in which these symbols are maintained through interaction with the environment (Green, 1982). Culture constantly is being modified through the interaction of a group with its environment, including other cultural groups and the social structures that influence those groups. Society uses diversity such as biological, psychological, and cultural characteristics, to differentiate between groups, assigning group members status and roles that determine their life chances, life-styles, and the quality of their lives (Berger and Federico, 1982). Via the mechanism of differentiation and stratification, society erects social structures that create further differences between these groups. Thus, social structures become both the cause and effect of diversity. Consistent with the ecological perspective that the necessary fit of the individual and family environment is assured when resources, such as food, shelter, money, education, recreation, and protection, are supplied at the appropriate time in the appropriate way (Germain, 1979), the transactional nature perspective views culture as a mediator in the individual and group interaction, functioning both as a marker for differentiation and as a coping response to stratification. Therefore, it is significant in the responses to environmental deficiencies and sufficiencies, in the existence of them, and their reciprocal interaction with one another.

Systemic Nature of Power

In terms of status, *power,* which is the capacity to influence for one's own benefit the forces that affect one's life space, obviously is a key factor in these dynamics. These dynamics define and give significance to the existence of majority groups, minority groups, and other groups that differ in terms of race, ethnicity, and other distinguishing characteristics. Via social structures, then, the majority or dominant group maintains its power by excluding subordinates who have been differentiated and stratified, by denying subordinates access to resources; by setting up expectations, tasks, and functions that affect the life-styles, life chances, and quality of life for both the dominant and subordinate groups; and by determining the way in which both groups view themselves and each other.

Power not only is significant to the creation and maintenance of designations of social group belonging, but also is critical to other levels of human functioning, which are directly affected through a systemic process. To the degree to which individuals, families, and groups perceive themselves as having or lacking power, power is critical to their manner of functioning. Additionally, social group status, which is a consequence of power, in turn is a factor in such self-perceptions. The systemic nature of power is evident as a factor in the interaction between two parties or more; in the context of which the interaction occurs; and in the goals, motives, and methods of the power-exercisers and in the motives of the victims (Kipnis, 1967).

Michael Basch (1975) contends that "throughout life, the feeling of controlling one's destiny to some reasonable extent is the essential psychological component of all aspects of life." (P. 513.) Thus, the perception of oneself as having some power over the forces that control one's life is essential to one's mental health. Powerlessness is painful and people seek to avoid feeling powerless by exhibiting behavior that will create a sense of power (McClelland, 1975). Power and powerlessness thus become critical in people's lives and are major issues in the five areas of human functioning: (1) individual–intrapsychic, (2) interpersonal–interactional, (3) familial, (4) ethnic–cultural, and (5) societal. As Barbara Solomon (1976) has noted, power and powerlessness are systemic phenomena, linking microsystem and macrosystem processes. Social workers who would base their interventions on a sound understanding of the dynamics of culture must become systems thinkers, being clear on the ways in which culture, power, and powerlessness operate in human functioning.

Culture, Power, and the Systemic Process

From an ecological and systems perspective, the application of equilibrium and feedback conditions to the feelings of power and powerlessness experienced by individuals and groups indicates a connection between people's responses to these conditions and the balance maintained in the particular system of which the individuals and groups are a part. Distortion or excess in the environmental resources necessary for effective functioning, such as protection, security, support, and supplies, can cause stress within the cultural group. For a family and its members, distortion or excess in environmental resources can result in disorganization, a malfunction in the organism or failure in development, and an inability to cope with the environment (Germain, 1979). Thus, poverty and oppression entrap people in a systemic process that is circular and reinforcing. When the larger social system fails to provide the necessary resources, the community becomes disorganized and unable to provide important supports for residents. The more powerless the community becomes because of a lack of resources and nutritive supplies, the more powerless will be the families within, hindered from meeting the needs of their members and from organizing to improve the community so that it can provide more support. When families are powerless in their efforts to protect themselves, the members will be blocked in attempts to acquire skills, develop self-esteem, strengthen the family, and improve the community. The circular, reinforcing process of these political, economic, and social forces creates a sense of powerlessness that undermines the skills needed to cope with them (Pinderhughes, 1983).

Bowen's (1978) concept of the societal projection process explains these dynamics. Bowen defines the *societal projection process* as one in which one group, the benefactors in a society, perceive and treat another group, the victims, as inferior or incompetent. This concept is of importance to people of color because minorities, as well as the poor, are among those whom Bowen identifies as victims.

> These groups fit the best criteria for long-term, anxiety relieving projection. They are vulnerable to become the pitiful objects of the benevolent, oversympathetic segment of society that improves its functioning at the expense of the pitiful. Just as the least adequate child in a family can become more impaired when he becomes an object of pity and oversympathetic help from the family, so can the lowest segment of society be chronically impaired by the very attention designed to help. No matter how good the principle behind such programs, it is essentially impossible to implement them without the built-in complications of the projection process. Such programs attract workers who are over-sympathetic with less fortunate people. They automatically put the recipient in a "one down," inferior position and they either keep them there or get angry at them. (P. 445.)

Based on this concept, it can be hypothesized that these victim groups are maintained in relatively powerless positions where they serve as a balancing mechanism for the system in which they exist. They provide stability for their benefactors because they are excluded and separated and are receptacles for most of the tension, conflict, contradiction, and confusion that exists within the various systems. Such stability is illustrated in the interactions between ghetto communities and suburbs, mental patients and caregivers, and prisoners and jailers. Because prisoners, mental patients, minorities, and the poor constitute a majority of the client population of social workers, are social workers the benefactors in the societal projection process? If so, are social workers also helping to maintain the social system equilibrium that victimizes clients?

In becoming systems balancers and tension relievers in the social system, victims must learn to live with stress, conflict, and contradiction. They must find ways to cope with the powerlessness that is mobilized. Coping responses vary from time to time and from victim to victim but become the essence of the culture developed by the group. Culture represents people's response to the political, economic, and social realities they face (Navarro, 1980)—responses in the form of values, social roles, norms, and family styles that grew out of efforts to achieve a sense of power. Such an understanding of culture and power allows appreciation for the creativity and complexity involved in cultural responses. The subtleties and nuances that characterize cultural differences, rich and varied as they are, become understood in terms of the strength they embody (Green, 1982).

Power in Families

A family's sense of power to control its destiny and to function effectively is affected by its fit with the environment. When there is a good fit and the environment offers support, security, protection, and supplies that the family can use in its effort to create an effective organization, members are able to reach their individual and group goals. When there is a poor fit and support is lacking, the family needs to compensate for this failure. Traditionally, the extended family and neighborhood systems, including the church, have been compensatory resources. When these supports have been unavailable, the family has been forced to rely almost completely on its own inner resources. In such a state of isolation, the family experiences stress and is vulnerable to malfunction in values and beliefs, boundary formation and environmental interface, rules, role relationships, communication patterns, and self-differentiation in family members.

Values and Power

Values are the guides for people's behavior. Families and groups that have to cope consistently with powerlessness may embrace values that ease their frustration and bring a sense of power. Such values include fatalism; high spirituality; living for today (the past is painful and there is no future); and valuing cooperative and sharing activities enabling survival and bringing a sense of power. These values constitute a source of strength. When families are confronted with stress and become overwhelmed, they may learn to value autonomy. This autonomy is not to be mistaken for self-actualization and development because it is derived from a sense of aloneness without any help; it must be seen as a source of strength and creative coping. Other values that families embrace when they have to cope with powerlessness, contradictions, and confusion include strength, toughness, ability to struggle, cunning, and power (Pinderhughes, 1982). In their struggle to cope with the racism, oppression, and poverty that have beset them, large numbers of Afro-Americans have adopted these values. While ensuring survival and facilitating a sense of power, some of these values, however, have proved costly because fatalism, ability to struggle, toughness, and power may not encourage the harmony, cooperation, and the reciprocal interaction that mark effective family and group functioning. Instead, they may create a vulnerability to dysfunction and conflict.

Flexibility and Power

The flexibility that families need to monitor interaction with the environment, either by rejecting anxious influences or by admitting needed resources, also is at risk. Powerlessness vis-à-vis environmental forces can compel the family to tighten its boundary to protect itself, which under extreme conditions can create such rigidity that the family cannot use help even if it should become available. The opposite effect also can occur: the family that attempts to extract supplies from external systems may maintain boundaries that are too permeable. Thus, the family cannot distinguish between forces that are noxious and should be rejected and those forces that are nourishing. Many social workers are familiar with families whose systems constantly are invaded by numerous human service providers. Many of these situations illustrate the societal projection process in which the helpers create or maintain the equilibrium that victimizes clients. The values, rigidly closed or overly open boundaries, all of which compensate for environmental failures and facilitate in family members some sense of power, also may result in greater vulnerability in the family's internal structure and process.

Vulnerability and Power

The systemic process that characterizes families operates in such a way that any one aspect of functioning affects and can be affected by all others. Thus, values affect boundary maintenance and both values and boundaries affect family rules, role relationships, communication patterns, and member connectedness, differentiation, or both. Effective family functioning requires that members acquire a strong sense of self-differentiation as well as a strong sense of connectedness. Strongly differentiated persons know their values and beliefs, can persist in their own behavioral intent, remain involved in close relationships, and can withstand stress and tolerate anxiety without becoming overinvolved with others. Stress from environmental pressures and the consequent powerlessness that can be experienced are better managed when members are well-differentiated. However, the nature of systemic process is such that great differentiation is threatened and overinvolvement is encouraged by the very stress against which such a coping defense is needed (Bowen, 1978).

Poor differentiation in family members makes for vulnerability to relationships characterized by isolation, overinvolvement, conflict, power flights, and dominance–submission in terms of power distribution. When the family system is characterized by either internal or external isolation, an emotional cocoon is created that, according to Guerin and Pendagast (1976) "intensifies emotional processes in the nuclear family, and significantly limits the relationships available to dissipate anxiety and emotional distress." (P. 452.) Intensified emotional processes more easily lead to conflict and promote the use of power tactics as a management mode. The value of power as a response to powerlessness is useful in such instances. Power in relationships is a central issue in severely victimized families, which are characterized by competition, put-downs, and negative interaction (Minuchin, 1968). The victims' entrapment in the systemic process becomes clear because the victims, as tension-relievers and anxiety-reducers for the benefactors of the social system, have been required to develop a high tolerance of conflict, confusion, contradiction, and paradox. When used within the family, the values of toughness, struggle, and power, which are developed to cope with external powerlessness, reinforce conflict and the use of power which, in turn, discourage negotiation and conflict resolution in relationships. Moreover, the American value system emphasizes power, money, possession, and ownership. These values, when applied to relationships, sustain domination as a mode. Victimized families, though isolated and excluded from the mainstream, identify with these values to some extent. Thus, their ability to engage in more harmonious relationships that are not characterized by dominance–submission is in jeopardy.

Communication and Power

Communication is another aspect of family functioning that is related to family power. Family therapists have maintained that victimized families exhibit a diminished ability to communicate and to share feelings—major handicaps for families. In contrast, other experts have noted that the style of communication in some ethnic groups has enabled them to cope well with the powerlessness associated with their systemic entrapment (Draper, 1979). For example, it is contended that the paradox, humor, subtlety, and deception that characterize Afro-American communication has demonstrated survival strength. Thus, the negativity and put-downs that so often are observed in Afro-American communication may not have the devastating effect that, at first glance, it appears to have. An example is the embracing of negatives that convey the opposite of what they appear to mean such as the adjective "bad" to mean "good." This behavior is calculated to transform impotence into an active force. Similar mechanisms that turn powerlessness into power are identified by Chestang (1972). *Aggressive accommodation* and *aggressive passivity,* which are exaggerated responses to powerlessness, can create a sense of power because they involve the use of initiative. Chestang (1972) has noted that these and other reversal mechanisms, such as victory in having pride (as opposed to pride in victory), "ward off the inconsistency, injustice and oppression" of the victim system and facilitate "a psychological unity for the adequately functioning Afro-American." (P. 4.) Thus, these seemingly paradoxical responses are adaptive for coping with the ambivalence, contradiction, and paradox with which Afro-Americans have been forced to live. Humor, paradox, subtlety, and deception are devices that assist them in communication, facilitating the contradictory task of managing rage and negative feeling while at the same time maintaining family solidarity and affection. Observers should be warned that they can only understand communication in these instances if they consider the context of the communication and the relationship between the communicators and the content. Communication that may appear to express disrespect to an observer of content only actually may be an expression of respect and confidence that honest feelings can be tolerated (Gurman, 1978).

Power and Individual Functioning

As individuals, people experience a host of feelings and engage in a range of behaviors that are reactive to being tension-relievers, anxiety reducers, and victims of powerlessness. This observation is based on the author's experiences with a number of experiential groups that have been conducted over the years. In these groups, members have examined their feelings and behaviors related to experiences of power and powerlessness as a result of family membership, ethnicity, class and racial identity, and male or female identity (Pinderhughes, 1984).

In the experiential groups, people who perceived themselves as powerless experienced anger, rage, and other emotions (Table 1). Behaviors that were responsive to these feelings of powerlessness aimed to provide a sense of power. For example, one behavior might involve a struggle not to accept the projections of the powerful that one is incompetent, dumb, crazy, a stud, sexual, or dependent. McClelland (1975) has noted that people do not desire dependency; instead, they may adopt dependency to get a sense of power or to be close to persons who actually have power. People also try to get a sense of power by assuming the negative attributions of the dominant society in an exaggerated way, for example, by being a super-stud. The process that creates these mechanisms is the same as the process that marks paradoxical communication. To ward off a sense of powerlessness, people adopt behaviors in which they identify with the aggressor (which leads to feelings of self-hatred); are guarded (seen by the powerful as being paranoid); strike out (seen by the powerful as being violent); and are oppositional, passive-aggressive, or autonomous (seen by the powerful as being stubborn). While being dependent, oppositional, passive–aggressive, and autonomous can provide a sense of power, these behaviors may encourage one to react rather than act and prevent one from developing the ability to assume leadership, exercise initiative, and make choices.

Table 1. Frequently Described Feelings and Behaviors Related to Difference in Power

View of the More Powerful	View of the Less Powerful
Feelings	**Feelings**
Having more comfort, more gratification	Having less comfort, less gratification
Feeling lucky, safe, and secure	Feeling insecure, anxious, frustrated, vulnerable
Experiencing more pleasure, less pain	Experiencing less pleasure, more pain
Having less tendency to depression	Having strong tendency to depression
Feeling superior, masterful, entitled	Feeling inferior, incompetent, deprived
Feeling hopeful	Feeling exhausted, trapped, hopeless, helpless, with few choices
Having high esteem	Having low self-esteem
Feeling anger at noncompliance in the less powerful	Feeling anger at inconsiderate control by the powerful
	Feeling anger at feelings of powerlessness
Having fear of loss of power	Having fear of abandonment by the powerful
	Feeling alone
Having fear of the anger of the less powerful	Having fear of the anger of the powerful
Having fear of retaliation by the less powerful	Having fear of own anger at the powerful
Having guilt over injustices that may result from power	
Having fear of losing identity as a powerful person	
Behavior	**Behavior**
Having opportunity to affect the external system for self	Lacking opportunity to impact the external system for self
Having ability to create opportunity	Lacking ability to create opportunity
Having ability to take responsibility, exert leadership	Lacking ability to take responsibility, exert leadership
Projecting onto the less powerful unacceptable attributes, such as being lazy, dirty, evil, sexual, and irresponsible, as justification for maintaining power and control	Projecting onto the power group acceptable attributes, such as being smart, competent, and attractive
Blaming the less powerful for assuming the projections	
Devaluing one's own pain and suffering	

Table 1. (Continued)

View of the More Powerful	View of the Less Powerful
Having distrust, being guarded and rigid because of vigilance needed to maintain power and control	Having distrust, being guarded and sensitive to discrimination, often seeming paranoid to the power group
Denying the more powerful position and its favorable effects on benefactors and unfavorable effects on victims	Denying the less powerful position and its effects
Displaying a paranoia resulting in delusions of superiority, grandiosity, unrealistic sense of entitlement, arrogant behavior, and tendency to distort reality with a consequent unreal assessment of the self and the less powerful	Displaying a paranoia resulting in the acceptance of a dependent position, passivity, and the assumption of stereotypes, such as a physical or stud image, dumbness, delinquency, and addiction, with a consequent unreal assessment of oneself and the more powerful
Isolating, avoiding, and distancing from the less powerful; taking comfort in sameness; becoming unable to tolerate differences in people; and lacking enriching cross-cultural experiences	Isolating, avoiding, and distancing from the more powerful
Displaying entitled, controlling dominating behavior	Using autonomous, oppositional, manipulative, and passive-aggressive behavior as a defense against powerlessness
Displaying rigidity in behavior; having to keep the power	Displaying rigidity in behavior: to control sense of powerlessness
Having a need for a victim, someone to scapegoat and control	Striking out, becoming verbally or physically aggressive to ward off powerlessness
Justifying aggression, and exertion of power or violence, dehumanizing behavior, and pleasure at human suffering	Identifying with the aggressor, leading to self-hatred, self-devaluation, aggressive violence, dehumanizing behavior, and pleasure at human suffering
Identifying with the less powerful, leading to a wish to repudiate power	Use of deceptions, secrets, half-truths, lies
Projecting aggression outside the group onto the less powerful to enhance group cohesiveness and unity (this behavior is assisted by a sense of entitlement)	Projecting aggression outside the group onto the more powerful to enhance group cohesiveness and unity (this behavior is reinforced by a sense of justice)

Table 1. (Continued)

View of the More Powerful	View of the Less Powerful
	Directing aggression within the ethnic group, resulting in conflictual relationships that are destructive to group cohesiveness
Experiencing conflict and confusion resulting from a sense of injustice versus a need to hold on to the power and a wish to share the power versus the fear of rejection by one's own ethnic group	Experiencing conflict and confusion resulting from the need to function in two worlds: that of the underpowered and that of the powerful

Sharing Power	Turning Powerlessness into Power
Developing a tolerance for conflict, ambivalence, and contradiction, which, when mastered, leads to flexibility, resourcefulness, creativity, and high self-esteem	Developing a tolerance for conflict ambivalence, and contradiction, which, when mastered, leads to flexibility, resourcefulness, creativity, and high self-esteem Sublimating aggression in adaptive ways

Adapted from Pinderhughes (1979). This table was developed from the author's experience in developing an experiential group process that facilitated awareness of the connection between cultural identity and one's sense of power.

In the experiential groups, when people perceived themselves as having power, their experiences were predictable. They felt secure, in control, and superior. Not all of the feelings were positive—some of the people expressed fear, anger, and guilt. Persons with power behave so that they may affect systems and create opportunities for themselves, take responsibility, and exert leadership. Having the power to define the powerless, they also may project onto the powerless their own unacceptable attributes, such as laziness. These tendencies often are related to their own internal drives that have been repressed, projected, and then are perceived as existing in the powerless. These projections are used to provide justification for maintaining power and control over these victims. Persons in power then can blame the powerless for assuming these projections. If the powerless fail to assume these projections, power people can perceive them as having done so anyway or can get angry at them (Bowen, 1978). Other behaviors that result from a position of power include controlling and dominating and expressing arrogance and displaying paranoia resulting from delusions of superiority, grandiosity, and an unrealistic sense of entitlement, with the consequence that one is unable to realistically assess one's own reality and that of the powerless. Holding on to the power encourages isolating, avoiding, and distancing from the victims of one's power, which results in a comfort with sameness and an intolerance of differences. This intolerance, in turn, results in rigidity and lowered self-differentiation. Having power can create the psychological need to have a victim, someone to scapegoat and control to maintain one's equilibrium. When these behaviors are exaggerated, they can lead to the justification of aggression against the powerless, to dehumanizing behavior, and, in extreme cases, to pleasure at human suffering (Ordway, 1973; and Pinderhughes, 1983). The systemic aspect of power is evident in the use of projections by the powerful to justify holding power over the powerless, in the opportunity for the powerful to arrange certain aspects of reality so that perceptions appear true, and in the trap of feeling guilty at the injustice of having power but of being unwilling to give up the power because of its benefits.

Relevance to Social Workers

The concepts concerning the dynamics of power have relevance for social work students and their mastery of ethnic minority content in several ways. First, these concepts have validity for every relationship that is marked by a consistent power differential. For example, they have applicability to the situation of women and men. Second, they allow a focus on the majority culture in transaction with that of ethnic minorities. Students can be helped to examine not merely these subordinate groups in isolation, such as identifying the symbols of their culture, but to consider the majority culture as well and the effect of the interaction between the majority culture and the culture of specific ethnic minority groups. One must focus on the strengths and adaptational aspects of ethnic minority groups and on the goals, dynamics, and interactional patterns of the majority group. Only a focus on power will permit this perspective, which has escaped careful scrutiny largely because of its negative connotation in American society (Kipnis, 1967). Third, these concepts facilitate student awareness of themselves from a power perspective. Whether they are members of the majority group or an ethnic minority group, students are encouraged to understand the importance to themselves of their status as benefactors or victims in the societal–projection process. This understanding has significance for social workers whose task is client empowerment—enabling clients to have some control over significant aspects of their lives. Empowerment requires that social workers help their clients understand the sources of their powerlessness and to develop ways of coping, including how to exercise power constructively. The paradox inherent in this task is made clear by the following question (Pinderhughes, 1983):

> In our effort to empower clients (who are also victims), can we as benefactors of the societal projection process which has maintained a sense of self worth and stability

for us while reinforcing powerlessness and low differentiation in victims, enable clients to gain power and relieve conflict without putting ourselves and our systems in conflict? (P. 337.)

The paradox suggested relates to the group identity of social workers who are white or male or middle-class or who belong to any other group whose members have occupied a consistently dominating role over another group. For all such persons are benefactors in the societal projection process and, thus, are vulnerable to participation in the social system equilibrium that victimizes clients. The advantages to the benefactor position appear to be many: avoiding awareness that the unacceptable attributions to victims, such as being sexual, lazy, and dumb exist in themselves; and deriving a sense of power, pleasure, positive self-esteem, and misperceiving themselves as competent and superior. This vulnerability can seduce social workers into exploiting the helping encounter for their own benefit so that they can use the power they have in the social work relationships to compensate for powerlessness elsewhere in their lives (Pinderhughes, 1983):

> And the more powerless we may *feel* in other areas of our lives (ethnic status, racial identity, class identity, family role, sexual identity, sexual preference, professional role, etc.), the more vulnerable we may be to using our professional role to gain a sense of power. Thus instead of empowering the client to cope with his realities and change his victim status, our helping efforts may very well be geared to reinforcing this status. (P. 337.)

Empowerment of clients and a change in their victim status means a change also in the status of benefactor. However, to change and to give up this status and source of power that has been syntonic can constitute a psychological loss. Thus, benefactors may get trapped in holding onto the status and power to avoid the pain and discomfort involved in giving status and power up. According to Ganter and Yeakel (1980), benefactors can free themselves from this entrapment and transcend the vulnerability to loss and pain if they understand the following:

■ The more that a sense of competence is based on the benefactor role, the less the competence is real anyway. The societal projection process does not increase differentiation and level of functioning in people; it only permits the appearance that this is so, reinforcing instead the need for benefactors to have a victim to maintain the appearance.

■ Benefactors pay a high price for their sense of power: fear, guilt, unrealistic entitlement, distorted view of the world, rigidity and intolerance in behavior, inability to grow, having a need for sameness, and an intolerance for difference.

■ If benefactors take back the projections they have made onto their victims, they can be assured of freedom from entrapment so that they can empower their clients. Freedom can be facilitated if they identify their own *power gestalt*—the significant experiences that have caused them to internalize feelings relative to the power or powerlessness within the social system, ethnic group, racial group, communities, profession and other systems in which power has been key. (P. 140.)

Awareness of the ways in which social workers have used and enjoyed power, its benefits and its costs, and the ways in which we have experienced powerlessness and defended against it prepare us to transcend the psychological loss of the benefactor role because we can understand the magnitude of our gain: freedom from entrapment, ability to grow, flexibility and creativity in functioning, and appreciation of difference (Pinderhughes, 1983; and Ganter and Yeakel, 1980).

Works Cited

Basch, M. As cited in E. J. Anthony and T. Benedek, eds., *Depression and Human Existence*. Boston: Little, Brown & Co., 1975.

Berger, R., and R. Federico. *Human Behavior: A Social Work Perspective*. New York: Longman, 1982.

Bowen, M. *Family Therapy in Clinical Practice*. New York: Jason Aronson, 1978.

Chestang, L. *Character Development in a Hostile Environment* (Occasional Paper No. 3). Chicago: University of Chicago School of Social Service Administration, 1972.

Curriculum Policy for the Master's Degree and Baccalaureate Degree Programs in Social Work Education. New York: Council on Social Work Education, 1982.

DeVore, W., and E. Schlesinger. *Ethnic Sensitive Social Work Practice*. St. Louis: C. V. Mosby Co., 1981.

Draper, J. "Black Language as an Adaptive Response to a Hostile Environment," in C. Germaine, ed., *Social Work Practice: People and Environments*. New York: Columbia University Press, 1979.

Ganter, G., and M. Yeakel. *Human Behavior and the Social Environment*. New York: Columbia University Press, 1980.

Germain, C. *Social Work Practice: People and Environments*. New York: Columbia University Press, 1979.

Green, J. *Cultural Awareness in the Human Services*. Englewood Cliffs, N.J.: Prentice-Hall, 1982.

Guerin, P., and E. Pendagast. "Evaluation of Family System and Genogram," in P. Guerin, ed., *Family Therapy, Theory and Practice*. New York: Gardner Press, 1976.

Gurman, A. "Contemporary Marital Therapies: A Critique and Comparative Analysis of Psychoanalytic, Behavioral and Systems Theory Approaches," in T. Paoline and B. Grady, eds., *Marriage and Family Therapy*. New York: Brunner/Mazel, 1978.

Kipnis, D. *The Powerholders*. Chicago: University of Chicago Press, 1967.

McClelland, D. *Power: The Inner Experience*. New York: John Wiley & Sons, 1975.

Minuchin, S. *Families of the Slums*. New York: Basic Books, 1968.

Navarro, V. Panel on Culture and Health Symposium on Cross-Cultural and Transcultural Issues in Family Health Care, University of California, San Francisco, November 8, 1980.

Ordway, J. "Some Consequences of Racism for Whites," in C. Willie, B. Brown, and B. Kramer, eds., *Racism and Mental Health*. Pittsburgh: University of Pittsburgh Press, 1973.

Pinderhughes, E. "Empowerment for Our Clients and for Ourselves," *Social Casework,* 64 (June 1983), pp. 331–338.

———. "Teaching Empathy: Ethnicity, Race and Power at the Cross-Cultural Treatment Interface," *American Journal of Social Psychiatry,* 4 (Winter 1984), pp. 5–12.

———. "Teaching Empathy in Cross-Cultural Social Work, *Social Work,* 24 (July 1979), pp. 312–316.

Soloman, B. *Black Empowerment*. New York: Columbia University Press, 1976.

CHAPTER 11

FRAMEWORKS FOR INTRODUCING RACIAL AND ETHNIC MINORITY CONTENT INTO THE CURRICULUM

LEON F. WILLIAMS

Since the early 1970s, it has been difficult to define the purposes and aims of social work without reference to racial or ethnic minorities as special populations with a major stake in the outcomes of social welfare services. As early as 1969, the social work profession—represented by the National Association of Social Workers and the Council on Social Work Education—established policies designed to combat and eliminate racism in the profession. As of the 1980s, a commonly held view among minority scholars and professionals is that the social work profession still has a distance to go before antiracism policies affect the problems of effective service delivery across racial and ethnic populations; the problems of minority content and emphasis in curricula of schools of social work; and the problems of the maldistribution of minorities among the personnel of agencies, schools, and recruits to the profession.

The reason for the lag in implementing antiracism policies are many and varied. However, for social work education the problem concerns a simple issue—whether content on racial and ethnic minorities, in fact, has achieved respectable status in the core of the social work curriculum in competition with the entrenched and normative core of content on therapeutic and psychological theories. Because schools of social work are responsible for training students for anticipated roles in the profession, minority content, particularly minority content associated with traditional minorities, such as blacks, Hispanics, Asians, American Indians, or other people of color, is proof of the commitment of the schools to these groups and to fairness in their representation.

Although most schools have courses devoted to cross-cultural and cross-racial content, efforts at mainstreaming this content without trivializing the plight of traditional minorities remains the single biggest challenge to social work educators. A content area that is not respected often is not well-developed or taught and not well-received in the marketplace of ideas. Thus, a less than scholarly regard for and rigorous attention to racism and oppression is tantamount in a practice-oriented field to the neglect of those groups that are victimized by racism and oppression. Such disregard, as Herrick (1978) has observed, may result in the promotion of institutional racism rather than in the preparation of practitioners to help them meet the needs of those victimized groups.

This chapter is a description of the efforts of one school to introduce content on racial and ethnic minorities in a manner that meets the criteria of scholarly analysis but in which the history, culture, life-styles, and experiences of people of color are respected. The content is designed to enhance student learning at all levels by providing a far-reaching but basic knowledge of racism and discrimination. Such knowledge is integral to social processes as divergent as the contribution of racism and discrimination to the development of personal identity, and the role they play in the making of national policies. Additionally, issues involved in curriculum planning are discussed and organizing frameworks of knowledge to establish general principles for including content on oppressed groups are described.

Problems and Issues

Content on racial and ethnic minorities can introduce hazards in curriculum planning in social work education, especially if such content is introduced with the intention of providing knowledge of the social context of social victims' lives and making such content an active part of the practice of social work. For example, competition may result when new content associated with racism, oppression, and the needs of special populations such as the handicapped and aged is pitted against old content in a curriculum already overloaded with required practice courses and content deemed inviolate by the faculty. Tension may be present between faculty who are people of color and majority faculty: the one group feeling pressured to respond, the other group feeling the response is not rapid enough. Outdated material in and the lack of attention to a curriculum that is related to practice issues and that affects racial and ethnic groups, which constitute a majority of the profession's clients, also raises the specter of less than excellence in academic and scholarly effort for a profession that has to rely on keeping abreast of the most recent trends in society for its very existence. Efforts to incorporate content on oppressed groups not only can introduce hazards into curriculum planning, but can create several unresolved issues in curriculum planning and in establishing educational program objectives that still must be resolved.

Given a commitment to equality and social justice for groups facing systematic discrimination and oppression, it may be difficult to choose the most appropriate theory and content, given that the field of race relations is over-burdened with theories that may be contradictory, vague, and ill-formed—theories that actually may constitute barriers to systematic analysis and under-standing of the problem (Blalock, 1967). Additionally, having identified racism and oppression as professional problems, what unitary theoretical frameworks could be devised that would promote needed changes in practice regarding the structural problems plaguing traditional minorities and other oppressed persons when the profession is divided at its core between individual versus social action perspectives on change?

Implementation of an educational policy requiring the inclusion of content on diverse at-risk groups confronts educators with a new challenge—to revamp the pedagogy. A new pedagogy would be associated with the victims of society, the content of which is nontraditional in that it does not lend itself to the value-neutral academic process that involves a rational and objective discussion of alternatives about which educators have little feeling one way or the other. Instead, the content is especially value-laden, evoking emotions and encouraging educators to take a position. How does a faculty strike a balance between the didactic–theoretical demands of the content and the expressive-emotional need of students and faculty exposed to controversial material? Material on oppression, domination, violence, and brutality elicits powerful sentiments that affect students' and faculty's belief–value systems and identities as people and future practitioners. When is knowledge of oppression and racism to be judged as adequate and sufficient for competent professional practice in a multicultural and multiracial society? Most importantly, when is it not? Can a student be terminated who has not achieved the requisite knowledge, values, and skills to work with persons of another race or culture?

Who has the expertise to teach the content? A culturally experienced minority scholar whose tenure and scholarship are suspect because of his or her association with the "minority course." Or the nonminority "expert" who has met publication criteria and has an established academic reputation? On the issue of group accommodation, which group or race gets primacy? Which is emphasized? Which group is given the limitations and time constraints of a curriculum to the group's detriment?

A partial answer to some of these issues lies in careful and systematic curriculum planning that addresses the social context of practice with minorities, the objectives of the school, the needs of various minorities, and the unifying and underlying themes that bind the groups together in their plight. This type of curriculum planning has not always been made by academics. According to Robinson (1969), social work educators have a tendency to avoid systematic curriculum planning in favor of *educational particularism,* a process in which educators conduct endless internal dialogue about methods of teaching, the nature of education, and the integration of content without discussing divisive issues. (P. 219.)

Dialectics of Racism: Analysis and Historical Overview

To a large extent, the failure of social work education to come to grips with racism and oppression stems from the knowledge base and ideological makeup of the social work profession. It has been said that social work is the liberal profession. This liberalism would have workers believe in an essentially pluralistic arrangement of power in the United States, open and responsive to citizen concerns, based on a consensus, capable of integrating conflict and difference, and, above all, moving in steady and acceptable ways and in a progressive fashion (Sternbach, 1971). Sternbach (1971) observed that *liberalism* is a professional creed characterized by contradictory beliefs in a social hierarchy; in role differentiation; in subordination of pleasure to action and performance; in the avoidance of conflict and theories of conflict; in the neutralization and assimilation of deviants; in the unequal distribution of rewards based on suspect criteria such as merit, credentials, skin color, and gender; and in the pursuit of self-interest. Theoretically, content on and the analysis of racism and oppression exposes a paradox in a profession that is both an agent of liberal reform and progressive change and functions equally well as an agent of repressive forces in society.

Because proponents of liberalism abhor conflict and seek consensus, racism, oppression, and domination issues create tension for the proponents. Liberalism is such that social workers find it difficult to name the forces of oppression. Social workers seek euphemisms—they prefer to study culture and ethnicity rather than racism, and the goals of education and practice are reduced to nostalgic cross-culturalism and ethnic sensitivity. As a result, if reports from students and faculty are accurate, many courses on ethnic minorities have incorporated the characteristics of consciousness-raising groups, sometimes lacking substance, quality, or an analytical focus. The student and faculty so need to feel at ease that comfort takes precedence over content and substance, in the author's view.

Social workers should be reminded that the impetus for the reification of ethnicity and ethnic status was provided by the neoconservative philosophies of Moynihan (U.S. Department of Labor, 1965) and Glazer (1975). Their theories of the culturally deficient poor (mainly blacks) fed into the white backlash of the early 1970s and brought about an *ethnic affirmation movement*—the buzzword for white ethnic resistance to the putative gains of blacks, women, and other oppressed groups under affirmative action. Theoretically, the rise in ethnic awareness can be correlated with the history of declining interest in combating racism and oppression, and, as such, must be viewed as a competing paradigm to the liberal social work position with regard to minorities.

Definition of Racism

In this chapter an operational definition of racism is used. According to Nasatir and Fernandez (1979), *racism* is a cultural ideology that espouses the view that one race of people is inherently superior to another race of people.

In the United States (and South Africa), the white population has developed and nurtured a cultural ideology that people of color, especially blacks, are inherently inferior. Whites have sufficient power and control of societal institutions to support this ideology even to the point where it is accepted by many members of oppressed populations. It makes no difference whether there is a scientific basis for the classification of people by race; the symbolic universe and dominant ideology is based on a belief in biological differences among groups and, thus, becomes part of the operating principles in allocation of rewards, goods, and services in society. The institutional component of racism involves a system of exclusionary rules, procedures, and regulations. Most often the rules were not formulated with the specific intention of excluding nonwhites; however, in a white, male-dominated society, most procedures and rules were established with white males as beneficiaries. According to Nasatir and Fernandez, this process has resulted in the almost total barring of people of color and females from equal and full participation in the society in which they are nominally full citizens. The focus of this definition of racism is on the dominance of one group and the inordinate power it has to establish what is normative in society. The definition incorporates the ideological aspects of racism, describing the root cause of the problem, its manifestations, and why it continues as a major force in society. The definition essentially approaches racism from a power and conflict perspective, adopting power and conflict as themes for a theoretical orientation to the problem of curriculum building. Jones (1981) noted that debates about theoretical orientations often are ideological in nature. In the case of content on racism and oppression, debates become vital.

The traditional view of racism has relied on and focused on individual prejudice as the root cause of racism in a prejudice ———▸ discrimination model (Feagin and Feagin, 1978). This view places certain constraints on action. For example, viewing the root cause of racism as primarily economic, serving to the material wealth and economic advantage of some people and to disadvantage and serious loss of economic opportunity for others, calls for different eradication strategies than if the cause were individual, egocentric, and psychological, or ethnocentric and cultural (Jones, 1981). The economic view should lead to social–structural interventions, the psychological to individual psychotherapeutic approachs, and the ethnocentric to group methods of psychotherapy education and human relations approaches.

The New Synthesis

Over the past decade, a new synthesis has emerged as a result of greater attention among theorists to structural and systems perspectives, or both, relative to the mechanisms that create and sustain racism and discrimination. The resulting theoretical frameworks are grounded in social system and institutional perspectives, employing interest group theories of power and domination in societies (Weber, 1946; Van Den Berghe, 1963; Dahrendorf, 1969; Blauner, 1972; Kinloch, 1974; Feagin and Feagin, 1978; and Alvarez, 1979). The individual prejudice perspective relied heavily on the study of the victims or prejudice and, in some cases, indirectly fostered a view of blacks, for example, as social and cultural inferiors—persons who had social defects or deficiencies that contributed to their disadvantage, which was the result of a legacy of slavery and racism. This was the culture of poverty thesis that dominated social science thinking for a time (Lewis, 1969; Glazer and Moynihan, 1963; and Moynihan, 1965). Meanwhile, the group and institutional dimensions of the problem went unexplored. The contradiction between the individual level explanation and that of the group and society was troubling, especially as overt signs of prejudice among whites diminished, the opportunity structure for blacks and other people of color either remained unchanged or had grown worse in certain critical areas (Feagin and Feagin, 1978). Theorists more often began to look to the social system for explanations. The concept of institutional racism was one of the earliest attempts to craft a satisfactory explanation for racism at the societal level. The concept appears to effectively bridge the gap between individual and social perspectives and, thus, represents a more universal theory. The concept of institutional or structural racism is associated with the findings of the Kerner Commission (1968) and the ideas of Carmichael and Hamilton (1967). Both perspectives used a unique view of racism that implicated institutions in racism whether or not they expressed or avowed racist principles. The effect of this orientation was to retain as central the critical role of racism to the problems of inequality, acknowledging the role of self-interested white society rather than the social inadequacies of those that society dominates and controls.

From Contact to Oppression

The recorded history of contact between various societies provides a basis for understanding how racism as a manifestation of social inequality became a routine part of a society that professes democratic and egalitarian ideals. Feagin (1978) has provided a cross-cultural model of the effects of aggressive colonialism on the founding and structure of Western societies. The migration of Anglo Europeans to Asia, Africa, and the New World yielded predictable results concerning intergroup contact and later between group accommodations. Feagin theorized that when previously isolated groups come into contact, the stage is set for one or a combination of three adaptations: (1) genocide or the wholesale slaughter of a people; (2) *egalitarian symbiosis*—the melding of two groups of equal status through intermarriage, which results in their sharing a common culture, biology, language, values, and history; and (3) a hierarchy or stratification system with one group being dominant and all other groups arranged according to ascribed statuses (class, race, and caste).

Figure 1. Modes of Group Contact

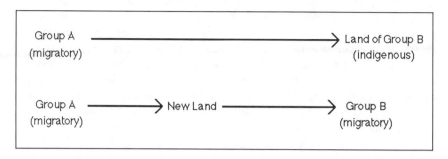

Adapted from Feagin, J. R. *Racial and Ethnic Relations.* Englewood Cliffs, N.J.: Prentice-Hall, 1978, p. 23.

According to Feagin (1978), migration is the major means of contact between previously isolated groups and follows a certain pattern (Figure 1). Eventually, power based on control of technological resources determines who has the rights to the land and who acquires indigenous status in the ongoing contact between the groups. According to Feagin, over the long-term, the range of adaptations in intergroup contact broadens to include the following possibilities:

■ continuing genocide;

■ continuing egalitarian symbiosis;

■ stratification replaced by inclusion along "anglo conformity" lines (the melting pot or assimilationist ideal);

■ stratification replaced by inclusion along cultural lines (separate but equal or cultural pluralism); and

■ continuing stratification with some acculturation, ranging from moderate to extreme internal colonialism.

Acculturation refers to the process of adopting the norms, values, and culture of the dominant group (assimilation), while *internal colonialism* refers to continued and forcible exclusion of groups through violence, coercion, segregation, and discrimination.

Feagin (1978) has indicated that the kind of migration generating race and ethnic relations can be seen as existing along a continuum from voluntary contact of a migrating group with an established society to that which is involuntary. The five basic types of migration in order of voluntariness are (1) slave importation, (2) the movement of forced labor, (3) contract labor movement, (4) movement of displaced persons, and (5) voluntary migration. The level of oppression faced by a group varies according to the motivation behind the initial contact, whether actively colonial or based on materialistic conquest, the stage of the development of the society, and the kind of adaptation and degree of voluntariness associated with the migration. Thus, as a group, people of color have had their status defined primarily through their experiences with violent conquest, slave importation, and forced labor, and with exclusionary procedures that perpetuate stratification by race, class, and caste. Yet the somatic aspects of race continue to be the most salient characteristics of these groups. White ethnic migrants from northern, southern, and eastern Europe came to the United States voluntarily seeking opportunities denied them in their own countries. Though many of them experienced American racism similar in quality to that faced by blacks, the dominant ideology was assimilationist through self-effacement, through acculturation, and through the device of adopting the racist views and attitudes of the dominant group. The adoption of racist attitudes of the dominant group distanced them from the faceless social category called negroes (Schermerhorn, 1974). Theoretically, large scale social movements were mounted by blacks, native Americans, and Hispanics to secure long denied civil, political, and economic rights. These movements resulted in a competitive outburst of ethnic fervor pitting the Poles, Italians, Irish, and Jews as defenders of the status quo, resisting the putative negative effects of affirmative action, against people of color.

Theoretically, one can surmise that the interethnic tension that marked the decades of the 1970s and 1980s had a dampening effect on civil rights and liberal reform because they are dependent on support from large sectors of the society. This conflict can be assumed to have contributed to the rise in overt racism and discriminatory acts that marked the period. The conflict between the various ethnic groups pitted those with the least against one another in a diversionary strategy not unlike that found under the policy of divide and rule used successfully by the British and Romans in their colonies.

One of the results of conflict between groups on the lower reaches of the society is to shield the socially privileged from scrutiny. In the face of racial jingoism and scapegoating, the privilege of the few is accepted as normal and goes unchallenged. In the United States, the basis for this privilege is rooted in the workings of *capitalism*—a system of private ownership of property that maintains an upper class elite that amasses the largest share of the society's wealth and income. This is an identifiable subgroup, bearing similitude of race, class, culture, religion, and family of origin. The existence of this group is strong evidence of a historical association between racism and capitalism.

Roots of Racism

The roots of racism lie within the capitalist system. According to Gordon (1977), the early merchants who found the slave trade profitable suggested and encouraged racist attitudes to help justify the selling of human beings. Having profited from the system of stratification based on biologic notions of inferiority that flourished under feudalism in the Old World, it was a simple step to use such justification to the exploitation and enslavement of nonwhites encountered in voyages of conquest. Thus, racism became an instrument of economic advancement based on exploitation of one's natural inferiors. Bennett (1966) noted that the commerce in slaves alone (involving shipbuilding, metalwork in fashioning leg irons and other restraints, and weapons manufacturing) was sufficient to fuel the industrial revolution and, thus, modern capitalism. As a consequence of slavery, theorists suggest that an elite mercantile class emerged, which garnered the lion's share of the economies of the western world based on the economic power accrued through this enterprise. The mercantile class had a sizable economic advantage, leading to the establishment of a capitalist class, which ultimately skewed the distribution of influence and power in the New World. As early as 1948, Cox (1948) saw racial stratification arising from the growth and expansion of the European economic system that began as mercantilism and ended as capitalism. The slave trade, beginning with Spain and Portugal, in his view, was "a way of recruiting labor for the purposes of exploiting the great natural resources of America." (P. 332.) The color of Africans was not important; they were chosen simply because they were the best workers to be found for the heavy labor in the mines and plantations across the Atlantic. A hereditary capacity for prejudice among white Europeans did not generate modern race relations. Rather, exploitation and the need for ethical and moral justification led to the system of race subordination. As profits and material wealth grew, so did the justifications, forming a historical dialectic that finds racism and capitalism as twin pillars of the American epoch.

Slavery can be viewed as the engine of domination that institutionalized and routinized the norms of black inferiority, of human degradation, of white masculine supremacy, and of paternalism through elite domination and control. Inequality became a norm, democratic ideals and institutions floundered as a racial stratification system arose that approximated colonial domination by a white male elite.

Institutional racism represents a residual social system in which racism is the major criterion for role assignments, role rewards, and for socialization and acculturation, depending on the shifting structure of a racial caste hierarchy. After colonial contact occurs, monopoly of political, economic, social, cultural, and psychological resources by an elite group develops, resulting in an American social system that is oppressive to nonwhites but also costly to whites as individuals and groups (Bowser and Hunt, 1981).

Given current theory, it is now possible to fashion a simple institutional or systems model of racism as a social dynamic, incorporating some of the major variables, and to demonstrate the relationship between various social and institutional elements that contribute to unequal life chances for persons of color (Figure 2).

In this model, racism and discrimination emerged in the United States as a result of colonial domination and slavery that influenced the beliefs, values, and ideals of the country, favoring an Anglo European, white, male elite that

Figure 2. A Model of Racism and its Effects on Society

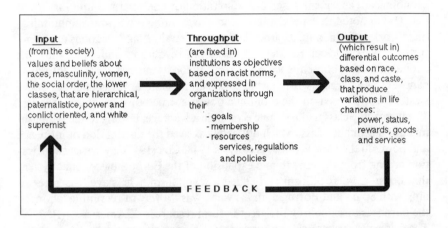

is perpetuated through a social hierarchy based on race (input). These pre-existing values were established as norms within the social institutions of the family, the economic, political, educational, religious, military, and welfare systems. Further, the race-based norms and values of these institutions were translated into major social organizations that regulate and distribute the society's goods and services and determine individual and group rights and entitlements. The organizations establish rules, regulations, policies, and procedures favoring dominant group white males directly and indirectly. These organizations reflect elite values and preferences in membership, in hiring, in participation, and in organizational support, leading to a differential distribution of goods, services, rewards, and entitlements based on race (output). For racial minorities or people of color, these differences generally lead to inequities. This inequity of result or output is used to justify (feedback) and support the claims to elite and dominant status for whites and inferior status for blacks and other persons of color (Williams, 1982).

Unequal Power and Racism

The author assumes that the issue of racism is primarily ideological at its roots with white supremacy as an ideal dictating the nature of power and the distribution of wealth in the United States. This assumption suggests that ideological frameworks dominate much of what is taught about intergroup relations, especially when the issues are about racial and cultural differences. The universal function of race, class, or caste distinctions in a society is to maintain the power of a dominant elite. Lowenstein (1976) has claimed that "...the relationship between men and women, between races, between different social classes, and between helping professionals and their clients are all variations of unequal power relationship in society." (P. 92.)

According to Kitano (1980), the groups in power are those that can discriminate effectively. Those persons can pass the laws and make the rules that help define who belongs inside the group and who stays outside. Thus, power can be identified as a major integrating concept around which to organize and give shape to a course or courses that addresses many oppressed groups in all their diversity. They have in common the fact that they all are generally at risk of unequal power relations. The author deliberately avoids the concept of powerlessness as contributing to a social deficit view of minority groups. All groups have power. It varies with their circumstance; for example, many black professionals and managers exercise relative power within the confines of their occupations, organizations, and institutions. However, minorities may have less power in the choice of where to live, the quality of education for their children, and in determining the overall health and well-being of their ethnic communities. Generally, only the dominant group has the capacity to define what power is and who has access to it and in what quantities.

Implications for Curriculum Structure

Debates over the introduction of content on racism and oppression into the curriculum, whether as one or more electives, or suffused through the whole curriculum as one course or more, generally become academic if one concedes that special skills are demanded of practicing professionals in a society in which race is a dominant variable. The issue then becomes how best to proceed? The Council on Social Work Education *Curriculum Policy Statement* (1983) conceptualizes the curriculum as essentially *foundation* (basic) and *advanced* (specialized). Content on racism and oppression appears to rightly belong in the foundation content area with human behavior, policy, practice, research, and field practice. One tends to think of foundation as content preparatory for advanced training for autonomous professional practice. In the foundation curriculum, power, theories of oppression, and inequality could constitute major integrating themes for content as varied as the effects of culture and race on human development and personal identity, issues of income maldistribution, practice within a crosscultural milieu, the distribution of social welfare services relative to certain subgroups, ethical issues in research with minority groups, considerations of social and distributive justice in social welfare policy, and the relative efficacy of various theories of human intervention as they pertain to various cultures and subgroups.

Given the integrating conceptions of power and oppression, one still requires an integrating mechanism, a curriculum model that would enable students to understand the interrelatedness of power and oppression across content areas, subsystems, issues, social problems areas, and methods areas. This interrelatedness is to be found in a curriculum structure that is anchored to a specific course devoted to racism and oppression that provides both an overview of

Figure 3. Model of Curriculum Organization

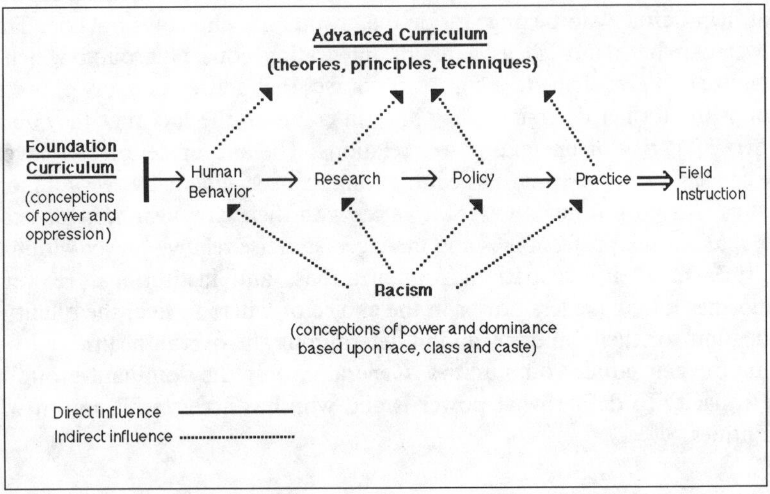

the problem in terms of history, its continuity and scope, and its implications for social work practice at all levels, and that offers an in-depth understanding of the theories that attempt to explain race-based inequality. This model of curriculum organization uses content on racism and oppression as an integrating mechanism for the entire curriculum but has a direct effect on the foundation (Figure 3).

A freestanding but required course on racism, containing the major integrating concepts of power and oppression, should have the effect of introducing students to and equipping them with analytical frameworks for understanding the operations of the negative social conditions within the racism course and in other courses in the foundation, especially if these themes are echoed in other courses. Students prepared in such a manner carry an internal agenda enabling them to challenge misconceptions, lapses, and disinformation in later courses and in the field. Additionally, students will be able to seek positive opportunities in research and scholarship related to minority groups in courses, from among faculty, and in field experiences. The aim of the course is to produce a student so attuned to value-laden, racially biased, categorical, and stereotypical thinking at such a level that antidiscriminatory attitudes and values become a part of their independent scholarship and individual practice.

Assumptions for a Course on Racism

The development of a course on racism at Boston College was guided by 10 assumptions related to a comprehensive view of racism as a dynamic of social processes involving people at the individual, group, and societal levels.

The 10 assumptions were:

1. Racism is combatable.

2. The elimination of race as a significant factor in the social system, on the societal, group, and individual level, remains the single most important challenge confronting Americans.

3. All groups are victims of institutional racism in either a direct or indirect manner; however, alleviating the distress for those most affected will produce positive and long-lasting changes for the society as a whole. No other approach will be as successful.

4. Racism is detrimental to the health, mental health, well-being, and safety of individuals, groups, and societies.

5. Racism has empirical outcomes that can be identified, understood, and changed. Racism does not arise out of mystical or magical or naturalistic functions in society, but is an invention designed to reach materialistic and power ends.

6. The solution to racism requires a change in society's institutional structure away from a racial foundation that is based on ascriptive criteria to one that is based on achievement, worth, and dignity.

7. The solution to racism requires collective action.

8. The ultimate beneficiaries of racism are a subcultural elite (white, masculine, and Protestant) that enjoys economic, social, and political power as a consequence of institutionalized norms of racism and domination.

9. Racism is both institutional and attitudinal. Developers of effective strategies against racism should recognize that it is both institutional and attitudinal and, in the light of the lack of success enjoyed by individual approaches that have favored victim centered social deficit and innate inferiority perspectives, should seek solutions that involve the macro system and social-structural changes.

10. For people of color, the goal of change in all instances must be empowerment: achieving parity, equity, equality, and liberation from oppressive social conditions through decolonization, increased economic opportunity, and major structural changes in the distribution of wealth and income. Because social welfare and social work occupy the vector between opportunity and exploitation for many groups such as the poor and minorities, changes must occur in those institutions as a primary objective for combating racism.

Course Content

The racism course is taught in several sections and relies on part-time faculty, mainly people of color representing various groups and women, who work under the direction of a full-time faculty member who coordinates the course and also teaches a section. The faculty assigned to the course meet as a team, share information and ideas, and exchange knowledge of current trends in the literature as well as teaching approaches.

The content of the course reflects its themes and is organized around several major headings:

- Introduction and Overview
- Major Theories of Prejudice and Discrimination
- The History of Racism in the United States
- The Institutional Approach to Racism
- Intergroup Contact and Oppression
- Social Work and Institutional Racism

The introduction to the course is informational and also sets the tone that this will be a serious attempt at scholarship and systematic analysis through the assumptions, discussion of textbooks, outline, bibliography, course assignments, and grading procedures. A key activity involves reviewing the assumptions on which the course is based. Most of the assumptions are factual, optimistic, and demythologizing in nature. The knowledge, value, and skill objectives of the course are both comprehensive and specific, conforming to the view that racism, while a major social problem, is reversible and combatable. Students in the course then are invited to examine and determine what is known about the problem of racism and prejudice based on the theories and discussions of various scholars and scientists. Each theory is examined for advantages as well as disadvantages in explaining continuities in race relations.

The history of racism is examined from the standpoint of five premises: (1) racism did not always exist and thus is not inevitable; (2) Europeans invented racism as a rationalization for exploiting nonwhites; (3) slavery in America marks a crucial period in the development of American society and, thus, the study of the division between blacks and whites is essential to an understanding of other forms of oppression and discrimination in the society; (4) Southern and Eastern European whites in many cases shared a similar history to that of people of color except for the voluntariness of their migration and their willingness to adopt the norms of dominant white society with regard to blacks; and (5) modern America appears as an extension of colonial domination and the materialistic pursuits of the early Anglo European settlers who now are institutionalized into the operating principles of the United States.

Intergroup contact and racial oppression are elements in the course that establish the theme of systematic inequality based on ascribed characteristics, such as gender, age, social class, religion, and country of origin, while holding racism as the most salient and intractable of the characteristics. The course examines the effects of a race, class, and caste hierarchy on the life chances of numerous groups, especially people of color, women, new immigrant groups, and old immigrants. The course gives particular attention to the similarities and differences between race based and gender based discrimination. Also examined are the issues of white victimization as the costs of racism to white people.

Finally, in the course the role of the social work profession in institutional racism is examined through the history and practices of the profession that contribute to or alleviate the problem of racism. The dualities in the philosophy and ideals of the profession are analyzed as they contribute to the profession's record with minorities. Attention also is given to the movement for change in the profession led by black workers and scholars, the surfacing of radical alternatives, and the effect of the Women's movement on the current practice stance and the distribution of power within the profession.

Teaching Methods

Recognizing that a major factor in understanding the material resides at the expressive–emotional level (as it should in a social work class), the faculty incorporated classroom discussion as a standard activity. A part of every class session is involved in discussing the concepts and ideas covered in that period; however, a free-floating discussion of other matters also is allowed. Additionally, each student may be asked to keep a diary or write a reaction paper. The diary is a kind of weekly log of private throughts about incidents, occurring either in the classroom or field, which relate to racism and discrimination. The reaction paper generally is a one- to two-page reaction to the content covered in each session. The faculty member comments on the papers and returns them. The diaries and papers are confidential, ungraded activities that serve the useful function of allowing students to express their feelings while allowing faculty to monitor the progress of the course.

A midsemester assignment allows students to observe examples of racism in operation. Students use a data collection schedule or questionnaire ("Inventory of Racism") to look for indicators of institutional racism in a social agency, preferably one in which they are in field placement. Without a preestablished hypothesis, students are to gather facts from their agency and write a brief report describing their findings based on facts alone. The goal of this exercise is to bridge the gap between the theoretical and anecdotal and the reality aspects of racism and discrimination.

In the final assignment, each student is asked to choose a group or issue in racism or oppression and write a major research paper on the subject. The expectation is that the students will develop their ideas carefully, relying on textbooks, lectures, discussion, and reading assignments. They devote the final part of their paper to an analysis of the role, if any, that social work plays in the solutions to the problem. Again, the emphasis is on critical analysis, using the models and theories developed around institutional racism to examine issues that have meaning to the students and to the profession.

Practice Outcomes

As this is primarily a theory course in social policy, the effect of the content on practice is more implicit than explicit. The curriculum model proposed, however, situates racism and oppression in the curriculum in a manner such that this content becomes a part of the basic theoretical knowledge that all students must take with them into practice not unlike the expectations one has of the practice and human behavior courses, for example. The developers of the course assume that sound theory is basic to good practice and that knowledge of the operations of racism and oppression are fundamental to effective social work practice in a diverse society in which race is a major factor in social status. The course does allow students to develop conceptual frameworks that would enable them individually and collectively to apply their knowledge of racism and oppression in actual practice—through assessment, evaluation, and intervention. In examining the various modes and methods of intervention used by the profession, the course leans toward generic solutions that cut across individuals, groups, communities, and settings and that are grounded thoroughly in those aspects of the profession's mission and values that are aimed at the relief of distress among its clients. Finally, the course operates from the premise that all social workers have a stake in combating racism and discrimination—white social workers as well as social workers who are people of color. All social workers should be able to function with equal efficiency with a number of groups in a manner in which race does not become a major variable in providing services.

The framework provided for introducing content on racial and ethnic minorities into the curricula of schools of social work is needed at this point in the development of the profession. Having made a commitment to non-discrimination and equity in practice, the test of that commitment rests on the success or failure of schools to inculcate students with the necessary knowledge, skill, and values to practice effectively with diverse populations. The student of today is destined to practice in a society in which matters of oppression and discrimination are going to be contested increasingly by their victims. The issue is not whether the social work profession will have a choice in the matter of its participation—that is assured—but whether it will exercise its choices in a manner that contributes to the field's longevity and the betterment of those it serves.

Works Cited

Alvarez, R., et al. *Discrimination in Organizations*. San Francisco: Jossey-Bass, 1979.

Bennett, L., Jr. *Before the Mayflower: A History of the Negro in America* (3d ed.). Chicago: Johnson Publishing Co., 1966.

Blalock, H. M., Jr. *Toward a Theory of Minority-Group Relations*. New York: John Wiley & Sons, 1967.

Blauner, R. *Racial Oppression in America*. New York: Harper & Row, 1972.

Carmichael, S., and C. V. Hamilton. *Black Power: The Politics of Liberation in America*. New York: Vintage Books, 1967.

Cox, O. C. *Caste, Class and Race*. Garden City, N.Y.: Doubleday & Co., 1948.

Curriculum Policy Statement. New York: Council on Social Work Education, 1983.

Dahrendorf, R. "On the Origin of Inequality Among Men," in A. Beteille, ed., *Social Inequality.* Baltimore, Md.: Penguin Press, 1969.

Feagin, J. R. *Racial and Ethnic Relations.* Englewood Cliffs, N.J.: Prentice-Hall, 1978.

Feagin, J. R., and C. B. Feagin. *Discrimination American Style: Institutional Racism and Sexism.* Englewood Cliffs, N.J.: Prentice-Hall, 1979.

Glazer, N. *Affirmative Discrimination: Ethnic Inequality and Public Policy.* New York: Basic Books, 1975.

Glazer N., and D. P. Moynihan. *Beyond the Melting Pot.* Cambridge, Mass.: Harvard University Press, 1963.

Gordon, D. M. (ed.). *Problems of Political Economy.* Lexington, Mass.: D. C. Heath & Co., 1977.

Herrick, J. E. "The Perpetuation of Institutional Racism Through Ethnic and Racial Content in Curriculum of Schools of Social Work," *Journal of Sociology and Social Welfare,* 5 (March 1978), pp. 527–539.

Jones, J. "The Concept of Racism and Its Changing Reality," in B. P. Bowser and R. G. Hunt, eds., *Impacts of Racism on White Americans.* Beverly Hills, Calif.: Sage Publications, 1981.

Kerner Commission. *Report of the National Advisory Committee on Civil Disorders.* Washington, D.C.: U.S. Government Printing Office, 1968.

Kinloch, G. C. *The Dynamics of Race Relations: A Sociological Analysis.* New York: McGraw-Hill Book Co., 1974.

Kitano, H. H. *Race Relations.* Englewood Cliffs, N.J.: Prentice-Hall, 1980.

Lewis, O. *La Vida: A Puerto Rican Family in the Culture of Poverty—San Juan and New York.* New York: Random House, 1969.

Lowenstein, S. F. "Integrating Content on Feminism and Racism into the Social Work Curriculum," *Journal of Education for Social Work,* 12 (Winter 1976), pp. 91–95.

Nasatir, D., and J. P. Fernandez. "The Use of Log-Linear and Hierarchical Models to Study Ethnic Composition in a University," in R. Alvarez et al., eds., *Discrimination in Organizations.* San Francisco: Jossey-Bass, 1979.

Robinson, A. "A Concluding Statement," in A. Robinson, ed., *Black Studies in the University.* New Haven, Conn.: Yale University Press, 1969.

Schermerhorn, R. A. "Ethnicity in the Perspective of the Sociology of Knowledge," *Ethnicity,* 1 (April 1974), pp. 1–14.

Sternbach, J. *The Dialectics of Social Work,* a monograph. Philadelphia: University of Pennsylvania, 1971. Mimeographed.

U.S. Department of Labor. *The Negro Family,* by D. P. Moynihan. Washington, D.C.: U.S. Government Printing Office, 1965.

Van den Berghe, P. "Dialectic and Functionalism: Toward a Theoretic Synthesis," *American Sociological Review,* 28 (October 1963), pp. 695–705.

Weber, M. "Class, Status and Parity," in H. H. Certh and C. W. Mills, eds., *Max Weber, Essays in Sociology*. New York: Oxford University Press, 1946.

Williams, L. F. "Measuring Racism: An Example from Education," *Social Work,* 27 (January 1982), pp. 111–115.

CHAPTER 12

USE OF ETHNIC MINORITY CONTENT IN TEACHING RESEARCH

PHILLIP FELLIN

The sequence of research courses in a school of social work should provide students with the opportunity to learn skills in the assessment and use of research knowledge for practice purposes. Ethnic minority content can be incorporated into the teaching of these skills. Experience in assessing empirical research on minority issues will provide a framework for understanding empirical knowledge presented in all areas of social work education and for applying the knowledge to practice situations. In this chapter, an approach for including ethnic minority content in the teaching of social work research is described.

The following major objectives of the research sequence in social work programs establish the context in which content on ethnic minorities may be introduced. The overriding objective of research teaching is to ensure that students understand the basic methodology of science, that is, philosophy of science and research processes. The model of scientific research taught to social workers customarily has been that of the behavioral and social sciences. While this knowledge objective is being pursued, a number of associated objectives related to skills development often are incorporated into course designs and direct the instruction and course exercises. Thus, students may be expected to develop a beginning capacity to engage in research on practice (the production of knowledge); to gain initial skills in the assessment of research for practice (consumption objectives); and to translate research skills, such as in conceptualizing, interviewing, and data analysis, into practice activities (contributions of research methodology to practice methods) (Tripodi and Epstein, 1978). In addition, the students are expected to develop an appreciation for scientific inquiry and for the relationship of research knowledge to competent practice.

One approach to teaching the basic information of research is through use of a "research consumption" perspective. This perspective involves reading and assessing research studies, with the goal of using the knowledge in social work practice and policy. A framework for teaching the assessment of research has been developed by Tripodi, Fellin, and Meyer (1983). Other similar frameworks have appeared recently in the literature, such as the works of Fischer (1981) and Kraybill, Iacono-Harris, and Basom (1982).

Ethnic minority content can be taught in research courses with an emphasis on research consumption. Ethnic minority content may be introduced by selecting examples of major types of research studies—exploratory, quantitative-descriptive, and experimental. For each of these types there are ethnic minority studies in the literature, such as exploratory studies on the self-concept of American Indian girls (Edwards, 1978); peer interviewing with Mexican American youth (Bloom and Padilla, 1979); quantitative–descriptive studies on black neighborhood diversity and anomie (Kapsis, 1978); ethnic agencies and service delivery (Jenkins and Morrison, 1978; and Jenkins, 1980); self-evaluation among blacks (Foster and Perry, 1982); self-esteem among American Indian, black, and white clients (Jayaratne et al., 1980); and experimental studies on racial and ethnic preferences of children (Teplin, 1976); and ethnic role taking (Aboud and Mitchell, 1977). Ethnic minority content also is introduced in terms of technical issues that arise when minority populations are studied, such as issues related to data collection, analysis of data, and application to practice (Billingsley, 1970; Banks, 1980; and Liu, 1982).

The assessment approach used in Tripodi, Fellin, and Meyer (1983) offers guidelines that assist the student in learning to classify, evaluate, and use empirical research for social work practice. This framework is a natural avenue for the introduction of ethnic minority content into research teaching.

This framework

■ can be used to teach students how a variety of research designs used for knowledge seeking can contribute to knowledge about ethnic minorities;

■ lends itself to the teaching of particular issues about research techniques, such as the reliability and validity of observations about ethnic minorities;

■ alerts students to issues on the analysis of data on minorities, the generalizability of the knowledge, and issues on stereotyping;

■ introduces substantive content on minorities; and

■ assists students in developing skills for the use of knowledge for practice with ethnic minorities.

Using the Assessment Framework

The instructor selects several exemplars of ethnic minority studies and examines them in class by classifying the studies, by evaluating their methodological qualities, and by showing how the findings may be used in the practice of social work. At the same time, students are asked to select and read ethnic minority studies from the literature that represent the major types of research. The students then complete written assignments dealing with assessment, as illustrated by the instructor's presentation. To illustrate the use of the assessment framework the classification, evaluation, and use of three minority relevant studies will be discussed: an experiment (Davis, 1979), a quantitative-descriptive study (Edgerton and Karno, 1971), and an exploratory study (Szapocznik, Scopetta, and King, 1978).

Classification of Research

The classification of research studies is the starting point in the assessment process. Classification allows for the recognition of major differences in the purposes and methods of various types of research studies. Students distinguish between three major types of studies: experimental, quantitative–descriptive, and exploratory. As they examine the study purposes of each of these types, they should think in terms of the nature of the knowledge sought by the investigator. (Tripodi's [1983] framework for distinguishing between knowledge levels is helpful in this exercise. He links the major study types to four distinct levels of knowledge, identified as (1) hypothetical–developmental, (2) quantitative–descriptive, (3) correlational, and (4) cause–effect.) The major purpose of an experimental study is producing cause–effect knowledge, although knowledge at "lower" levels also is produced. Quantitative–descriptive studies produce correlational and quantitative–descriptive knowledge, and likely contain hypothetical–developmental knowledge. An exploratory study produces hypothetical–developmental knowledge; by virtue of its design characteristics, it is restricted to this level of knowledge.

Experimental Studies. Briefly put, experimental studies verify hypotheses. These studies attempt to establish cause and effect relationships by using designs that control or minimize the influence of variables other than those specified to be tested in the hypotheses. Experimental studies are expected to meet the following criteria: manipulation of one or more independent variables, the use of control groups, and randomization procedures for assignment to experimental and control groups. Experimental studies can be classified further by setting (field experiments and laboratory experiments).

The Davis (1979) study on the racial composition of groups is an example of an experimental study with a minority focus. The Davis study examines how racial balance, the ratio of black members to white members, can influence the treatment group. Using a laboratory experimental design, Davis tested implicit hypotheses about racial differences and their effects on the subjects' preferences regarding ratios of blacks to whites in groups. The relevance of this study to social work practice is evident in the Davis study questions and findings. They are related to the tasks of social work practitioners in determining the ideal composition of a group; and more generally, to an understanding of the racial factor in group treatment.

Quantitative–Descriptive Studies. Studies that pursue correlational knowledge or quantitative–descriptions but do not meet the design criteria for experiments are classified as quantitative–descriptive studies. The specific purposes of quantitative–descriptive studies differ, and usually can be distinguished in terms of subtypes, according to their purposes, such as the testing of hypotheses, describing characteristics of populations, or seeking to identify relations among variables. A variety of designs and data collection techniques are used in these studies, with the most familiar being the social survey.

The research by Edgerton and Karno (1971), "Mexican–American Bilingualism and the Perception of Mental Illness," exemplifies a quantitative–descriptive study with a minority focus. These investigators examined selected relationships between bilingualism and attitudes toward mental illness. Interviews were carried out in households of Anglo and Mexican American residents in two east Los Angeles communities. The researchers did not intend to test a priori hypotheses, but sought to relate a number of factors to respondents' attitudes toward mental illness. A major purpose of the study was to identify variables with predictive value, and the researchers achieved this objective in relation to the variable, "the language in which the respondent took the interview." (P. 232.) Intended to bear on the access and use of mental health clinics, the study is relevant to social work because it deals with the significance of language in the Mexican American culture, and the need for mental health professionals "who possess both fluency in Spanish and sensitive understanding of the culture of the Mexican–American poor." (P. 236.)

Exploratory Studies. Individually or collectively, articulation of concepts, the development of hypotheses for further investigation, and increasing one's familiarity with a selected phenomenon are the purposes of exploratory studies. Research procedures in exploratory studies generally are less systematic than those employed in quantitative–descriptive or experimental studies, and the data frequently are qualitative. Information is gathered often on a small number of cases, or a single case, with a variety of observational techniques. A mixture of purposes and methods is common in an exploratory study; such a study has features of both exploratory and quantitative–descriptive types.

Szapocznik, Scopetta, and King (1978), in their study, provided an example of an exploratory study on an ethnic minority topic. Their investigation of "culturally sensitive treatment" addressed cultural variables, acculturation, and procedures for matching clients (especially Cuban immigrants) and treatment methods. A Spanish Family Guidance Clinic staff interviewed Latin heroin users. Research methods included interviews of the clinic's Latin paraprofessional counselors to elicit their perceptions of their effectiveness in working with Latin clients. Preliminary findings were used to develop a second stage of study, with more rigorous methods used to investigate basic value orientations between Cuban immigrants and Anglo Americans. The implications of basic value orientations between Cuban immigrants and Anglo Americans for delivery of mental health services are relevant particularly to social work practice.

Ethnic Minority Research Issues. Students benefit from using studies in the classification of research. Students learn to recognize and legitimate differences in research designs while obtaining knowledge about ethnic minorities and to recognize variations in the nature of the knowledge produced by research. Using such studies emphasizes the knowledge available at various levels. Classifying research is relevant particularly to gaining knowledge about ethnic minorities; it permits the introduction of a number of issues raised by minority researchers. The first issue centers around determining the kind of minority research needed and the research knowledge that is most useful. Hill (1980) has suggested that those in search of knowledge about minorities would benefit most "by placing greater emphasis on quantitative–descriptive and exploratory studies than on experimental studies." (P. 193.) He noted that an inordinate emphasis on traditional experimental designs may leave a deficit in information about ethnic minorities. Hill has urged that the knowledge on minorities be generated from the full range of study designs, particularly exploratory studies "designed both to develop and refine concepts and hypotheses that more adequately reflect the circumstances of racial minorities." (P. 192.)

In contrast to Hill's view on the usefulness of different research designs, Gary (1981) has expressed the view that in the area of research "dealing with health care problems confronting the Black Community,...[there is an] over-utilization of exploratory and descriptive studies instead of more experimental designs." (P. 163.) Given these contrasting views, the general issue of levels of knowledge that are appropriate can be debated, and consideration can be given to whether some areas, such as mental health, have need for more knowledge from experimental studies, and others may need more knowledge from other levels such as quantitative–descriptive and exploratory studies.

In this vein, the student can be introduced to the subject of quasi-experimental designs. In studying minority relevant topics, especially those related to policy research and program evaluation, the conditions for true experiments may not be possible. Yet, approximations to these conditions through quasi-experiments may be employed to generate knowledge relevant to minority concerns (Blalock and Blalock, 1982; Campbell and Stanley, 1963).

A second issue highlighted through the classification of research concerns the relative advantages and disadvantages of using secondary data to study minority populations. A strong case can be made for the contributions of secondary analysis of data to the understanding of ethnic minorities, especially with the existence of data from the U.S. Census, national studies of university research centers, and so forth. Consideration also can be given to the potential deficiencies of these data if reliability and validity are not discussed. Examples of the use of secondary data in relation to minority populations are the Gary (1981) report on "The Health Status of Black Americans," the Walter (1982) study on the use of social indicators on minority groups, and the research by Gilbert, Specht, and Brown (1974) on demographic correlates of citizen participation.

Minority researchers have identified a third issue that can be discussed in the context of a classification system. This involves the relative merits of studies that focus on a single ethnic minority group, on a comparison of a majority group to one or more minority groups, or a comparison of culturally similar minority groups. Wong's (1980) discussion of the characteristics of comparative, cross-cultural methodologies in social work research on minorities offers a useful approach to the initial classification of minority studies. Wong has emphasized the contributions comparative minority studies can make to the challenging and testing of assumptions or myths about individual and group behavior of ethnic minorities.

The reading and classifying of exploratory studies allows for discussion of the method and perspective of ethnomethodology. The research instructor can introduce this topic through reference to the works of Watts (1981) and Washington (1982). For example, Washington (1982) defined *ethnomethodology* as the "study of the patterned, socially transmitted lifestyles of cultural and social groups." (P. 104.) He also indicated how it can be used "to understand the significance of ethnicity in defining functional behavior, social needs, and social competence." (P. 195.) Washington (1982) noted that this study approach has special meaning for practice with ethnic minorities; it looks at historical and sociocultural factors in seeking to understand the social world of the ethnic minority. This perspective, in turn, has implications for practice, especially as social workers combine micro and macro practice strategies in working with ethnic minority populations.

Finally, in the exercise of classifying research studies, the issue of how to classify studies included in literature reviews of research on specific topics arises. These reviews typically address a specific social problem or a particular conceptual framework. Examples of this kind of review are found in the work of Montiel (1973) and Allen (1978). One of the principal problems in dealing with reviews is they usually do not include sufficient information for classification purposes. As a consequence, ascertaining the levels of knowledge provided by the studies is difficult. This does not mean that these reviews are without merit; they may direct the student to studies that can be assessed.

The classification exercise helps students differentiate between types of research studies and the levels of knowledge related to them. This exercise also helps students think about criteria for selecting research relevant to social work practice. Special issues related to research on ethnic minorities can then be dealt with in this context.

Evaluation of Research

Following the classification of research studies, students consider guidelines for the systematic assessment of the methodological qualities of studies, that is, problem formulation, research design and data collection, data analysis, and conclusions. Instructors should assist students in determining the extent to which the researcher has reduced uncertainty about the topic under investigation. Students should determine the soundness or quality of the research, in order to decide how much confidence to place in the ideas, findings, and empirical generalizations derived from a study. The framework for this evaluation takes into account the appropriateness of the different methods employed in the major types of research.

The use of illustrative studies from minority research can lead to systematic examination of risks inherent in the conduct of all research when considering the chain of activities required, such as sampling—Who is studied?; measurement—How are people and behavior observed?; data collection—uniformity (reliability) and accuracy (validity) of measurement affected by field operations; handling of raw data—converting responses and observations into variables, editing field notes or interviews; and analysis of data—What are meaningful categories to be used for reducing the data to an understandable scope?

The evaluation of research studies on ethnic minority content can follow the same format used for the evaluation of all research studies. When evaluating research, whether experimental, quantitative–descriptive, or exploratory, the same features of the research—such as clarity in formulation of the research questions, logic of the research design, operationalization of concepts used, and so forth—require attention. These features often are most vivid when evaluating experimental studies, but the questions raised are applicable to other types of research studies.

Experimental Studies. The evaluation of an experimental study starts with a consideration of the way the investigator formulated the research problem. The evaluator examines the theoretical framework for study, the citation of the literature, presentation of concepts, hypotheses, and assumptions of the study. The special concern about ethnic minority studies is the extent to which there may be conceptual problems, that is, the use of concepts that are not "culturally sensitive" (Jackson, Tucker, and Bowman, 1982), and that focus only on negative attributes of minorities. Minority researchers raise serious questions in the literature about the use of "standard" concepts that may have little relevance to the ethnic minority experience.

As the student examines the research design and data collection procedures of the experimental study, issues about measurement become significant. There are a number of specific designs that can be used in experiments, and they vary in the degree to which controls for internal and external validity are possible (Campbell and Stanley, 1963). These forms of validity can be examined, with special reference to any issues specific to research on ethnic minorities; for example, the race of the experimenter or the actual measurement process.

In addition to using customary guideline questions on data analysis and conclusions (dealing with such things as evidence supporting study hypotheses and appropriate use of statistical tests), evaluators must attend to the conclusions of the study. Frequently, the experimental study is limited to a small, select group of subjects; therefore, there are questions about the generalizability of the findings. While the features of the experimental design may minimize threats to internal validity, evaluators should question external validity and limitations of generalizability.

The Davis (1979) study is used as an example because it deals with racial balance as its major focus, and it relates to a social work practice issue—"What is the ideal racial composition of a treatment group?" Davis examined the concepts of race and color, perceived racial differences, social distance, cross-racial contact, and how these concepts were related to group composition. Evaluative judgments can be made about his conceptualization of the study problem using his literature review. The appropriateness of his use of an experimental design is then considered. From Davis' description of the research questions and practice problems, accepting this design as useful for an initial exploration of the problem seems reasonable. As he noted, a next step might be to study the research questions in a field experiment with clients rather than students as subjects.

The study design used by Davis involved randomly assigning 80 black and 80 white undergraduate students to two groups in which experimental conditions differed "in respect to the racial balance of the list from which a subject was to select group members." (P. 209.) Davis recognized the potential effects of the race of the experimenter on the subject's responses, and employed a black and a white experimenter. Only after the study did he examine issues related to the validity and reliability of the data. He noted that the race of the subject and the gender of the subject "probably" affected the responses.

Davis' analysis of data is presented clearly; he provided the empirical data in tables that display findings for each of his research questions. Although his research questions were enumerated clearly, the hypotheses they embodied mainly were implicit. However, the questions are examined in the analysis of data and subjected to statistical tests. His commentary related the findings to other research; he cautioned the evaluator not to overgeneralize the findings. Additionally, he noted practice implications that can form the basis for classroom discussion about research use.

Quantitative–Descriptive Studies. The variety of subtypes of quantitative–descriptive studies results in the evaluations of the studies to take somewhat different directions, depending on whether the purpose of the study is to test hypotheses, evaluate programs, describe populations, or identify relationships between variables. Not infrequently, a study will combine two or more of these purposes. Often the quantitative–descriptive study design calls for some type of sample survey, using survey questionnaires or interviews for the collection of data. It is especially in regard to social surveys that minority researchers have articulated issues specific to ethnic minority research.

In examining the problem formulation of a quantitative–descriptive study, traditional concepts from psychology and sociology may be problematic for studies involving ethnic minorities, especially, according to Jackson et al.

(1982), when the conceptual framework reflects "the white, middle-class values of the researchers." (P. 17.) Equally problematic is the way concepts are operationalized, often creating measurement issues concerning reliability and validity. In the literature a number of deficiencies relative to data collection with minority populations, such as instrument designs and content exist. The instruments do not ensure that all respondents understand and respond to the questions in a similar context and do not take into account the influence of the language or the propriety of the questions used. These factors could bias the results. Hill (1980) noted that

> there is no reason to assume that scales and indexes which were validated on whites measure the same concepts, such as self-esteem, powerlessness, aggression, or socioeconomic status, among minorities. (P. 193.)

Closely related to these concerns about the nature of the data instrument are issues about data collection procedures, such as the potential bias caused by the race of the interviewer and the respondent (Welch, Comer, and Steinman, 1973; and Schuman and Converse, 1971), interviewer-respondent interactions, and response inaccuracy. Given the identification of conceptual and methodological issues salient to minority group studies, the research instructor can draw from the literature to discuss the ways researchers have attempted to improve the quality of data in the investigation of minority populations, such as back translation, random probe, converging operations, extensive pretesting and input from members of the minority community, use of bilingual minority interviewers, and special interviewer training (Cardenas and Arce, 1982; and Jackson, Tucker, and Bowman, 1982).

Evaluators also must pay special attention to sampling when evaluating quantitative–descriptive minority studies. Evaluators must be alert to the efforts the researcher has made to minimize the negative influence of low-response rates. The nature of the study population, the population from which the sample is drawn, is another important issue. Not infrequently, this population is difficult to specify, as documented by Cardenas and Arce (1982). Yet another concern emerges when the sampling procedures are systematic, but drawn from a relatively small, geographically limited population, placing restrictions on the extent to which the findings can be generalized. Jackson, Tucker, and Bowman (1982) and Cardenas and Arce (1982), as well as other minority researchers, have argued for the availability of national samples of minority populations, so that more valid generalizations can be made with reference to black and Hispanic populations and to variations of subcultural groups within these populations.

With regard to data analysis and ethnic minorities, Hill (1980) identified and examined practices by social researchers that may distort findings. One such practice is placing an emphasis on the use of proportions in data analysis, when reference to absolute numbers might be more meaningful. Second, generalizations about minorities may overemphasize differences based on statistical tests and ignore similarities between groups. On the other hand, the researcher may minimize differences between the majority and minority group; examples of such are found in some policy-oriented studies.

The Edgerton and Karno (1971) study was designed to produce knowledge that would help explain an underrepresentation of Mexican Americans in psychiatric treatment facilities in the Southwestern states. Evaluators can use this study to examine some of the special issues in the evaluation of a minority-relevant quantitative–descriptive study. The authors sought to discover if the use by Mexican Americans of such facilities could be related to "differences in their perceptions of, or attitude toward, mental illness." (P. 231.) The authors used vignettes in the interview situation to obtain data, and allowed respondents to choose the language for participation in the interview. When few differences between Anglo and Mexican Americans were found, the authors limited their next analysis to the Mexican American sample. They related the variables of age, sex, religion, education, occupation, and number of years in the United States to responses toward mental illness and found no significant differences. However, there were six areas in which differences were found in the Mexican American sample when individuals interviewed in Spanish were compared to those interviewed in English. The response categories that showed differences included: (1) depression, (2) juvenile delinquency, (3) schizophrenia, (4) the inheritance of mental illness, (5) the effectiveness of prayer, and (6) familial orientation. Based on these findings, the authors concluded that "the more commonly described cultural traits of Mexican-Americans . . . are applicable . . . only to those persons who speak mainly or only Spanish." (P. 235.)

In examining the Edgerton and Karno study, the research instructor is able to recognize the advantages of the random sampling procedure, and that the sample size was sufficiently large (444 Mexican American and 224 Anglo American respondents) to make comparisons between the two study groups, and also within the Mexican American group. At the same time, the generalizability of findings is limited to the two communities studied.

The six vignettes used in the interviews are reproduced in the text of the study report. This provision allows students to examine a measurement technique that may have had potential bias effects. Most of the findings are in narrative form, with no tables showing quantitative data. When the claim of statistical significance is made, there is no citation to the type of statistical tests employed. These aspects of the report limit the evaluation of the quality of the data and the meaning of the findings. Still, the research instructor can use this study to consider alternative approaches to use of statistics, data analysis, and data presentation.

Exploratory Studies. The evaluation of exploratory studies can be made from at least two viewpoints. First, the researcher may choose this research approach with the primary goal of developing, clarifying, or modifying concepts and ideas to create researchable hypotheses for further study. On the other hand, the researcher may not have further research in mind at all, and may choose this design because of its immediate promise of generating useful and practical knowledge. The exploratory study generally allows for a wider set of sources of information, and the collection of both qualitative and quantitative data, and the opportunity to explore a subject in depth.

In evaluating an exploratory study, assumptions about the significance of the variables under investigation must be identified. The reader of the study decides whether the assumptions are appropriate; however, this requires some knowledge of the topic of research. For minority studies of an exploratory nature, the potential biases in the process of data collection are magnified (Glasgow, 1981). This is the case because rigorous and systematic procedures are not required or expected. As a result, we expect the researcher to inform us of the data collection procedures and to take precautions to minimize bias in the collection process.

Evaluators face a dilemma when evaluating the analysis of the findings of exploratory studies. Perhaps a researcher knew little about the subject under study; he or she then chose an exploratory model for the investigation. Having acquired some new knowledge, the researcher may be inclined to over-value it and make unwarranted generalizations from limited data. In the instance of minorities, evaluators must be cautious and not ignore the diversity within such groups. Evaluators should pay particular attention to the study of minority factors in areas where little research has been conducted. A review of a number of exploratory studies will give the reader a sense of the range of exploratory designs and findings, and in turn, skill in estimating the soundness of the research.

The Szapocznik, Scopetta, and King (1978) study begins with an anthropological kind of exploration of Latin clients of a Spanish Family Guidance Clinic. Clinic staff interviewed 50 Latin heroin users to determine why there was a low number of Latin clients in Anglo American-oriented drug abuse programs in Miami. The client interviews suggested that a strong family structure was an important factor in explaining the low incidence of narcotic addiction among Latins. In addition the data suggested that low use of services resulted from Anglo American facilities not being acceptable to the families of Latin clients.

In a related research effort, one of the researchers interviewed Latin paraprofessional counselors in the clinic. This information led to the identification of cultural variables in the Miami Latin population that were thought to be relevant to treatment. Using information from the exploratory studies, anthropological and clinical, one of the researchers developed a more systematic study of a sample of Cuban immigrant and Anglo American subjects and their acculturation patterns. With the data and implications of these studies, the stage was set for developing a procedure for creating and matching culturally sensitive treatment to the Cuban immigrant client population.

A major limitation of the Szapocznik, Scopetta, and King (1978) study is that the authors provided little information about the procedures used to carry out their exploratory studies. They reported some of their findings in a narrative manner, especially in terms of concepts of culture, value structures, and acculturation, and relate these findings to practice issues. Despite the limited information provided by the report, the research instructor still can use this type of study to consider alternative ways of improving the quality of the data, and how cultural and ethnic variables can operationalized. For example, an alternative could be a value questionnaire to compare Cuban and Anglo American adolescents.

Evaluators gain knowledge about major types of research designs, of a variety of research techniques, and varying types of research knowledge. The evaluation framework allows them to identify special design and methods issues related to minority studies. The emphasis is on differential assessment so that maximum use of knowledge is possible. Evaluators also can benefit by taking advantage of as much knowledge as possible, and using it in their practice.

Use of Research

Once students engage in exercises of classifying and evaluating research, the next step in assessment is considering how to use the knowledge for social work practice directly, or to understand a practice-related issue. Principles and guidelines for use are well developed in *The Assessment of Social Research* (Tripodi, Fellin, and Meyer, 1983). As noted in that work, two questions are central to use: what knowledge does the research offer, and what activity of social work practice does it concern?

In considering what knowledge the research offers, Thomas (1964) identifies criteria that lead to judging the usefulness of scientific knowledge, such as the extent to which the knowledge is relevant to social work. Thus, content that deals with topics such as the effects of interventions of social work practitioners and knowledge that helps them understand human behavior, the social environment, social welfare policies and services, social service organizations, and characteristics of clientele, community and society are of interest to evaluators. Other factors that make knowledge useful relate to its power (for example, the level of knowledge, such as cause and effect) and its referent features (accessibility, manipulability, and cost and ethical considerations). These ideas are all helpful in considering the utility of ethnic minority studies.

Use of an Experimental Study. The Davis (1979) study has immediate content relevance for the social worker; it addressed the ways in which racial balance can influence the treatment group. Considering that social workers frequently work with integrated groups, the topic is relevant to direct practice. The Davis study also is relevant to the process of serving clients through the use of groups. Finally, according to Garvin (1981), the composition of groups is of primary concern to the social worker. Because the selection of individuals for treatment groups can be made with the race of clients as a significant factor, social workers should view the variable of race as engineerable, that is, it can be manipulated in practice. In considering the use of the Davis (1979) study, evaluators must remind themselves that it is a laboratory experiment, and that the findings "may not correspond exactly with those of clients under the conditions of professional practice." (P. 213.)

The Davis (1979) study was limited in its generalizability. However, findings suggest guidelines for placing white and black persons into treatment groups. The importance of the race of the group leader for the group is suggested, as well as the meaning of the assignment of a single out-group member (in terms of race) to a group. The study provides conceptual knowledge useful for practice in its development of the concepts of racial balance, and of the nature of the group; that is, the degree of intimacy in the group's proposed activity.

The Davis study is a useful example of the opportunities and the difficulties of using research knowledge for practice. The study is sound enough to be useful, and although limited in scope, is rich in implications for practice. This is demonstrated in Davis' (1979) statement of implications:

> In brief, someone who is to form a group that might contain both black members and white members would be wise to consider the following questions concerning the nature of the group: (1) Is it to be organized for work or play? (2) Is it to be informal or formal? (3) Is it to be large or small? and (4) What race should the group's leader or leaders be? (P. 212.)

Further insights into practice implications of biracial groups can be gained by the student's reading of Davis' "Note to Group Workers" (1980), an outgrowth of his research study.

Use of Quantitative–Descriptive Study. The title of the Edgerton and Karno study (1971), "Mexican-American Bilingualism and the Perception of Mental Illness" alerts social workers to the potential relevance for practice with ethnic minorities. The study addressed the nature of the services and the use of mental health professionals in the delivery of services. The authors identified relationships that may exist between bilingualism and attitudes toward mental illness (correlational knowledge). The data for the study were quantitative, although ethnographic field studies provided additional qualitative data to the researchers. The study reported quantitative–descriptive data, with little or no difference between Anglo and Mexican American respondents and their significant perceptions of mental illness. However, the authors reported data that did show significant differences between Mexican American respondents who are bilingual and those who speak only Spanish. In this analysis evaluators must focus on the meaning of the language used in the interview. Thus, an interesting issue is raised: "Whether persons who live in different worlds of language also live in different worlds with regard to mental illness." (P. 233.) The findings suggest they do and that more commonly described cultural traits of Mexican Americans were not applicable to all Mexican Americans, but mainly to those who spoke only Spanish. Practitioners thus can be alerted not to stereotype their Mexican American clients.

Edgerton and Karno (1971) have provided some directions for using the findings in their discussion of the importance of language as a distinguishing factor in relation to perceptions of mental illness. They have concluded that there is a need for Spanish-speaking professionals for some clients. Because the match of professionals to clients can be manipulated in some social agencies, the implication is that practitioners should identify and consider the language world of the client when assigning cases.

Use of an Exploratory Study. To consider the usefulness of an exploratory study, evaluators should consider several questions:

■ To what extent does a study enhance sensitivity to problems, clarify concepts, and stimulate interest in the topic of study?

■ Have the concepts been operationalized in a way useful for practice?

■ Can the concepts be referred to particular behaviors?

■ Does the research stimulate practice questions?

In the Szapocznik, Scopetta, and King (1978) study, the relevance to social work practice is clear; the study deals with the concept of matching treatment modalities with client variables. The study has particular relevance to the treatment of Cuban immigrants. The quest for information started with the concerns of a social agency to match clients to treatment modes. The study points to ways of "adapting the treatment to the client rather than by socializing the client into a preselected treatment mode." (P. 117.)

With information from quantitative–descriptive studies, reference to the literature, and their own exploratory study, Szapocznik, Scopetta, and King examined acculturation as a special problem of Cuban immigrants. The researchers developed the concept of a "psychosocial model of acculturation" to study further Cuban immigrant families. Their study has advanced our understanding of acculturation. It must be noted that the clarity and soundness of this concept, its foundation in the literature on immigrant populations, the rigor of the quantitative–descriptive operations, and the process of reaching conclusions are subject to the limitations of exploratory studies with respect to both internal validity and generalizability. Therefore, evaluators must be cautious when using the research as a basis for proposing a treatment model. The research can sensitize practitioners to some possible features of minority populations for whom programs of mental health are offered.

From a utilization point of view, the Szapocznik, Scopetta, and King study has implications for treatment and the delivery of mental health services. Especially relevant are the notions of mutuality of patient–therapist expectations, cultural sensitivity, and family systems theory. The researchers combined quantitative and qualitative data and offered conceptual clarifications, descriptions of Cuban clients, and an example of how ethnic minority studies can be used to develop direct practice treatment models.

Cautions about Use of Research. Generalizations have particular salience in regard to use of knowledge about ethnic minorities. As Mullen (1978) has noted, social workers look to "summary generalizations" to guide them in the development of practice guidelines. Rothman (1974) similarly approached community change, and demonstrated how research findings could be used to develop generalizations, which in turn form the basis of action guidelines for practice. Yet, it is with regard to generalizations that the dangers of misinterpretation, overgeneralization, and stereotyping must be recognized (Garvin, 1976). Discussions in the literature about stereotyping and myths in regard to ethnic minorities provide a basis for exploring these dangers.

The work of Herzog (1970) sets the stage for this discussion: "among the potentials of social research is its ability to contribute to the making or the breaking of social stereotypes." (P. 110.) She also cited areas such as research about delinquency, familial stress, and employed mothers in which stereotypes have been created. She attributed the generation of stereotypes to "premature generalizations, insufficient qualifications, uncritical and unverified citation of findings, and lack of replication." (P. 118.) In addition, she indicated that these faults place limits on the possible contributions of social research.

Moore (1973) and English (1974) provided further illustrations of stereotyping through their research on minorities. Moore (1973) has contended that "academic research has sustained stereotypes and even generated them, impeding minority efforts at a meaningful self-definition." (P. 73.) English (1974) concluded that "the scientific investigation, study and description of black families have been characterized by myths, stereotypes, and unvalidated generalizations." (P. 39.) English attributed this characterization to a number of factors, including a "focus on pathology, and on crude theories of race and race relations." (P. 39.)

Given these legitimate concerns about the causes and consequences of stereotyping, social workers can make a case for the usefulness of research based generalizations about ethnic minorities. McGoldrick, Pearce, and Giordano (1982) confronted the issue of stereotyping in regard to ethnic differences in family patterns and family therapy. They recognized the dangers of stereotyping in the presentation of ethnic generalizations, but concluded that one must take this risk and develop frameworks "to move past the stereotypes, as starting points to learn more." (P. xvi.) They suggested that ethnicity training with students need not avoid generalizing about cultural differences, but that consideration of several groups and comparisons within groups can help in the definition and acceptance of ethnic differences.

Norton's (1978) development of the "dual perspective" approach to ethnic minority content highlights the need for valid knowledge about the majority societal system and the minority client system. However, Norton has cautioned that

a racial or minority label does not presume monolithic thought, values or behavior for all members of any group. Although there appear to be certain common characteristics that seem deeply embedded because of shared experiences, individuals and groups do react differently. The specific situation must be observed within its practice milieu. (P. 9.)

Solomon (1976) offered a similar point of view concerning the application of scientific knowledge to practice. She noted "generalizations are patently developed for the social scientist and not for the practitioner." (P. 29.) According to Solomon, the generalizations of science provide the practitioner a set of alternative explanations, and the practitioner must use practice skills to determine which possibility holds in the individual case. Solomon has indicated that scientific generalizations are useful, within limits of "illumination," but not for direct application.

These positions about generalizations and stereotyping have special implications for social work. To confront them in courses about research alerts the students to special opportunities and precautions they must take in using research on ethnic minorities.

The research assessment model for including ethnic minority content into research teaching should not be viewed as a rigid instructional plan. The instructor may use variations of the model through a range of instructional modes:

■ research studies on ethnic minorities in the social work and behavioral science literature;

■ literature pertaining to methodological issues relevant to the study of ethnic minority populations;

■ literature on the use of research knowledge for social work practice, and

■ literature on alternative strategies for teaching social work research.

These areas of the literature serve as a basic resource for the enhancement of the assessment model as a mechanism for including ethnic minority content in the social work curriculum.

Works Cited

Aboud, F. E., and F. G. Mitchell. "Ethnic Role Taking: The Effects of Preference and Self-Identification," *International Journal of Psychology,* 12 (January 1977), pp. 1-17.

Allen, W. R. "Black Family Research in the United States: A Review, Assessment, and Extension," *Journal of Comparative Family Studies,* 9 (Summer 1978), pp. 166-188.

Banks, W. M. "The Social Context and Empirical Foundations of Research on Black Clients," in R. L. Jones, ed., *Black Psychology* (2d ed.). New York: Harper and Row, 1980.

Billingsley, A. "Black Families and White Social Science," *Journal of Social Issues,* 26 (1970), pp. 127-142.

Blalock, A. B., and H. M. Blalock. *Introduction to Social Research* (2d ed.). Englewood Cliffs, N.J.: Prentice-Hall, 1982.

Bloom, D., and A. M. Padilla. "A Peer Interviewer Model in Conducting Surveys among Mexican American Youth," *Journal of Community Psychology,* 7 (1979), pp. 129-136.

Campbell, D. T., and J. C. Stanley. *Experimental and Quasi-Experimental Designs for Research*. Chicago: Rand McNally, 1963.

Cardenas, G., and C. Arce. "The National Chicano Survey: Recruiting Bilingual Interviewers," in W.T. Liu, ed., *Methodological Problems in Minority Research*. Occasional paper #7. Chicago: The Pacific/Asian American Mental Health Research Center, 1982.

Davis, L. "Racial Composition of Groups," *Social Work*, 24 (May 1979), pp. 208–213.

Edgerton, R., and M. Karno. "Mexican American Bilingualism and the Perception of Mental Illness," *Archives of General Psychiatry*, 24 (March 1971), pp. 286–290.

Edwards, E. D. "Enhancing Self-Concept and Identification with 'Indianness' of American Indian Girls," *Social Work with Groups*, 1 (Fall 1978), pp. 309–318.

English, R. "Beyond Pathology: Research and Theoretical Perspective on Black Families," in L. Gary, ed., *Social Research and the Black Community*. Washington, D.C.: Howard University Press, 1974.

Fischer, J. "A Framework for Evaluating Empirical Research Reports," in R. M. Grinnell, Jr., ed., *Social Work Research and Evaluation*. Itasca, Ill.: F. E. Peacock Publishers, 1981.

Foster, M., and L. R. Perry. "Self-valuation Among Blacks," *Social Work*, 27 (January 1982), pp. 60–66.

Garvin, C. *Contemporary Group Work*. Englewood Cliffs, N.J.: Prentice-Hall, 1981.

———. "Ethnic Analysis and Social Work Intervention." Unpublished manuscript, University of Michigan School of Social Work, Ann Arbor, 1976.

Gary, L. "The Health Status of Black Americans," in A. E. Johnson, ed., *The Black Experience*. Chapel Hill: University of North Carolina School of Social Work, 1981.

Gilbert, N., H. Specht, and C. Brown. "Demographic Correlates of Citizen Participation: An Analysis of Race, Community Size, and Citizen Influence," *Social Service Review*, 48 (December 1974), pp. 517–530.

Glasgow, D. *Black Underclass*. New York: Vintage Books, 1981.

Herzog, E. "Social Stereotypes and Social Research," *Journal of Social Issues*, 26 (1970), pp. 109–125.

Hill, R. B. "Social Work Research on Minorities: Impediments and Opportunities," in D. Fanshel, ed., *Future of Social Work Research*. Washington, D.C.: National Association of Social Workers, Inc., 1980.

Jackson, J., M. B. Tucker, and P. Bowman, "Conceptual and Methodological Problems in Survey Research on Black Americans," in W.T. Liu ed., *Methodological Problems in Minority Research*. Occasional paper #7. Chicago: The Pacific/Asian American Mental Health Research Center, 1982.

Jayaratne, S., et al. "Self-Esteem and Locus of Control Among American Indian, Black and White AFDC Recipients," *Journal of Social Service Research,* 3 (Spring 1980), pp. 239-252.

Jenkins, S. "The Ethnic Agency Defined," *Social Service Review,* 54 (June 1980), pp. 249-261.

Jenkins, S., and B. Morrison. "Ethnicity and Service Delivery," *American Journal of Orthopsychiatry,* 48 (January 1978), pp. 160-165.

Kapsis, R. "Black Ghetto Diversity and Anomie: A Sociopolitical View," *American Journal of Sociology,* 83 (1978) pp. 1132-1153.

Kraybill, D. B., D. A. Iacono-Harris, and R. E. Basom, Jr. "Teaching Social Work Research: A Consumer's Approach." *Journal of Education for Social Work,* 18 (Fall 1982) pp. 55-61.

Liu, W. T., ed. *Methodological Problems in Minority Research.* Occasional paper #7. Chicago: The Pacific/Asian American Mental Health Research Center, 1982.

McGoldrick, M., J. K. Pearce, and J. Giordano, eds. *Ethnicity and Family Therapy.* New York: Guilford Press, 1982.

Montiel, M. "The Chicano Family: A Review of Research," *Social Work,* 18 (March 1973), pp. 22-31.

Moore, J. "Social Constraints on Sociological Knowledge: Academica and Research Concerning Minorities," *Social Problems,* 21 (October 1973), pp. 65-77.

Mullen, E. J. "The Construction of Personal Models for Effective Practice: A Method for Utilizing Research Findings to Guide Social Interventions," *Journal of Social Service Research,* 2 (Fall 1978), pp. 45-63.

Norton, D. *The Dual Perspective: Inclusion of Ethnic Minority Content in the Social Work Curriculum.* New York: Council on Social Work Education, 1978.

Rothman, J. *Planning and Organizing for Social Change.* New York: Columbia University Press, 1974.

Schuman, H., and J. Converse. "The Effect of Black and White Interviewers on Black Responses in 1968," *Public Opinion Quarterly,* 35 (Spring 1971), pp. 44-68.

Solomon, B. *Black Empowerment.* New York: Columbia University Press, 1976.

Szapocznik, J., M. Scopetta, and O. King. "Theory and Practice in Matching Treatment to the Special Characteristics and Problems of Cuban Immigrants," *Journal of Community Psychology,* 6 (1978), pp. 112-122.

Teplin, L. "A Comparison of Racial/Ethnic Preferences Among Anglo, Black and Latino Children," *American Journal of Orthopsychiatry,* 46 (April 1976), pp. 702-709.

Thomas, E. J. "Selecting Knowledge from Behavioral Science," in E. J. Thomas, ed., *Building Social Work Knowledge.* New York: National Association of Social Workers, Inc., 1964.

Tripodi, T. *Evaluative Research for Social Workers.* Englewood Cliffs, N.J.: Prentice-Hall, 1983.

Tripodi, T., and I. Epstein. "Incorporating Knowledge on Research Methodology into Social Work Practice," *Journal of Social Service Research,* 2 (Fall 1978), pp. 65–78.

Tripodi, T., P. Fellin, and H. J. Meyer. *The Assessment of Social Research* (2d ed.). Itasca, Ill.: F. E. Peacock Publishers, 1983.

Walters, R. W. "Race, Resources, Conflict," *Social Work,* 27 (January 1982), pp. 24–30.

Washington, R. O. "Social Development: A Focus for Practice and Education," *Social Work,* 27 (January 1982), pp. 104–109.

Watts, T. D. "Ethnomethodology," in R. M. Grinnell, Jr., ed., *Social Work Research Evaluation.* Itasca, Ill.: F. E. Peacock, Publishers, 1981.

Welch, S., J. Comer, and M. Steinman. "Interviewing in a Mexican American Community: An Investigation of Some Potential Sources of Response Bias," *The Public Opinion Quarterly*, 37 (Spring 1973), pp. 115–126.

Wong, P. "Social Work Research on Minorities: Toward a Comparative Approach," *Journal of Education for Social Work,* 18 (Fall 1982), pp. 69–76.

CHAPTER 13

GROUP APPROACH TO TRAINING ETHNIC-SENSITIVE PRACTITIONERS

ANNE CURRIN ADAMS and ELFRIEDE G. SCHLESINGER

L ike other members of American society, social work students are products of socialization processes that internalize deeply ingrained prejudices, stereotypes, and negative images of members of minority groups. Minority group members are not excluded from this process. Nevertheless, most individuals come to social work with cognitive awareness of the destructive consequences of negative treatment of minorities. Many educational efforts are made to help students harness and make use of this awareness. Not all educational objectives are met because some students do not have an opportunity to explore the source and nature of the unspoken biases that affect interactions between people who are of different races or backgrounds.

This chapter is a description and analysis of an elective course entitled "Bias and Discrimination: Awareness of Attitudes." The major objective of the course is to heighten student sensitivity and skill in interacting with colleagues and clients from different ethnic backgrounds. The concepts and procedures taught are derived from the assumption that capacity for empathic personal involvement with people from a variety of groups is prerequisite for social work practice. Course instructors identified and used a number of conceptual formulations that highlight the sources of strength and stress of diverse groups and applied group work approaches to classroom teaching. The model presented in this chapter is the result of a five-year effort to incorporate a number of conceptual formulations with a teaching and learning approach that draws on the student life experience—both in the past and in the context of the learning environment—as a way of acknowledging and moving beyond deeply held stereotypes.

Conceptual Formulations

Norton's (1978) view of the "dual perspective" and the concept of the "ethnic reality" (Devore and Schlesinger, 1987) have facilitated efforts to trace the source of racism and identify the socialization processes by which images of self and others are internalized. Norton has suggested that all people are a part of two systems. The dominant or *sustaining system* (Chestang, 1976) is the source of power and economic resources, and confers status. Embedded in the sustaining system is the *nurturing system,* which comprises the physical and social environment of family and community. It is in the nuturing system that the individual sense of identity is developed.

The analysis by Devore and Schlesinger (1987) points to an intrinsic component of the sustaining system—the stratification structure. At each level of the class structure, social class and ethnicity converge to generate "ethclass" (Gordon, 1964). Although social class is a major factor in determining the basic conditions of life, ethnicity—conceptualized here as the *ethnic reality*—functions to define and differentiate the experiences, attitudes, behaviors and dispositions of various groups at the same social class level.

Ethnic groups are defined or set off by race, religion, or national origin, or some combination of these factors. Members of such groups conceive of themselves as being alike by virtue of common ancestry and experiences, and are so regarded by others (Gordon, 1964; Shibutani and Kwan, 1965; and Devore and Schlesinger, 1987). Those ethnic groups that are most devalued by the larger society usually are referred to as minority groups. The term *minorities of color* refers to those members of American society who are victims of racism—blacks, Puerto Ricans, Chicanos, American Indians, and Asian Americans. People develop a perspective—whether or not clearly articulated—of their "place" in the stratification system, and whether that "place" is valued or demeaned.

Students who elect to take the "Bias and Discrimination" course usually come with or quickly acquire cognitive understanding of the social facts. However, the reality often is denied affectively. Many present with a stance that says "we are alike, regardless." Emotional acknowledgment of the real status differences and that they have been imperceptibly incorporated into the ego can be disquieting. This is especially true for members of majority groups. Such acknowledgment is unwittingly perceived as negation of past struggles to surmount such unworthy stances.

The concept of an alternative generalized other—roughly equivalent to the nurturing system—focuses cognitive attention on the role played by this system in intensifying or managing negative societal orientations to minority and low-status people. To help students handle these "facts," concepts are introduced that pinpoint the processes by which people come to develop a unique sense of self, at the same time as they incorporate societal responses and expectations, and come to act in accord with these.

Mead's (1934) discussion of the "generalized other" is characterized by Norton (1978) as "taking on the attitude of the wider society in regard to oneself." (P. 4.) This attitude is useful as a way of alerting students to the systematic source of bias. The concept of an alternative generalized other—equivalent to the nurturing system—focuses cognitive attention on the role played by this system in intensifying or managing negative societal orientations to minorities.

The degree to which minority group members internalize negative or positive self-images is in part a function of whether their nuturing environment has been able to provide love and care, and to sufficiently buffer against the destructive definitions often conveyed by the larger society. Analogously, the nature and intensity with which members of majority groups incorporate racist and other prejudiced perspectives is related to whether and how these perspectives are conveyed by significant others. For both sets of members, the primary groups that are important in their lives play an intermediary role in the process. They determine, in large measure, the institutions and individuals with whom their members interact. They also serve as role models in respect to response to societal themes about oppression. Given the pervasive devaluation of underclass and minority groups in the society, few people—whether members of minority or majority groups—are likely to emerge unscathed. For the former, this translates into varying degrees of doubt about self-worth and persistent discrimination. The latter almost inevitably harbor some degree of negative appraisal of those who are "different" or considered "lesser."

Coupling the sociological concepts with review of life experiences can help group participants come to grips with the fact that few "escape" the impact of societal forces without conscious and ongoing struggle. Exploration of the concept of the ethnic reality suggests how primary groups—an important component of the nurturing system—transmit ethnic and class-based behavior as well as biases. While exploring, students review how their family and community systems use group language, rituals, religion, and modeling of deeply ingrained coping styles to link themselves to the group and its values.

This process helps students grapple—both cognitively and affectively—with the methods members of ethnic groups use to internalize group identification. Reference to these concepts can help students develop appreciation for diverse groups—their struggles, their difficulties, and their strengths. Such appreciation is essential in social work practice. Norton (1978) used the term *dual perspective* to refer to a stance, an "attitudinal and cognitive approach" that facilitates the efforts to simultaneously understand and compare the values, attitudes, and behaviors of the larger social system with those of an individual's family and community system. Norton suggests that the approach embodied by this perspective calls for the social worker to know and be empathic toward the majority societal system and the client system. The model of practice derived from the view of ethnic reality provides a framework for acquiring the type of knowledge needed to function in the terms suggested by the dual perspective. The course helps students develop a dual perspective.

Group Work Approach

Assumptions

Social group work traditionally has sought to modify attitudes and behaviors using cognitive and affective processes. Researchers view small group experience as having the potential of replicating in a microcosm major elements of what is experienced in the larger society. A major component of the historical tradition of social group work embodies a problem-solving focus. No single, unified model of group work has emerged (Garvin, 1981).

A number of traditions and orientations are identified in group work literature. The social goals approach, referred to by Vinter (1965), is linked to social work's struggle for human rights and social justice. The socialization approach is focused on enhancing the social development of those who enter a group voluntarily. Resocialization or remedial approaches assume the existence of some problem or deviance. The latter usually have objectives of "remedying" or "resocializing" those who exhibit dysfunctional behaviors (Garvin, 1981). Although the approaches to group work practice vary in objectives, conceptual underpinnings, and style, a number of elements are integral to most. These include efforts to achieve group objectives through sharing, the development of cohesion, and viewing the group as a mutual aid system in which aid is solicited to solve problems in both contextual and interpersonal situations.

The approach described in an educational context in this chapter synthesizes and makes explicit three objectives. The first objective is related to fundamental social work values that justify efforts and compel participants to minimize bias and its effects. In the second objective, that growth and change in this and all other areas have intrinsic value is a given. The third objective is derived from and based on the assumption that, though universal and pervasive, biased perspectives are deviant and dysfunctional.

The approach described draws on the dynamics generated when life experiences are shared and uses the mutual aid system as a vehicle for facilitating conflict resolution. The major objective is to create a learning environment to modify biased attitudes and discriminatory practices among social work students.

In the group approach, there is an emphasis on the generation of controversy as a means of developing open and clear statements of the issues as well as to ensure a problem-solving emphasis. As practitioners, students are confronted with the antiempathic potential of their socialization and encouraged to use the forum of the small group, with whatever the diversities in ethnicity, gender, or other personal differences, to consider a restructuring of their views about others. As the group struggles with various issues, the leader is responsible for the timely introduction of theoretical material to explicate points of view and further develop the search for understanding. The healthy resolution of controversial issues is an ultimate goal of the group process, along with the acquisition of knowledge, the development of empathic understanding of cultural diversity and the development of practice approaches for cross-ethnic, cross-cultural intervention.

Attributes of the Instructor/Group Leader

To use the learning and teaching approach a course instructor needs knowledge and skill in a number of areas. He or she must be well versed in group dynamics and skilled in practice techniques in social group work intervention. The instructor must be able to serve as a role model in a number of areas and demonstrate professional respect for differences and alternative and conflicting viewpoints. The instructor must be able to model those components of social work ethics and values that lead to the commitment to improve skills in practice with ethnic minority populations.

Also crucial is the ability to convey, in attitude, stance, and verbalization, understanding of the different rates of personal growth. This takes the form of responding to individuals and the group in a way that acknowledges variations in time, depth, and purpose. Social group workers always are faced with the responsibility to make dual assessments of both the individuals in the group and the capacity of the group for work based on the stage in which the group is functioning. How much time it takes for students to recognize certain behaviors or stereotypical responses, and the depth at which they grasp the salient issues of the course is evaluated differentially. The instructor considers each student as an individual, his or her past experiences, and personal and current struggle.

The depth to which a given topic can or should be explored is connected with the objectives of the group as well as the professional determination of the constructive and purposeful nature of the interchange. Closely related to this is the skill involved in demonstrating a major practice principle—observing the uniqueness of all individuals. The instructor must recognize that members bring a variety of experiences and are at different levels of self-awareness about the issues that are the focus of this course. In so doing, the instructor must be able to set the stage for helping students to invest energy in maximizing their unique potential.

A differential perspective on the purpose of a given process exists. The instructor's decision to apply group work skills or periodically use more traditional or didactic teaching styles should be based on whether the focus will be affective or cognitive.

The instructor must deal well with tension and conflict, and understand that the healthy resolution of tension and conflict is the work of the group. If the leader is fearful of this area, much of the group's potential for growth likely will be diminished. The instructor also must be able to hear and tolerate statements that reflect bias. Students often come to school harboring many stereotypes. Further, out of naivete, many do not recognize these as such. Consequently, students may express stereotypical beliefs and attitudes openly without awareness that they are offensive to others. Therefore, the instructor needs skill in helping students appreciate the purposes to be served by "permitting," for the purposes of learning, the expression of biased attitudes.

Another important consideration in using this course format is the responsibility of the dual role of instructor and group leader. Unfortunately, a clear dichotomy cannot be made. Rather it is an issue of continual assessment depending on where the group is developmentally at a given time, its capacity to tolerate content or process, as well as which is in greater need of attention. Criteria for assessment include such factors as timing, intensity of the emotional climate, accuracy and sophistication of the knowledge base of the group members around the issues being debated, and the implications to group movement in the choice of content over process or vice versa. In addition, the leader must be open with the group about the duality of roles and the issue of academic accountability (evaluating the group members' work and professional development). Issues of attendance and participation are areas of student accountability. Students contract with the instructor regarding whether a grade of good or excellent will be assigned. The difference between the two grades is based on the submission or quality or both of a given amount of written work. It is important that the academic requirements do not negate the student's room to grow and to recognize that the nature of the course is to encourage students to take risks. They should not be penalized by the grading procedure for taking risks.

Use of Group Process

Identifying Experiences with Difference

In the early stages of the learning group, it is helpful to begin by examining the degree of exposure to difference the students have had throughout their lives. Such discussion usually surfaces barriers within the social structure that persistently inhibit interaction between people different from each other. The instructor, consciously using the leader role, should identify quickly the diversity within the group and help the group members recognize how little they really know about each other. Intrinsic to this stage is pinpointing any indications of stereotyping. For example, to begin the interaction the instructor may pose the following question:

> I wonder if we could all focus on, and some or all of us share, the first time we recall having awareness of the differences in people, other than male/female differences? What was the situation, and what do you remember about your feelings at the time?

People generally draw on childhood memories relating in the telling of the actual experience a host of issues regarding how prejudice is taught and institutionalized, how biases are socialized and generationally transmitted and reinforced, and how stereotypes are created and maintained. The students' tendency to begin the process of sharing by focusing on childhood experiences generates a group atmosphere of light-hearted humor.

Since childhood experiences are perceived as being largely out of one's control, this kind of content is easier to deal with in this early phase of group life. The leader recognizes this as preliminary to more difficult considerations. She or he may tell the participants that the group is destined to grapple with similar issues in more depth, as well as to struggle with more controversial and potentially conflictual problems. For instance, the instructor may choose to raise consciousness regarding the etiology of subtle nuances such as the use of terms like "you people" or "you know how they are." It may or may not be a time to introduce the group to the reality that even less acceptable terms may surface in the heat of group discussion. If the instructor perceives this as a constructive time for this work, reference to literature and the concepts described earlier place the private experiences of this group of individuals into the social context.

Establishing Group Norms

The instructor contracts with the members to work on developing norms whereby the group learns "to live with" statements that reflect unpopular, prejudicial, or stereotyped ideas expressed in the group. Though many of the group members are surprised or distressed by this stance, the leader presents it as an important vehicle for accomplishing the group's work. In this process, reference to "you people" and other such terms highlight biased thoughts and discriminating practices as inevitable consequences of socialization experiences. The instructor points to the limited experience most have with people with different backgrounds. Review of the kinds of stereotypes with which we "all grow up" can help members realize that no one is likely to move beyond them unless the group permits free expression for the purpose of examination. At all times, emphasis is on living with biased ideas as a way of illustrating how ingrained these are, even in those who abhor them. Thus acknowledged, the group can use its potential for honest confrontation and meaningful problem exploration to facilitate growth.

Acknowledging Bias

Accepting the fact that "we all harbor prejudices" facilitates the next step in the learning process. Though acknowledged as an inevitable fact of everyone's experience, prejudiced attitudes and behaviors are nevertheless social problems that need to be addressed. Prejudiced attitudes and behaviors debase individuals and, in the case of social workers, inhibit effective practice. Hence this learning group is one method of problem resolution, and all of the group members are the target of attention.

It is common for the group to establish an "us against them" stance, thus denying personal involvement in the perpetuation of oppression. There also is a tendency to focus discussion on racism and sexism on an intellectual level. The leader continually must refocus the group's discussion to include a personal emphasis. For example, a male group member may make a comment to the effect that "the literature shows sexism to be particularly rampant in the corporate structure." Others may suggest that "racist institutions inhibit the advancement of minorities." All convey a sense—both verbally and nonverbally—that these problems exist "out there." The leader cuts through this effort to depersonalize the issue by asking the members to reflect on how they and the institutions they value play a part in the process. They may be asked to reflect on how racism and sexism are expressed in the social agencies in which they function.

This does not deny the validity of intellectual pursuit of knowledge of the socialized "isms." Rather, it is the commitment to the development of individuals as practitioners capable of sensitive practice in these areas that compels the joining of intellectual and personal involvement.

The experience of sharing, comparing, and discussing life experiences with a diverse group of colleagues takes the concept of the dual perspective to the essential additional step—the experiential level. The hands-on approach, vital in practice, is an essential component of the educational endeavor that seeks to help students integrate social theory for use in practice. In a summarizing paper on the course, a student captures the essence of this conceptual integration that the sharing of life experiences in the group provided for her.

> And you...in that precious moment when your newborn daughter was placed in your arms had the joy of that moment blighted by thoughts of how you could protect her from the effects of racism...and...mother's fears causing her to overprotect and overcontrol. Or adoption practices among the poor black population to insure survival of family members with the associated pain of giving up children after caring for them an extended period of time. Hearing all this from all of you made it too vivid and too real. Reading only Chapter VI on *Child Rearing Practices in the Black Urban Community* (or some such title in some such book) would have been much less disturbing.

As is the nature of groups, the quality and emotional intensity of the shared life experiences increases as the group becomes cohesive. The leader's role is to reach for the issues and the emotions within the experience that help students identify commonality in their life experiences at the same time as they are exploring differences (the former is an important means to group cohesiveness and should not be neglected in the zeal to have students face the realities of the prevalence of bias and discrimination); gain insight into the cultural and racial reality of others as a means of developing an empathic response in practice with diverse cultures; examine personal readiness for practice in various service arenas; and discover areas of interest that can and should be pursued more intensely through self-study. This may result in individual students selecting topics of particular concern to them, reading additional references and presenting material to the groups. The subjects cover a broad spectrum of groups and issues that have tended to result in discriminatory stances. Examples are homosexuality, the physically handicapped, or ethnic minority groups whose experiences usually are not considered in an ethnic context.

Oppression as a Universal Victimizer

Oppression can be viewed as a universal victimizer; all members of society are deprived when oppressive acts are sanctioned or tolerated. This kind of perspective comes as "news" to many. Those who are members of majority groups are surprised to learn that they may be viewed as "victims" when oppression deprives them and society of the potential contributions of members of minority groups. Thus viewed, oppression in the view of a member of the majority is to be minimized not only for "their" sake, but "for mine."

Social work students are victims in special ways. Their profession does not countenance oppression and the "isms" overtly. When social work students are victims of oppression, they are hampered from carrying on their work effectively. Yet, by virtue of the socialized nature of racism, sexism, and the host of other "isms" that oppress various groups, it is possible, indeed likely, that people will be drawn into perpetuating conditions to which they are ideologically opposed. Throughout the learning process these realities need to be acknowledged and reinforced. As life experiences, practice incidents, and classroom experiences are being shared, the leader looks for examples in the student's experiences that underscore the concept of joint victimization and victim perpetuation of the problem. Shared plight and shared values, clearly identified, encourage the development of cohesiveness and reliance on mutual aid as a means of problem solving.

As in all social groups, the leader seeks opportunities to strengthen and reinforce mutual aid, an important group dynamic. It is not uncommon, with class groups organized around this model, to have students solicit the group's help in efforts to change after reaching a level of consciousness regarding behavioral or verbal manifestations of bias. Students may request help in correcting their continual use of terms such as "you people" when referring to a particular minority group; deeply held view that minority people's only access to positions of authority in agencies or schools is the result of affirmative action; belief that a person's major qualification for a particular position is his or her race or sex; and unduly solicitous behavior toward the handicapped or the elderly. When such help is requested, students must receive visible evidence of support for achieving a major group objective—self-awareness. The fact that enhanced self-awareness has led to efforts to "give up" behavior to which the student is ideologically opposed needs to be stressed. Such responses encourage other students to engage in closer self-examination and similar risk taking.

When the group helps an individual make these kinds of changes, it functions in a manner akin to the "alternative generalized other" or primary group.

The fact that the group has become sufficiently cohesive to engage in this process illustrates the capacity of the nurturing system to affect behaviors and attitudes. Once more, a critical concept is more readily learned when linked to direct experience.

Conflict and Controversy

Instruction on ethnic minority life, social injustice, and efforts to heighten related self-awareness are emotionally charged. There is considerable potential for conflict to develop among members of the class. The greater the degree of heterogeneity among class members in terms of race, ethnicity, age, socioeconomic background, religion, or sexual preference, the greater is the likelihood that they will have conflicting attitudes and life stances and respond in "conditioned ways," both to the content and the process of the course. The instructor must be sensitive to the members of different groups who respond differently to the public expression of conflict and controversy. Students must learn that regardless of their dispositions, the capacity to deal with conflict and controversy is integral to practice.

Instructors should approach the learning group and the teaching task with the expectation that conflict and controversy are integral to practice. Additionally, instructors should seek to determine the nature of conflicting ideas and their etiology. Because group members more than likely have been socialized into viewing conflict as negative and undesirable, they usually are uneasy when evidence of potential conflict surfaces. Group members are likely to repress, deny, rationalize, intellectualize, and employ other means of avoiding conflict. Many clues, both verbal and nonverbal, will indicate that tension is mounting. The leader, by attending to the content of the group's discussion, and by making linkages between the material and previous discussions of this group, can develop hypotheses concerning the nature or central cause of the conflict. Hence, the leader can have salient material or topics derived from the group around which members can work, learn, and grow. However, before engaging the group around this material, an important assessment must be made.

The leader is sensitive to the probability that this is the first time participants will be experiencing encouragement around expression of honest feelings that are going to be uncomfortable for someone else. Reticence is natural and the resort to defense mechanisms likely. The leader understands why defense mechanisms are being used and seeks to enhance group functioning by enabling the participants to be in conflict. The immediate goal is to turn the conflict into controversy, a more manageable state. Johnson and Johnson (1975) explain the difference this way: "controversy is a form of conflict among group members. . . a discussion, debate or dispute in which opposing opinions clash." (P. 237.) This attention to conflict is consonant with the developing norm of establishing a climate for the acceptance of unpopular statements by members.

According to Johnson and Johnson (1975),

> Controversy among group members is essential because it is only through controversy that involvement, creativity, commitment to task accomplishment and to group maintenance, and high quality decisions can evolve. Emotional responses to controversy may be positive (excitement, enjoyment, stimulation, curiosity, commitment, involvement, liking for other members) or negative (anger, distrust, resentment, fear, hurt, rejection), depending upon how the group handles the differences of opinions among members. (P. 237.)

The leader initially focuses on the content of the conflictual statements and the actions or postures of the participants. The aim is to establish the parameters of the controversy—the topics to be thrashed about. The leader also attends to the emotional aspects of the messages being conveyed. He or she attempts to assess the potential for reaping a positive emotional response from engaging in the controversial debate, by assessing the intensity of the negative feelings and degree that they are personalized or targeted to a particular person, and the degree to which the intense negative or emotional feelings are consonant with the social reality. After deciding that "good" can come of this heated debate the leader should relate the controversial topic or topics—being careful to broaden the problem statement to ensure maximum investment of all group members. This attempt at a universalization of the issues usually reduces the intensity of strong negative feelings directed at a single member of the group.

In the case of a high level of negative intensity between two subgroups, the leader should acknowledge the conflict, help to identify the essence of their struggle, and the social costs or benefits of their polarized views. The leader should present only enough material to minimize the group's fear of the negative emotions that are at the core of the conflict. In this way the group can mobilize to engage in struggling with the controversial issues embodied therein. Following this the leader's role is to facilitate the exchange by concentrating on the process in which the group is engaged. According to Hinton and Reitz (1971) the leader's role is to

> listen in order to understand rather than appraise or refute, assume responsibility for accurate communication between members, be sensitive to unexpressed feelings, protect minority points of view, keep the discussion moving, and develop skills in summarizing. (P. 33.)

For example, in one session of the course, while students were expressing what they believed to be the basic causes of discrimination, a black student mimicked (without humor) the way a white and older student expressed herself. The group participants became quiet, tense, and apprehensive as evidenced by their body language. The issues that seemed paramount were the statements by the white student that, although unintended, demeaned and deemphasized the struggle of minority groups within the society; and the anger of the black student, which was relayed covertly and ambivalently. The leader verbally acknowledged the change in atmosphere and suggested that fear and apprehension about whether what had happened should be permitted and the possibility of not understanding what had provoked the confrontation were the causes. Group members examined the content of the statements of both participants and expressed how they would want such issues handled. The result was a great deal of sparring between participants.

Three subgroups developed: (1) black, (2) white, and (3) mixed. The mixed subgroup represented the class members who saw problems with the presentations of both students. The instructor attempted to get issues clearly stated; took the risk to suggest some unstated issues; and suggested that from a professional stance there were problems with the behavior and content messages of both students. The struggle precipitated by this event became the work of the group, sometimes subtle and sometimes overt, throughout the term. The success reaction on the first encounter was to bring the issues to the surface. Hence, the group learned it could survive conflict, if not resolve it. Resolution came many weeks later when the student who had mimicked the other shared an article with the class. The article, an analysis of a clinical syndrome, reflected the first student's problem. The problem resulted from racial oppression rather than a psychopathological origin, as the article clearly explicated. The analysis, in turn, evoked understanding from the other class member as to what had triggered the anger.

As the group becomes accustomed to debate, a normative pattern is established that may be described as a "climate of mulling over things." Thus, over the course of a term, a given topic such as the one previously noted is likely to receive a second and even a third review. Over time, there is an increase in group member references to previous discussions, even those of a more painful nature. This in itself is a measure of the group's developing strength in coping positively with the emotional aspects of conflict.

Utility of the Course

The shortcomings are clear. This is an elective course of which only a single section is available per semester. In addition, the degree of sophistication in relation to clinical issues that the group can achieve is determined largely by their previous, ongoing and subsequent opportunity to become familiar with human behavior, social policy, and research issues directly related to this content. In no way should such a course be construed as sufficient in terms of meeting the requirement of the inclusion of content on ethnic minorities, women, and other oppressed groups.

There is, however, some opportunity to deal with practice issues and theories. One of the drawbacks of practice theory is that in general it is based on research and experience with majority populations. As a result, it has been difficult, at times, to apply the skills and procedures of practice successfully with various populations, such as oppressed minorities who are at high risk for poverty, inadequate education, poor housing, poor health, and inadequate support systems. An ongoing effort within this course is to foster creative thinking regarding the adaptation of practice knowledge to the various clinical realities, which take on new meaning as students gain understanding of many of the ethnic issues. To be sure, time is a huge constraint. However, students are encouraged to integrate the combined theoretical and experiential knowledge gained in this course with other practice and core course assignments and discussions.

The nature of group discussion, particularly in the middle and end phases of the learning group, often centers on practice experiences in the field and alternative ways of approaching intervention. Thus, the students begin to make pragmatic use of the course content and the experiential design.

This model of teaching for the preparation of ethnic-sensitive practice enables students to add the ethnic reality to their understanding of behavior. In addition, students generally gain a deeper understanding of self-awareness as a concept in professional development.

Works Cited

Chestang, L. "Environmental Influences on Social Functioning: The Black Experience," in P. Cafferty and L. Chestang, eds., *The Diverse Society: Implications for Social Policy*. New York: Association Press, 1976.

Devore, W., and E. G. Schlesinger. *Ethnic-Sensitive Social Work Practice*. Columbus, Ohio: Merrill Publishing Co., 1987.

Garvin, C. D. *Contemporary Groupwork*. Englewood Cliffs, N.J.: Prentice-Hall, 1981.

Gordon, M. M. *Assimilation in American Life*. New York: Oxford University Press, 1964.

Hinton, B. L., and H. J. Reitz. *Groups and Organizations: Integrated Readings in the Analysis of Social Behavior*. Belmont, Calif.: Wadsworth Publishing Co., 1971.

Johnson, D. W., and R.F.P. Johnson. *Joining Together, Group Theory and Group Skills*. Englewood Cliffs, N.J.: Prentice-Hall, 1975.

Mead, G. H. *Mind, Self and Society*. Chicago: University of Chicago Press, 1934.

Norton, D. G. *The Dual Perspective*. New York: Council on Social Work Education, 1978.

Shibutani, T., and K. M. Kwan. *Ethnic Stratification*. New York: MacMillan Publishing Co., 1965.

Vinter, R. D. "Social Group Work," in H. L. Lurie, ed., *Encyclopedia of Social Work* (vol. 15). New York: National Association of Social Workers, Inc., 1965.

CHAPTER 14

AN APPROACH FOR ADDRESSING RACISM, ETHNOCENTRISM, AND SEXISM IN THE CURRICULUM

IVOR J. ECHOLS, CAROLYN GABEL, DONNA LANDERMAN, and MIGDALIA REYES

The goal of social work educators for more than a decade has been to increase recognition of the importance of training social workers to work with minority populations and developing strategies to confront racism, ethnocentricism, and sexism. The social work profession advanced toward achievement of that goal in 1970 when the Council on Social Work Education (CSWE) declared that as a priority it would develop educational programs that addressed the concerns of minority groups.

> In a pluralistic society composed of different racial, ethnic, and socio-economic groups, the goal of social work education must be to train social workers to meet the needs of its total client systems. Most social workers, minority and non-minority alike, work at one time or another with members of at least one minority group: American Indians, Asian Americans, Blacks, or Latinos. These groups should be understood in context of not only the problems that often accompany their minority status, but the richness of their heritage and the potential for their beneficial contribution to society. Social work education must teach its students to understand, appreciate, and be sensitive to cultural differences (Norton, 1970). (P. 1.)

CSWE reported that courses addressing minority concerns already were being taught in a number of schools of social work. However, the goal of increasing recognition of the importance of these concerns in social work training only could be achieved by incorporating content addressing racism, ethnocentrism, and sexism into the entire social work curriculum. Thus, CSWE prescribed an infusion model that would provide specific information about different minority groups. Additionally, CSWE suggested a systems approach, the dual perspective, in which the client and his or her social system would be the focus. The

217

dual perspective would involve links between the two systems and would require both an attitudinal and cognitive approach.

Under the stimulus of extensive writing by several social work authors including Crompton (1974), Oliver (1979), Arnold (1976), and Scott (1971), a pattern of specialized courses based on content reflecting the history of both blacks and Puerto Ricans emerged. Most of the literature espoused incorporation and infusion, but the practical application suggested the creation of separate courses that would focus on introducing the history of these racial groups into the curricula—a topic that is not evident in the social work literature.

In this chapter, curricula mandates that prompted one school of social work to develop courses that focused on oppressed groups are described. Additionally, the results of three group independent studies on black women, Puerto Rican women, and white, antiracist women are discussed and the groups' objectives and experiences are examined. Recommendations are offered for infusing content on racial and ethnic minorities—especially women, ethnocentrism, and sexism—into the social work curriculum.

Curricula Mandates

Like activists in the civil rights movement who pressed for the inclusion of content on blacks, Puerto Ricans, and other minority groups in the curriculum, women, as a result of the Women's movement and a renewed consciousness of the oppression of women in the United States and in social work practice, pushed for curricula that addressed women's issues. In 1978, CSWE mandated that schools of social work address issues of sexism ranging from faculty and student equity to nonsexist curricula that include content on women as an integral part of the curriculum and permeate it in totality (*Handbook of Accreditation Standards and Procedures,* 1984).

Schools did respond to the mandates. For example, the University of Connecticut School of Social Work administration indicated that the primary goal of the school continued to be infusing content on racism, ethnocentrism, and sexism into the curriculum. Additionally, the school developed discrete courses and substantive areas of study in which the focus is issues of oppression and on oppressed groups.

These areas include "Puerto Rican Studies," "Black Studies," and "Women's Studies Substantive Areas," all of which offer a variety of specialized courses that focus on Puerto Ricans, blacks, and women (*Reaccreditation Report,* 1982). Concerned women faculty and students of different racial and ethnic groups recognized the need for additional courses to address the experiences of black and Puerto Rican women as well as the need to provide students with experience-based learning to help the students combat racism and ethnocentrism. As a result of the efforts of the faculty and students, three group independent studies on black women, Puerto Rican women, and white women's antiracism were developed.

Independent Study on Black Women

Reasons for Development

In fall 1980, a black woman student who was enrolled in courses offered in the "Women's Studies Substantive Areas" expressed concern that the content did not focus adequately on minority females. Although she ackowledged the general relevance of the materials for women and felt that issues of sexism were explored, she decried the lack of understanding of the special plight of minorities, especially black females.

For instance, an increasing black population in the United States has brought a larger share of problems for black women. Of the five million black families existing in 1980, more than two million were headed by women. Numerically, black women constitute the largest group of the poor. Black females had a median annual income of slightly more than 50 percent of that of white males; they ranked fifth on the scale of income, behind all males and below white females (*U.S. Census of Population,* 1980). The problems of economic survival, employment advances, and life quality are important issues.

Black women who aspire to become professionals do not escape the economic, employment, and other life problems by virtue of personal achievement, but rather become more sensitized to the vulnerability of their race, sex, and class. Angela Davis has suggested that black feminism has reflected a bourgeois ideology and has failed to recognize that working class women and black women were linked to men by class exploitation and racist oppression that did not discriminate between the sexes (Davis, 1980). Thus, Davis has summarized an ongoing struggle among black women who seek to reconcile their self-realization and personal strivings with their responsibility to their race and community. Black women who enter professional training bring to that experience personal feelings, community expectations, and the cumulative effects of racial discrimination, all of which serve to shape what they are and what they will become as they assimilate the knowledge and seek to meet the requirements of a study curriculum. Even though the chosen endeavor may be a helping profession, that of social work, and may be traditionally elected by a preponderance of females, the crucible of learning often ignites doubt, denial, and hostilities. Also, because the end product may involve the delivery of services by these women to a substantial number of minority clients, the gaps between human need, available resources, and agency provisions present formidable challenges and barriers to self-fulfillment and success. In fact, the definition of success may be a socially determined state of having satisfactorily returned positive contributions to one's own community and one's ethnic institutions.

As a result of the black woman student's efforts and the support of women faculty in light of the problems black women face, the independent study on black women was formed and was first offered in spring 1981.

Purpose

The independent study on black women provides a curricular mechanism for responding to accumulating demographic data about this target population. Furthermore, the linkage between societal conditions for black women and the demands of black women for a responsible social work practice for both clients and professionals seems appropriate to overall social work educational goals.

Goals

The goals for the independent study on black women were determined jointly by interested black women students who constituted the first self-selected enrollment and a faculty member. The goals were to further exploration of the needs and aspirations of black women, to challenge value conflicts and barriers in professional training for social work, to make community and client service delivery consonant with self-determination and minority perspectives, and to offer recommendations to the school of social work curriculum.

One of the goals of the "Women's Studies Substantive Areas" was that students from two other groups, Puerto Rican women and white women antiracists, should be combined with the black women's group for exchange and communication of experiences and findings. The first black women's independent study group in 1981 held a two-day invitational two-part symposium in which each group reported its findings. Additionally, two invitational speakers participated: (1) the faculty coordinator and (2) a research analyst from the Connecticut Permanent Commission on the Status of Women. At times, black women participating in the symposium expressed some apprehension about giving up "their autonomy"—there were increased feelings of ownership about their work. The discussion following the first symposium was at times defensive in tone. However, the faculty who were involved are not deterred by what they believe was a realistic reaction to the stimulus of bringing to a more conscious level the range of frustrations, disappointments, and challenges faced by the black women students.

Benefits

The black women who have participated during the years of the independent study have described many benefits of the study. For many of them, the encouragement to read from a variety of sources was a legitimate investment in their own history. Students read from Robert Staples' (1973) work on black families, Robert Hill's (1978) research on the dynamics of change among black Americans, and Lerone Bennett's (1968) history of the black experience. Many of the students had taken the required course on human oppression and, thus, had a frame of reference for assessing the impact of the material on the experiences of black women. Barbara White's (1981) work, the works of black sociologist Joyce Ladner (1973), and the emerging works of Bonnie Thorton Dill (1976), Director of the Center for Research on Women, Memphis State University, Tennessee, also helped students to apply social science findings to their personal experiences and opinions. It often is assumed that minorities know about their own culture, and, therefore, can recall information upon demand. This is not a valid assumption. For each group that has participated in the independent study, by the end of the semester, the group has become what the author terms a *support group*. Participants who shared many of their anxieties about themselves learned about the possibilities and limitations of the social work profession in meeting human needs that appear indigenous to the society.

Enrollment

Since the inception of the black women's independent study, student enrollments have included female students who elected to take the credit to explore the literature and to explicate issues based on their findings. The student who had initiated the development of the independent study group has served as convener, and the steering and evaluating of the group became her special project.

Independent Study on Puerto Rican Women

Like courses concerning black women, a need exists for specialized courses that address the issues of Puerto Rican people, in general, and Puerto Rican women, in particular.

Reasons for Development

Poverty in Puerto Rico has resulted from the colonial status in which that nation has been placed by the United States; many Puerto Rican peasants, farmers and other Puerto Ricans living on the island have been forced to migrate to the United States to attempt to escape poverty. The experience of many of the Puerto Ricans who migrate to the United States provides the incentives that attract Puerto Ricans to the United States for secondary level jobs. Approximately 2.1 million Puerto Ricans live in the United States (*U.S. Census of Population,* 1980). Poor housing, high levels of unemployment, low levels of formal education, increased incidence of mental illness, and resentment of the justice system and crime all too often characterize Puerto Rican communities in the United States. Puerto Ricans, North American citizens by birth since 1917, are members of a young, multiracial society that suffers not only from problems of inequality in the United States, but also from racism, prejudice, and discrimination. Nevertheless, little of the information on and attention given to oppressed groups during the past decade has been focused on Puerto Ricans (Morales, 1986).[1]

In July 1980, as a result of the efforts of Julio Morales, NIMH awarded the University of Connecticut School of Social Work a Puerto Rican Studies Project grant. A specialized training model on the provision of social services to Puerto Rican clients and client systems, which included the development of an area of specialization in Puerto Rican studies and the recruitment of Puerto Rican and Latino students to the school's program, was created. Also developed and implemented through the Puerto Rican Studies Project was a program training component to reach human service providers throughout the state and region.

Guaranteeing that the particular needs and problems of Puerto Ricans are addressed in a school of social work program, however, does not assure necessarily that the concerns of Puerto Rican women are identified effectively. The development of appropriate programs, services, and relevant policies and practice issues for this oppressed group may be overlooked. The Puerto Rican women shares with Puerto Rican males the experiences of being a member of an ethnically and racially oppressed minority group in the United States; however, the Puerto Rican woman experiences other levels of oppression based on class and sex. For example, Puerto Rican women compose the highest percentage of female single-headed families in the United States and are more likely to fall under the poverty level (82.2 percent) than are Puerto Rican male-headed families (49.7 percent), white North American women single-heads of household (40.3 percent), or black women with similar responsibilities (65.7 percent) (*U.S. Census of Population,* 1979, 1980).

Purpose of Independent Study

To address issues faced by Puerto Rican women, the University of Connecticut School of Social Work developed through the Puerto Rican Studies Project an independent study program during spring 1981. The purpose of the group independent study on Puerto Rican women was to not only examine factual information and technical assistance on the provision of social services to Puerto Rican women, but also to serve as a support and consciousness-raising group, where emotional and intellectual issues could be shared and discussed.

---

[1] Material appearing here is extracted from the Puerto Rican Studies Project proposal (or continuing grant proposal report) prepared from 1979 to 1983 and submitted to the National Institute of Mental Health (NIMH) by Morales. Additional information on the University of Connecticut School of Social Work Puerto Rican Studies Project Training model can be obtained from M. Reyes, Chair of the Puerto Rican Studies Project, University of Connecticut School of Social Work, 1798 Asylum Avenue, West Hartford, CT 06117.

Formalization into a Course

The independent study was formalized into a course in 1982 to allow non-matriculated students to access content on Puerto Ricans and to develop a permanent curriculum that addressed the concerns and problems of Puerto Rican women students and clients. Initially when the course was proposed to the faculty for approval, a controversy arose regarding the requirement that students who enrolled in the course needed to know Spanish. The rationale for this requirement was based on the fact that often Puerto Rican women who seek social services and are in crisis are unable to communicate in English; therefore, at times they receive inappropriate services from social service providers. Furthermore, much of the literature that addresses this population is in Spanish. Also, Puerto Ricans need a course in which they can express themselves comfortably in the language with which they are most familiar. Puerto Ricans throughout history have resisted assimilation, cultural genocide, and losing their sense of culture, heritage, and language (Maldonado, 1972).

Course Highlights

Despite opposition, the "Puerto Rican Women and Their Reality" course was adopted by the University of Connecticut School of Social Work in May 1982 as proposed, and became an elective in the overall general curriculum. It is the only course on Puerto Rican women taught at any graduate school of social work. Highlighted in the course is the double oppression that Puerto Rican women may face when seeking to maintain identity as Puerto Ricans and as women in a society that may discriminate against both. Additionally, the cultural aspects of traditional Puerto Rican socialization processes of males and females are considered. A feminist ideological perspective and cultural sensitivity mechanism is used in the course content and is encouraged in the discussion format. Equal emphasis also is placed on issues of racism, classism, and heterosexism. Also examined in the course are social work practice issues as they relate to Puerto Rican women. Students are encouraged to provide services to Puerto Rican women.

Enrollment

Students enrolled in the course have been predominantly Puerto Rican women, although non-Puerto Ricans and men have enrolled in the course. Some women in the course have expressed their preferences for a women-only space. Other students have expressed the importance of having more men, particularly Puerto Rican and Latino men, access the course content. Recently, the number of males registering for the course has increased. Most of the students who have taken the course have stated that the course should be made a requirement in the "Puerto Rican Studies Substantive Area."

Independent Study by White Women on Antiracism

Background

The white antiracism independent study group offered at the University of Connecticut School of Social Work was developed out of antiracism education traditions outside the social work field; however, it is supported clearly by literature within social work. For example, experienced-based training models for effectively challenging racism have been developed by the Peace Corps, religious groups, and most recently within the Women's movement (Terry, 1970; Crompton, 1974; and Dawson, 1976).

Additionally, many women, particularly those in rape crisis and battered women's organizations, have begun to address racism within their work and training (Cross et al., 1979; Smith, 1979; and Landerman and McAtee, 1980). The approach for antiracism education at the University of Connecticut School of Social Work is based on the work of white women at the YWCA Sexual Assault Crisis Services (SACS) in Hartford, Connecticut (Landerman and McAtee, 1980).

The course is based on the assumption that racism is a white problem and that whites need to play a unique role in overcoming racism. The infusion of racial and ethnic minority content is a critical aspect of challenging racism in the social work curriculum. However, along with the knowledge of the historical, cultural, political and social aspects of ethnic and racial minority groups, white students also must have an opportunity to explore their values and fear toward people of different cultures. For this reason, the education of white social workers must be different from that of Third World students. Social work education for whites must help students to both intellectually and emotionally experience their role as whites in a society and to develop antiracism skills. G. Winefred Kagwa, an African black woman who teaches about racism in a United States school of social work, has stressed that learning on only a cognitive level is incomplete. For teaching to truly reach students, it must touch them as a whole, on cognitive and emotional levels (Kagwa, 1976).

In fall 1980, a white feminist student who had developed and participated in the antiracism groups at SACS suggested that an independent study modeled on the SACS feminist antiracism group be introduced at the University of Connecticut School of Social Work. In spring 1981, 10 women participated in the first independent study. The student who suggested the creation of the independent study and a white feminist faculty member instructed the group.

Format

The most basic characteristic of the independent study group was that it consisted solely of white women. Such group composition created an atmosphere of security, safety, and trust that allowed participants, guided by the leadership of skilled group facilitators, to express, recognize, and change racist attitudes and behaviors. At the University of Connecticut School of Social Work, antiracism independent study groups always comprised white women. Mixed race/sex groups limited the effectiveness that this model created. The model served to encourage white students to identify components of racism, while at the same time allowing them to take risks that were conducive to trusting and learning.

One of the important steps that white students must take in learning about racism and their role in combatting it is to recognize themselves as white. While blacks, Puerto Ricans, and other racial and ethnic minorities are forced by racial oppression to be aware of themselves as members of racial groups, whites generally are not aware of their whiteness. Racial identification has been recognized as an important concept among minority social workers—whites who wish to become antiracist also should recognize this important concept (Brown, 1976).

First, whites must recognize that racism in North American society exists, and they must see its effects. Second, whites must recognize that they, as whites, contribute to racism. This often is the most difficult step. It means taking responsibility as a white person for racism. Third, whites must act to combat racism. The purpose of antiracist groups is not simply to become more enlightened, but to act and not just talk (Young, 1982). While there might be resistance in schools to all-white classes, there is no reason why homogeneous groups cannot meet periodically as small groups in a multiracial class on racism or in a group independent study format.

Another format characteristic of the independent study group is that the group learning experience be emotional and personal, as well as intellectual. Techniques such as participating in consciousness-raising groups used during the Women's movement have contributed to this study group format. Predominantly white members of the Women's movement spoke to counteract the myths about them. A similar approach is effective for white women confronting their racism.

Application

The SACS and the University of Connecticut School of Social Work white antiracist group format has been used primarily with feminist groups. However, the University of Connecticut School of Social Work has experimented with incorporating the approach of creating racially homogeneous discussion groups into the required "Human Oppression" course. Does the current composition of the groups lend to the groups' effectiveness or do different groups for white men and white women need to be developed because of the gender differences of socialization and of women understanding the connections with their own oppression? The viewpoint of one participant from SACS, which is shared by the University of Connecticut groups, gives a sense of the groups' effectiveness:

It hits home a little harder when we dig into our own past and see how closely we've lived with racism and never even knew it. I don't expect a black woman to educate me about *my* racism when I see how thoroughly it is a part of my white experience in the world. My responsibility in combatting racism starts with looking at my life (Landerman and McAtee, 1980). (P. 16.)

Instructors

It is obvious that instructors need group work skills to offer the independent study on white, antiracist women, which is different from the traditional lecture format of many classes. Additionally, the traditional power relationships of the teacher/student relationship become dismantled. Effective teaching of such a class mainly requires an openness and willingness to learn along with the other group members. It requires an awareness of the dynamics of racism and the connection of whites to racism.

Benefits

Students and faculty participating in the independent study generally found the experience challenging, supportive, and an effective way to develop antiracist abilities individually and in social work practice. Students also increased their understanding of other areas of differences based on their class, religion, ethnicity, and sexual preference, and an understanding of the connections between all forms of oppression.

By taking advantage of educational techniques developed outside of social work, social work educators can develop effective, experience-based learning opportunities for white social work students to combat racism and ethnocentrism.

Recommendations

The following recommendations combine the objectives and experiences drawn from the group independent studies on black women, Puerto Rican women, and white, antiracist women:

■ Develop a curriculum and support for educational experiences and informational learning about institutional and personal racism, ethnocentrism, sexism, and other types of diversity.

■ Obtain support for the ideology and process from as many groups as possible by building and maintaining strong representation of faculty and students from diverse racial, ethnic, and other oppressed groups who are committed to antiracist and feminist education and activities.

■ Obtain community cooperation and involvement throughout the curriculum development process as well as plan to be supportive of community efforts with the same common goals and issues.

■ Offer content that acknowledges the oppression of groups and individuals within the society, and challenge victim-blaming ideology and practice.

■ Recognize and respect the differences of diverse groups and their right to explore their differences and similarities. At the same time, however, develop a format that unites students from separate homogeneous independent study groups to work collectively on racism, ethnocentrism, and sexism.

■ Work to incorporate the concept of homogeneous groups based on race, ethnicity, and gender into required courses such as "Human Oppression."

■ Recognize that a dearth of literature in these areas exists, and produce materials that add to knowledge and understanding.

■ Use both the models of infusion of content on oppressed population groups throughout the curriculum and in special substantive areas of studies and of discrete, homogeneous, small groups to extend curriculum and further the aims of social work in educating for change.

Summary

The social work profession, based on its history, evolution, and commitments, has a responsibility to educate all students to be competent in responding to racism, ethnocentrism, and sexism whether the evidences are overt racial injustices; inherent inequality in social systems; narrow and introverted thinking leading to exclusive, subjugating social policies; or discrimination against women who by the biological fact of gender become targets for scorn, abuse, and devastating social and economic discrimination. In a practice-based profession, the education not only must be cognitive in design, but must offer genuine, open opportunities to experience, feel, and process the content in a way that personalizes the learning so that it becomes retrievable in interpersonal transactions.

There is a growing academic movement to forge links between women's studies, black studies, Puerto Rican studies, and other areas of specialized study. The underlying assumptions are that these groups experience oppression in society; hence, sexism, ethnocentrism, and racism are linked and remedies for all can be generated by using the collective strength to educate new professionals in these areas. The social work profession, which preponderantly comprises women and which serves women and children as the largest constituency, should give a high priority to developing theory and practice that are informed and specially targeted toward the needs of women of all racial and ethnic groups.

Historically, issues of women of color have not been given attention and support. There is a developing field of information to address these omissions, such as the courses developed at the University of Connecticut School of Social Work. The format of small independent study groups provides a structure that not only increases knowledge but also creates a separate space to share personal experience and gain support for common struggles.

It is critical that social work education maintain a strong commitment to the infusion of content on racial and ethnic minorities and women throughout the social work curriculum. However, it must be recognized that this approach alone is inadequate to challenge racism, ethnocentrism, and sexism in social work education and practice. Separate discrete courses also must be available that address specific areas like black and Puerto Rican women. In addition, white students need experiential-based learning to confront their racism in small homogeneous groups. It is only with a racially and ethnically diverse faculty and student body that support a feminist ideology that schools of social work will have the resources to develop cooperative efforts that will challenge racism, ethnocentrism, and sexism.

Works Cited

Arnold, H. D. "American Racism: Implications for Social Work," *Journal of Education for Social Work,* 6 (Fall 1976), pp. 7–12.

Bennett, L. *Before the Mayflower.* Chicago: Johnson Publications, 1976.

Brown, P. "Racial Social Work," *Journal of Education for Social Work,* 12 (January 1976), pp. 28–75.

Crompton, D. "Minority Content in Social Work Education: Promise or Pitfall?" *Journal of Education for Social Work,* 10 (Winter 1974), pp. 9–18.

Cross, T., et al. "Talking about Racism: CR Guidelines," *Off Our Backs,* 9 (November 1979), pp. 17–23.

Davis, A. Y. *Women, Race and Class.* New York: Random House, 1980.

Dawson, D. M. "Anti-Racism Training: A One-Day Workshop on White Racism," pp. 5–7, and A. M. Freedman, "Hang-Up on Black and White: A Training Laboratory for Conflict Indentification and Resolution," pp. 45–48, in H. L. Franklin and J. J. Sherwood, eds., *Intergroup and Minority Relations.* La Jolla, Calif.: University Associates, Inc., 1976.

Dill, B. T., who has published in *Signs,* 1976.

Handbook of Accreditation Standards and Procedures (rev. ed.). New York: Council on Social Work Education, Commission on Accreditation, July 1984.

Hill, R. *The Illusion of Black Progress.* Washington, D.C.: National Urban League Research Department, 1978.

Kagwa, W. "Utilizing Racial Content in Developing Self-Awareness," *Journal of Education for Social Work,* 12 (Spring 1976), pp. 21–27.

Ladner, J. (ed.). *The Death of White Sociology.* New York: Random House, 1973.

Landerman, D., and M. McAtee. *White Anti-Racism Work,* National Institute of Mental Health Rape Prevention Report. Hartford, Conn.: YWCA Sexual Assault Crisis Service, 1980.

Maldonado, D. M. *Puerto Rico: A Socio Historical Interpretation.* New York: Random House, 1972.

Morales, J. *Puerto Rican Poverty: Migration to Elsewhere.* New York: Praeger Publishers, 1986.

Norton, D. G. (ed.). *The Dual Perspective: Inclusion of Ethnic Minority Content in Social Work Curriculum.* New York: Council on Social Work Education, 1970.

Oliver, J. "A Pragmatic Model for Integrating Minority Content in the Social Work Curriculum: Toward Developing an Alternative Incentive Network," *Journal of Education for Social Work,* 15 (Fall 1979), pp. 100–107.

Reaccreditation Report, Curriculum Study (vols. 1 and 2). West Hartford, Conn.: University of Connecticut School of Social Work, 1982.

Scott, C. "Ethnic Minorities in Social Work Education," in A. M. Pins et al., eds., *The Current Scene in Social Work Education.* New York: Council on Social Work Education, 1971.

Smith, B. "Some Thoughts on Racism," *Aegis: Magazine on Ending Violence Against Women,* (March/April 1979), pp. 15–19.

Staples, R. *The Black Woman in America: Sex, Marriage, and Family.* Chicago: Nelson Hall, 1973.

Terry, R. W. *For Whites Only.* Grand Rapids, Mich.: Wm. B. Eerdmans Publishing Co., 1970.

U.S. Census of Population, 1980. Advanced Report. Washington, D.C.: U.S. Government Printing Office, 1980.

———. 1979. Washington, D.C.: U.S. Government Printing Office, 1980.

White, B. "Black Women: The Resilient Victims," in A. Wick and S. J. Vandiver, eds., *Women Power and Change.* Washington, D.C.: National Association of Social Workers, Inc., 1981.

Young, V. Toward an Increased Understanding of Whiteness in Relation to White Racism, pp. 1–30. Unpublished manuscript, Amherst, Mass., 1982.

CHAPTER 15

INFUSION OF
MINORITY CONTENT
IN THE CURRICULUM

LEON W. CHESTANG

S ocial work educators during the past decade have grappled with a number of issues related to the integration of racial and ethnic minority content in the social work curriculum. These issues are epitomized in the furor that characterized discussions of the black experience during the late 1960s and the early 1970s, but they reflect similar issues raised by other oppressed ethnic groups.

During the 1960s, these issues often centered on the debate about whether the black experience offered substantive information and if the black experience should be viewed as a legitimate area of scholarly inquiry. Another debate involved the assertion that the inclusion of minority content detracted from the limited time available to teach the primary focus of a course.

Currently, many social work students are challenging the requirement that they devote attention to racial and ethnic minority content. These are important issues, and their resolution will require continuing diligence and study. Still, a sufficient and growing body of knowledge exists that can guide the pursuit of a meaningful resolution of these issues.

This chapter is premised on the belief that a strategy to facilitate the infusion of content on racial and ethnic minorities is needed. To be effective, such a strategy should relate this content to the purposes of the field of social work, propose a structure by which this content can be infused and integrated throughout the entire curriculum, and illustrate learning experiences by which this can be accomplished. Each of these objectives will be addressed, but the main focus will be on proposing a framework that promises to facilitate the integration of ethnic and minority content in social work courses, regardless of central objectives or themes.

Professional Purpose and Minority Content

Social work is concerned with helping people with problems of social functioning. This concept directs attention to the various contexts in which human activity occurs, including interpersonal interactions; social roles; families; institutions, such as schools, social organizations, and neighborhoods; and communities. Because the profession also is interested in the relationship between these contexts and their reciprocal influences on each other, the concept of social functioning urges social workers to understand social processes such as the origin, development, and implementation of social welfare policy and social structures such as institutions and organizations.

Social work's interest in matters such as those previously outlined is shared by members of a host of other professions. However, social work has defined a peculiar focus: it is concerned with phenomena from the point of view of people in the situation (Bartlett, 1970). Within this perspective, observations are made, concepts defined, and generalizations formulated. This idea links humans with the contexts and conditions of their lives, calling attention to the reciprocal and interactive exchanges between and among people and their environments. Because this idea suggests the significance of the meaning events have for people, it emphasizes and validates the importance of personal and group experience.

The idea of people in a situation is not only the distinctive feature of the profession's focus, but it also suggests the theoretical basis for the link between minority content and professional purpose. It provides a compelling rationale for infusing minority content throughout the social work curriculum. This perspective should defuse the debate about the substantive nature of the black or other racial or ethnic group experience as well as the related questions about the legitimacy of these as areas of scholarly inquiry. In addition, this perspective can help to deal with students' negative attitudes toward having to devote attention to this content and provide a practical and theoretical answer to those social work educators who argue that including content on blacks and other minorities detracts from the time available to teach the material that is the focus of the course.

In what follows, specific principles that can guide the development of courses in the five core areas of knowledge mandated by the Council on Social Work Education (CSWE) *Curriculum Policy Statement* (1983) will be addressed. The purpose of this chapter is to set forth a conceptual scheme for infusing minority content in the social work curriculum. It does not attempt in any detailed way to specify substantive content either for the knowledge area or the particular racial group used to exemplify the process. Much substantive information is available in the literature, easily accessible to the reader. It is hoped that the strategy offered in this chapter will facilitate the infusion of minority content regardless of the knowledge area or the ethnic minority group being addressed.

Conceptualizing a Course of Study

Educators must surmount both attitudinal and intellectual barriers to integrate minority content into curricula. The attitudinal barriers were alluded to earlier and have been discussed in the literature. The discussion in combination with the mandates of CSWE (*Curriculum Policy Statement,* 1983) has resulted in significant penetration of these barriers. Similarly, significant progress has been made in resolving the intellectual impediments of infusing minority content. What remains is the development of a strategy to ensure continued progress in this area.

The strategy proposed here urges social work educators, regardless of the course being designed, to clarify and to specify three major dimensions of course construction related to the infusion of minority content. The three dimensions to be discussed in turn are (1) the organizing framework, (2) the organizing concept, and (3) the organizing principle. This strategy rests on the assumption that conceptualizing a course involves identifying the elements of a particular area of knowledge and relating the elements to each other. Regardless of the knowledge area, these elements involve key concepts that describe, clarify, and explain the phenomenon under study. Attention to these dimensions provides a structure for infusing minority content and keeps it closely tied to the broader considerations of the course. Thus, it avoids the gratuitous quality that inevitably attends when this content is presented in one or two class meetings or when a representative of a minority group is invited to give an occasional guest lecture.

The Organizing Framework

Many social work educators conceive of core courses in social work curricula too narrowly. The bases for this tendency often are related to limitations of time, the need to cover large bodies of knowledge, and the instructor's personal interests and competencies. When it is recognized, however, that the failure to develop a sufficiently broad conceptualization of a course impedes the infusion of minority content, it is possible to take steps to move beyond these impediments. Identifying and setting forth the organizing framework of the course is a crucial step in this process of infusion.

The organizing framework is the conceptual model of the course summarizing its essential dimensions and its terrain (Figure 1). The organizing framework identifies the elements of a course at a conceptual level and tells what is to be studied. This author has noted elsewhere, for example, that the "terrain" of human behavior in the social environment must include the study of human development and the person's interaction with the environment (Norton, 1978). (P. 12). Certain specific topics follow from such a study, including the development of the human life cycle, which involves people's basic needs and drives related to the life stages, and the role of the environment on the life cycle, reactions to stress, and the ways people cope.

Figure 1.

Organizing Framework
(an ecological
systems model)

Substantive Area (Human Behavior in the Social Environment [HBSE])	Portrays HBSE content as fit between	Ethnic/Minority Content (Black Americans)
Role of environment on	1. An active, growing human being	Perspective of nurturing environment
1. Human development through the life cycle	2. Changing properties of immediate settings in which person lives	1. History of the group
2. Role of environment on a. life cycle b. reactions to stress c. adaptation d. ways people cope	3. Effects of relations between these settings	2. Social and psychological values 3. Acculturation experiences 4. Racial and ethnic experiences
3. Basic human needs and drives related to life stages	4. Effects of larger contexts in which these settings are embedded	5. Socioeconomic experiences
	Organizing concept (ego development and functioning)	
	Ego defined as: A set of functions of the personality which 1. Develops in interaction with the environment 2. Becomes increasingly complex over the life cycle. *Organizing principle* (describes relations between and among major concepts covered in the course; for example, human social functioning is the result of constitutional factors, significant relationships within family and factors in the social environment such as race, class, and culture.	

Experiential and Cognitive Learning

The infusion of information on minorities requires blending information from the group's perspective on such matters as the history of the group, acculturation experiences, racial and ethnic experiences, and socioeconomic experiences. These categories are not exhaustive, but they illustrate the kind of information usually included in Human Behavior in the Social Environment (HBSE) courses. Norton (1978) points out that for such a course to integrate minority content, knowledge about the specific ethnic group in its "nurturing environment" must be included. This content "can take many forms of organization depending on the minority or ethnic group being considered." (P. 12.) The point of emphasis here, however, is that the organizing framework can provide the vehicle for linking the general course content to a specific minority or ethnic group.

The ecological systems model, an organizing framework, can be used to order minority content in human behavior courses. From this perspective, Bronfenbrenner (1979) has claimed that

> human development involves the scientific study of the progressive, mutual accommodation between an active, growing human being and the changing properties of the immediate settings in which the developing person lives, as this process is affected by relations between these settings, and by the larger contexts in which these settings are embedded. (P. 21.)

As an organizing framework, this model outlines the structure of the body of knowledge covered by the course and clarifies how the elements are related to each other. Thus, the organizing framework integrates the elements and gives unity to the subject matter. Clearly, these functions provide important aids to the instructional and learning processes. From the instructor's point of view, sequencing, coherence, and increasing complexity are protected. From the student's point of view, clarity, logic, and understanding are likely. One sees these functions in operation as the student learns that people's basic needs and drives affect their motivation, adaptation, and coping. The student also recognizes that these processes are affected by the social context (environments) in which the developing person lives. As can be seen readily, content on ethnic minorities is crucial to understanding these processes. The student can then understand how one's ghetto or barrio experience or reactions to discrimination and prejudice influence adaptation.

The unity of the subject matter is underlined by the organizing framework through its portrayal of each element of course content as inextricably linked to the other; the omission of any link results in inaccuracies in understanding, gaps in knowledge, and insufficient skill. The organizing framework serves two other critical functions. First, it provides a scheme for analysis, comparison, and criticism, skills essential to the competent practice of social work and effective student learning. The second attribute of the organizing framework is that it clarifies the difference between teaching a theory and teaching an area of study. In relation to the organizing framework, a specific theory becomes an element of the course while the area of study usually is more inclusive, encompassing several theories. If the educator is confused on this point, he or she will focus on a single theory and compromise the comprehensiveness of an area of study (for example, psychoanalytic theory in HBSE). This not only limits the opportunity to include minority content but may block a more comprehensive view of the subject matter related to other themes as well. A human behavior course focused on psychoanalytic theory, because this subject is so broad and complex, often leaves little opportunity to consider the role of the environment on human development and social functioning. Conversely, a course using a broader organizing framework would consider psychoanalytic theory as one element to be included among many other theories of personality development. Considered in this fashion, psychoanalytic theory provides one among a number of other perspectives on personality development. What the foregoing suggests, then, is that an organizing framework is an ordering device with important consequences for the structure and content of a course as well as for the nature and kind of knowledge and skill the student is expected to acquire.

The Organizing Concept

The organizing concept sets forth the core conceptual idea of the course. It is the theme around which all other aspects of course content revolve. Throughout the course, it is examined, elaborated on, expanded, and explored. The organizing concept selected for a course, therefore, must be central to understanding the structure of an area of study, its relationship to other areas of study, and the professional purposes served by it. The organizing concept is illustrated by the concept of ego development in an HBSE course. Students must understand this concept as more than an abstraction. This requires understanding that the ego is a set of functions of the personality, that it develops in interaction with the environment, and that it becomes increasingly complex over the life cycle.

Opportunities to structure minority content into such learning are many. Students learn that there is variation in the ways in which the ego adapts, integrates, chooses, and defends itself. Further, students learn how the environment interacts with biological and cultural factors and the social structure to influence the character of ego development and operation. As the course progresses through the life stages, one can see how race and ethnicity influence ego development. Approached in this way, the infusion of minority content not only is achieved, but the student gains a fuller appreciation and understanding of the subject matter addressed in the course.

The effective use of the organizing concept can aid the inclusion of minority content in a course, but it is important that this content also be ordered so that appropriate linkages and syntheses are made. For this purpose, a separate organizing concept specifically designed for this is useful. Chestang's (1976) formulation of "duality in black culture and coping" and Norton's (1978) concept of the dual perspective are illustrative. Norton defines the dual perspective as

> the conscious and systematic process of perceiving, understanding, and comparing simultaneously the values, attitudes, and behavior of the larger societal system with those of the client's immediate family and community system. It is the conscious awareness on the cognitive and attitudinal levels of the similarities and differences in the two systems. (P. 3.)

Because this perspective requires substantial knowledge and empathic appreciation of the majority system and the client's nurturing environment, it "allows one to experience each system from the point of view of the other." (P. 3.)

Solomon's (1976) concept of "empowerment" also is relevant. Empowerment "refers to a process whereby persons who belong to a stigmatized social category throughout their lives can be assisted to develop and increase skills in the exercise of interpersonal influence and the performance of values social roles." (P. 6.)

Either of these ideas—duality in black culture and coping, the dual perspective, or empowerment—can be used to further solidify the structure of minority content in a given social work course. These concepts, of course, are not exhaustive of the possibilities. Others that come to mind are oppression and racism. The main point here, however, is that an organizing concept specifically addressing minority content orders such content and provides a rationale for its inclusion in the course.

The Organizing Principle

The organizing principle describes the relations between and among the major concepts covered in a course. These relationships should result in a statement of the fundamental assumption or hypothesis of the body of knowledge addressed.

Consider, as an example, the following organizing principle used by this author in a course titled "Race, Culture, and Social Functioning": "Human social functioning is the result of the interaction of constitutional givens, significant relationships within the family, and factors in the social structure and social environment such as race, class, and culture." As this statement indicates, the student's attention is directed to the key dimensions of knowledge to be examined and understood in the course. The statement also contains a point of view that defines what is significant to the area of study: constitutional or biological attributes, relations in the family, and social factors that impinge on the person are important in order to understand black social functioning. It is important to note also that the statement links these elements by hypothesizing that the interaction among them influences the quality and character of social functioning.

The statement directs the student's attention to key dimensions of knowledge and the links among them, but it does not say specifically what the nature of these connections are or how they come about. That is the function of the many subprinciples and hypotheses that will be covered in the course. The organizing principle is the grand idea of the course, serving as the anchor for the related ideas that give it vitality. It is stated at a high level of abstraction because it is intended to subsume a large body of information.

Enough has been said to show the relevance of this idea to structuring minority content into a course. It bears repeating, however, that structuring minority content into a course through an organizing principle enhances the probability that the student's understanding and application of knowledge will accurately reflect the fundamental assumption inherent in the area of study.

Before leaving this topic, it may be useful to distinguish the organizing principle from the organizing framework. The organizing framework summarizes and describes the general types of information essential to knowledge in an area of study. The organizing principle makes this knowledge concrete by moving it to a level of greater specificity. The organizing framework offers a broad outline of the subject matter; the organizing principle relates its specific elements into a coherent statement of its most fundamental assumption.

Designing Learning Experiences
to Infuse Minority Content

The organization of course content should reflect the purposes of the course. Because social work is concerned with understanding and intervening in human problems, courses ordinarily include facts, concepts, theories, and principles that bear on these matters. A major point of this chapter is that knowledge of racial and ethnic minorities is an integral component of any area of study in social work.

Techniques and approaches for ensuring the infusion of ethnic and minority content in the social work curriculum will be discussed. Two areas of learning thought to be central to the infusion will be considered: (1) attitudinal responses and (2) substantive knowledge, including its application.

Attitudinal Responses

Although students bring a host of attitudes toward minorities from their family and life experiences, the instructor sets the tone for their attitudes toward the relevance and importance of minority content as components of professional knowledge and competence. A norm permitting open class discussion and conflict around opinions and controversial ideas among the students and between the instructor and students must be set. This means, for example, that in a course on social welfare policy, a student must be free to express the view that affirmative action results in injustices to members of the dominant society. Further, it means that the instructor must protect this student's right to have his or her say. Similarly, students holding other points of view must have the same protection and rights. The instructor's role, after ample opportunity for class discussions, is to relate these various points of view to the orientation and purposes of the profession. Again, the organizing framework, concept, and principle can be used to analyze the various points of view in relation to their fit with the accepted knowledge and perspective of the profession.

Inherent in this approach is the acceptance of controversial ideas and conflict as natural and essential aspects of learning. This especially is necessary because the material is laden with emotional, social, and personal implications. But this is not acceptance of controversy and conflict for their own sake. For attitudinal change and learning to occur, controversy and conflict must be considered in the light of professional development and competence, and the instructor must link controversy and conflict to the objectives of the course.

A brief illustration of one technique follows. In an effort to help students acquire an emotional understanding of what "taking the attitude of the other" means, this author engages them in the following experiential exercise:

Issue 1: Identify three of your most dearly held values. Prioritize these three values.
■ Tell how you learned these values.
■ Tell how these values are reflected in your functioning and your family's functioning.
■ How has your perspective (the meaning of or ways of living out these values) changed on the application of these values?
■ What values about family life do you hold which were not learned in your family?

Issue 2: What does it mean "to take the attitude of the other?"
■ Identify an attitude commonly held by black (or other ethnic group) people that you *do not* share. Be specific.
■ Describe the process you would go through in order to take this attitude for yourself.

This exercise requires students to confront their values and to come to terms with their attitudes. The exercise also provides a lesson in the difficulty and the advantages of taking the attitude of the other. Through it, students move beyond cognitive self-awareness to emotional awareness of the feelings and attitudes of persons whose life experiences often are vastly different from their own.

Substantive Knowledge

It is not possible to detail what the students need to understand and intervene in the problems of the various minority groups encountered in social work. It is possible, however, to outline briefly the kinds of information relevant to the core courses students need. Knowledge of human behavior has already been alluded to in this chapter. Much of that information also is pertinent to social work practice, social welfare policy, and field instruction courses.

In addition to an analytic perspective derived from a broad organizing framework focused on the interaction between person and environment, students need specific information from a minority perspective, including, but not limited to, the work of minority scholars. It is important for students to understand the feelings, attitudes, values, and perspectives that grow out of minority group experiences including how these experiences and perspectives result in life-styles, coping strategies, world views, and attitudes. Further, these results have implications for the minority person's behavior and attitudes toward social welfare policies and programs. These factors have implications for research courses in social work. In addition, it is essential for students to appreciate and understand how the questions posed, the research designs used, and the interpretation of data affect the minority person's view that such research might contribute to or alleviate the negative valuation of minorities in society.

In the course on race and culture, it was helpful to focus the course content exclusively on theories and research that specifically address issues relevant to the black experience and areas of interest to the profession. Such issues included childhood, the role of women, the role of men, family functioning, race relations, and social intervention. By examining systematic theories and empirical research, students learn how to analyze critically their own views as well as the methodology and findings of research. They come away from the course with a clearer view of the minority experience, greater skill in assessing the negative valuation of minorities, and increased awareness of their roles in the helping process. A greater respect for the content is expressed because it is seen as more substantial than the opinions and preachments of colleagues or the instructor. Students believe that their attitudes and knowledge have been influenced by data.

Finally, the student needs an opportunity to apply learning regarding the minority experience and perspective. This can be done in both classroom learning experiences and in field instruction. In the classroom, the annotated bibliography on a specific student-selected question or issue provides an excellent opportunity to review information for the light it sheds on the question or issue raised by the student. The annotated bibliography is useful especially if the student is asked to provide a summarizing narrative that precedes or concludes the bibliography. This requires the student to become involved in the issues he or she has read about.

The term paper is a familiar device for assessing student learning. Whatever the subject area, content on minorities can be infused if the instructor explains that a comprehensive discussion of the subject must include attention to the meaning, perspective, and impact of the general issue on a particular minority group or minorities in general.

Using another technique for infusing minority content, the oral report, the student examines an issue and reports on the state of the art, findings, or conclusions. Again, the instructor expects that this dimension of the subject matter must be covered for the work to be completed. The advantage of using the oral report as an application device is that the student shares a point of view on the material and interacts with colleagues on the topic.

Field instructors are in an excellent position to help students see examples of the minority experience and perspective. As students engage clients in information gathering, and as they arrive at diagnostic assessments and plan interventive strategies, they can be helped to use their knowledge and appreciation of the minority perspective to carry out these steps in the helping process. Faculty liaisons may find it necessary to help field instructors to include this dimension in their work with students. Field instructors also should encourage students to discuss openly their reactions, including gaps in understanding, biases, and fears in work with minorities. In this way, the norm suggested for the class is carried through to the field, and the student's integration of ethnic and minority content is enhanced.

Although the relevance of minority content to education for social work is acknowledged, its infusion into the entire curriculum has proceeded with varying degrees of success. Efforts to achieve such infusion have been characterized by a disjointed approach such that minority content is taught apart from the core courses or it has been "tacked on" to a few class sessions. In other instances, it has been give an obligatory nod by inviting representatives of minority groups to present a "guest lecture."

Approaches such as these fail to achieve the educational objectives of this content, and, therefore, limit the opportunity for students to acquire the knowledge and skill necessary for competent professional practice. To reach educational objectives, a structural approach to the infusion of minority and ethnic content is proposed. This chapter has described such an approach to help educators build this content into the design of their courses. However, although the conceptual formulations discussed can become useful strategies for infusing minority content, the achievement of this goal rests on the conviction of social work educators about the relevance of this information and their willingness to strive consistently to integrate it throughout the curriculum.

Works Cited

Bartlett, M. *The Common Base of Social Work Practice*. New York: National Association of Social Workers, Inc., 1970.

Bronfenbrenner, V. *The Ecology of Human Development*. Cambridge, Mass: Harvard University Press, 1979.

Chestang, L.W. "Environmental Influences on Social Functioning: The Black Experience," in P.S.J. Cafferty and L. W. Chestang, eds., *The Diverse Society: Implications for Social Policy*. Washington, D.C.: National Association of Workers, Inc., 1976.

Council on Social Work Education. *Curriculum Policy Statement*. New York: Council on Social Work Education, 1983.

Norton, D. *The Dual Perspective*. New York: Council on Social Work Education, 1978.

Solomon, B. B. *Black Empowerment*. New York: Columbia University Press, 1976.

CONTRIBUTORS

Ann Currin Adams, MSW, Associate Director of Social Work, Community Family Planning Council, New York

Pallassana R. Balgopal, DSW, Professor, School of Social Work, University of Illinois at Urbana-Champaign

Dorcas D. Bowles, EdD, Acting President, School of Social Work, Atlanta University, Atlanta. Dr. Bowles also maintains a private practice. She has taught at the Boston College School of Social Work in both the master's and doctoral programs. She was Professor of Social Work and Associate Dean at the Smith College School for Social Work in Northampton, Massachusetts. She served as principal investigator of the Ethnic Minority Manpower Development Grant funded by the National Institute of Mental Health. She received her MSW from the Smith College School for Social Work and her EdD in mental health administration from the University of Massachusetts—Amherst.

Leon W. Chestang, PhD, Dean, School of Social Work, Wayne State University, Detroit

Mary E. Davidson, PhD, Director, School of Social Work, Southern Illinois University at Carbondale

Melvin Delgado, PhD, Professor, School of Social Work, Boston University

Ivor J. Echols, DSW, Professor, School of Social Work, University of Connecticut, West Hartford

Phillip Fellin, PhD, School of Social Work, The University of Michigan, Ann Arbor

Carolyn Gabel, MSW, former Assistant Professor, School of Social Work, University of Connecticut, West Hartford

Carolyn Jacobs, PhD, Associate Professor and Acting Chair, Research Sequence, Smith College School for Social Work, Northhampton, Massachusetts. Dr. Jacobs has been on the faculty since 1980 and carried primary responsibility for the curriculum development component of the Ethnic Minority Manpower Development Grant funded by the National Institute of Mental Health. She received her PhD in social welfare from Brandeis University, Waltham, Massachusetts.

Shirley Jenkins, PhD, Professor, The Columbia University School of Social Work, New York

Donna Landerman, MSW, Consultant, Hartford, Connecticut

Brenda G. McGowan, DSW, Professor, The Columbia University School of Social Work, New York

Elaine B. Pinderhughes, MSW, Associate Professor, School of Social Work, Boston College, Chestnut Hill, Massachusetts

John Red Horse, PhD, Associate Professor, School of Social Work, Arizona State University, Tempe

Migdalia Reyes, MSW, Assistant Professor, School of Social Work, University of Connecticut, West Hartford

Elfriede G. Schlesinger, PhD, Professor, School of Social Work, Rutgers University, New Brunswick, New Jersey

Marta Sotomayor, PhD, President and Chief Executive Officer, The National Hispanic Council on Aging, Washington, D.C.

Leon F. Williams, PhD, Associate Professor, Graduate School of Social Work, Boston College, Chestnut Hill, Massachusetts

Maria E. Zuniga, PhD, Professor, School of Social Work, San Diego State University